THE ARCTIC MELT

IMAGES OF A DISAPPEARING LANDSCAPE

Diane Tuft 2017

3 Park Avenue, 27th floor
New York NY 10016, USA
Tel.: 212 989-6810 Fax: 212 647-0005
www.assouline.com
ISBN: 9781614285861
Edited by Justin A. O'Neill
Design by Jihyun Kim
Printed in China

DIANE TUFT

THE ARCTIC MELT

IMAGES OF A DISAPPEARING LANDSCAPE

Foreword by Joe Romm
Haikus by Diane Tuft

ASSOULINE

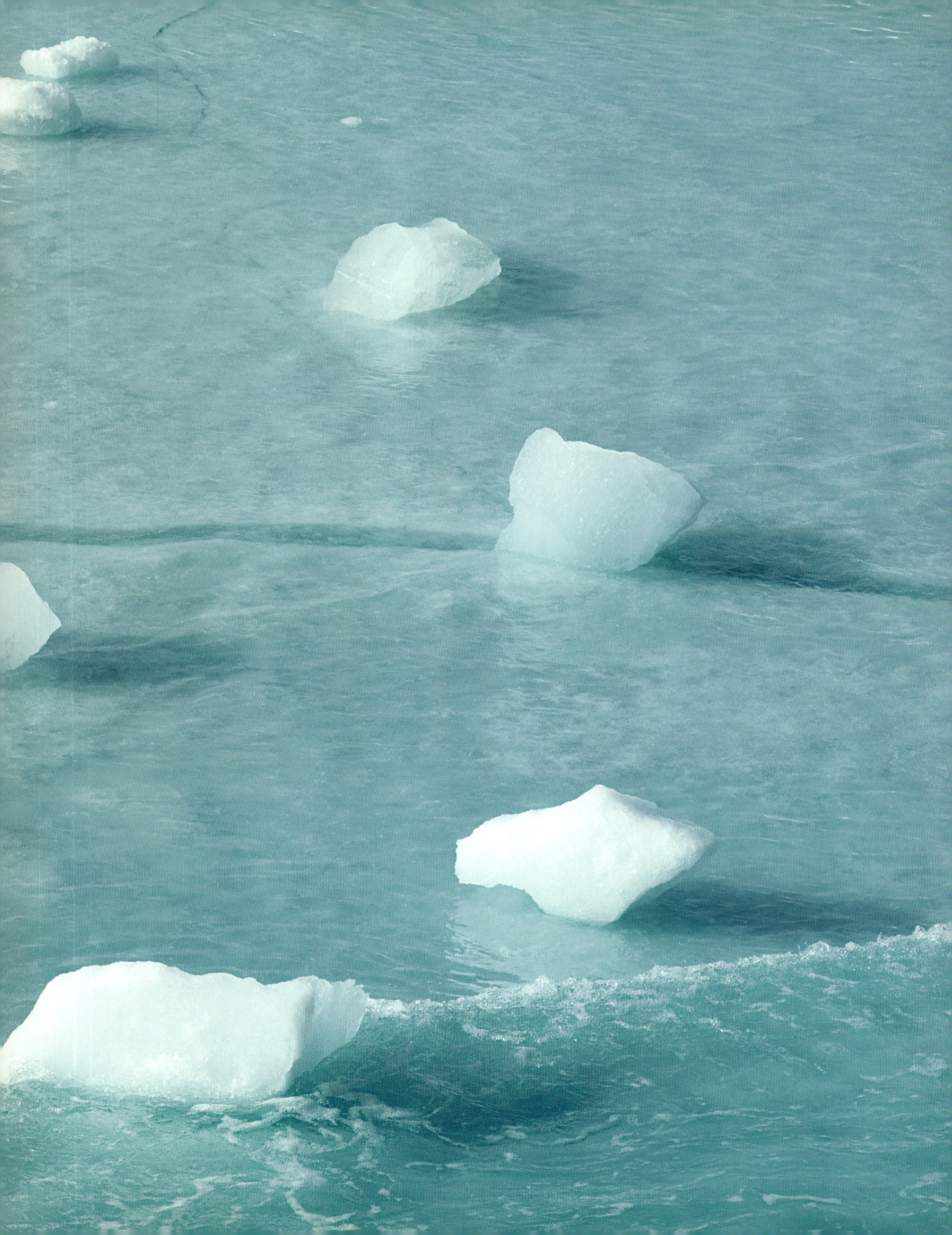

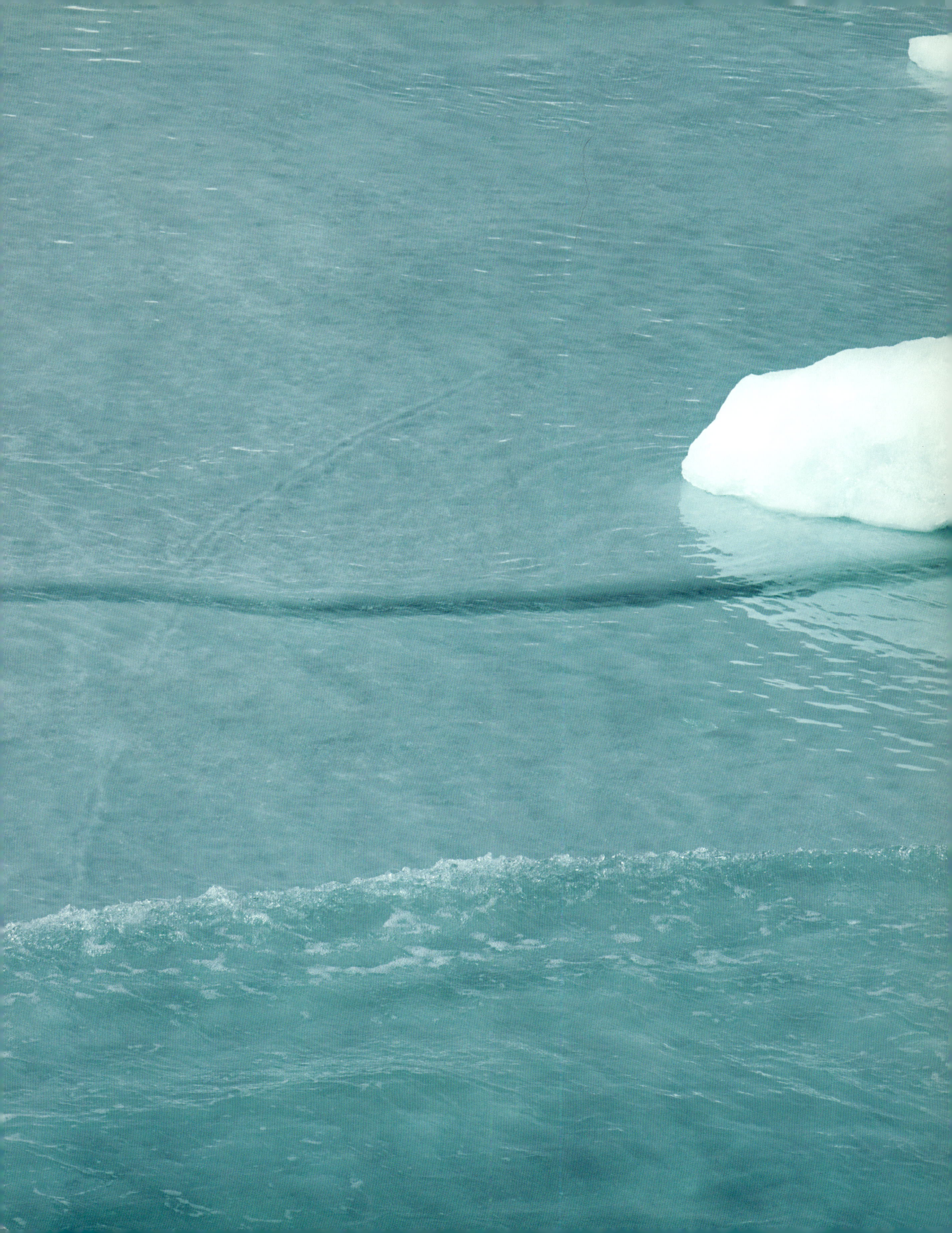

ARTIST'S PREFACE

metamorphosis
a snowflake an ice crystal
each alone unique

illumination
kaleidoscope splitting light
refract and reflect

ultraviolet
infrared radiating
absorb or disburse

open corridor
individuals combine
and so on until

endless white vista
icebergs dancing in oceans
snow embraces trees

glaciers rise and fall
fragile moments transforming
water messages

STATES OF WATER, ISFJORDEN, NORWAY.

previous pages THE NORTH POLE, ARCTIC OCEAN, 90 DEGREES N, 0 DEGREES C.

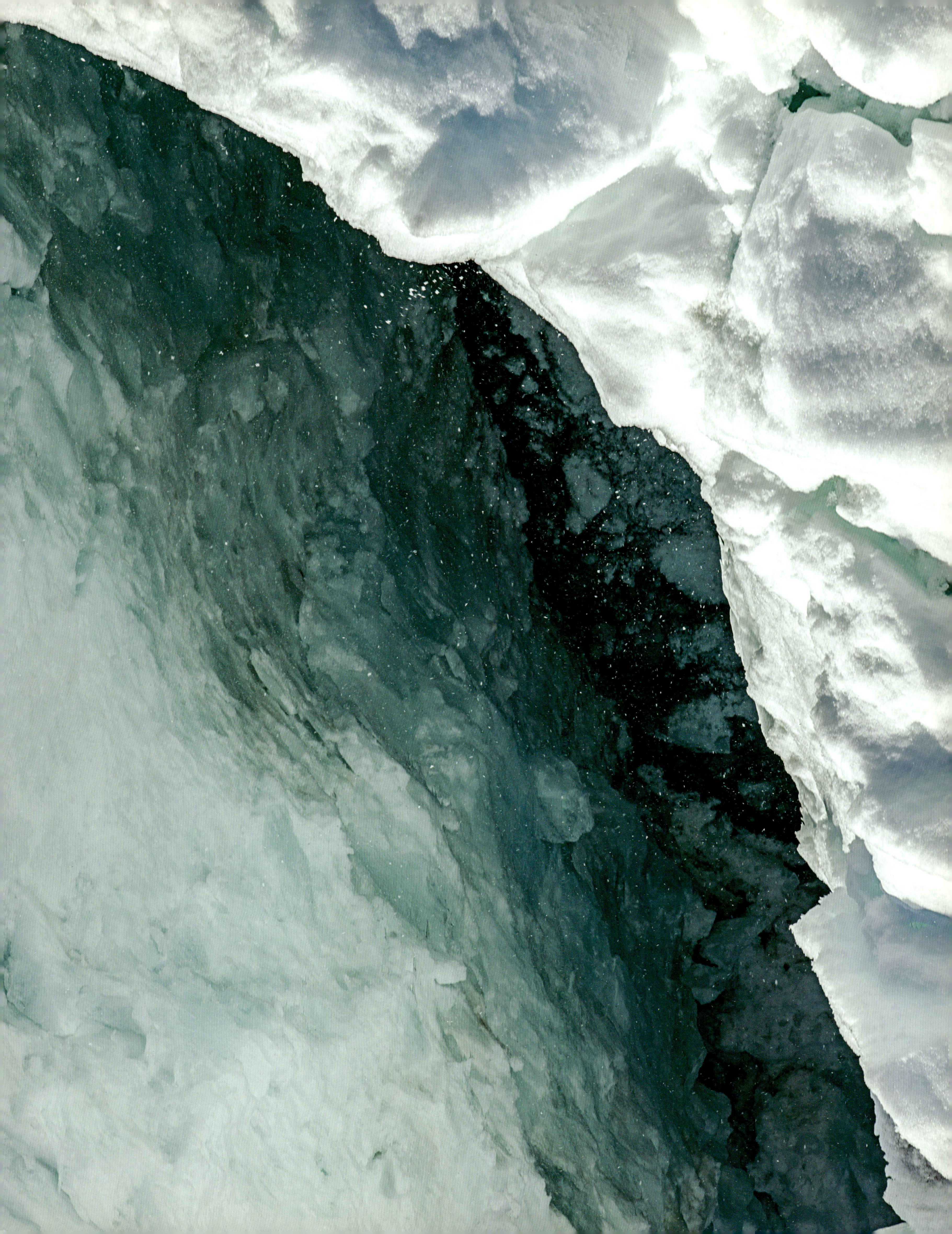

My attachment to frozen water began with my first photographic series, *Distillations* in 1998. Snow and ice became the palette that I would use for the next eighteen years to visually record atmospheric effects on the Earth's landscape. Each snowflake and ice crystal is unique. When combined with another, they form an ever-changing palette. While exploring the Arctic this past year, I was transfixed by the panoramic vistas, with shapes and patterns that appeared as sculptures formed naturally by wind, air, temperature, moisture, and atmospheric conditions. As the sun changes its position, the colors of the ultraviolet, infrared, and visible-light spectrum are reflected, refracted, and absorbed within these ice sculptures.

The Arctic is melting faster than any other place in the world. I felt compelled to photograph its splendor before the effects of global warming cause this landscape to disappear. In order to get a comprehensive picture of the fragility of the Arctic, I traveled to the mountain glaciers of Svalbard, Norway, the Arctic Ocean's sea ice, and the icebergs and ice sheet of Greenland.

I began my Arctic exploration on June 4, 2015, at 78 degrees North in Svalbard, an archipelago in the Arctic Ocean located halfway between mainland Norway and the North Pole. Most of Svalbard's twenty-three thousand square miles remain untouched by civilization, and the majority of its twenty-six hundred inhabitants live in Longyearbyen, the world's northernmost settlement. After great difficulty arranging to rent the only helicopter in Svalbard, I was able to access the region's mountain glaciers and surrounding waters.

Circling the Konglomeratfjellet, a mountain in Wedel Jarlsberg Land that towers above the almost ten-mile Recherchebreen glacier, I became mesmerized by the strong ultraviolet shadows cast by the low sun. Through my camera lens, the glacier's pristine snowdrifts became soft gentle forms. The turquoise-blue meltwater ponds of the archipelago's Nathorstbreen and Wahlenbergbreen glaciers became otherworldly shapes. Viewed from above, remnants of snow on the Wordiekammen, a geological formation made of limestone rocks, appeared to outline the area, defining it from the surrounding blue-green of the Isfjorden inlet. Ice floes in Isfjorden created patterns of cracked ice resembling abstract paintings. Terracotta rivers of ancient Devonian sandstone branched throughout the valleys of the Abrahamsenbreen glacier.

Beyond the beauty of Svalbard, I was also aware that it is home to the Arctic's only international science research center, Ny-Ålesund. On a previous photographic journey to Antarctica, I had spoken with climate change scientists at the U.S. scientific research center, McMurdo. I was now interested in discussing the effects of climate change on the Arctic.

Because accessing Ny-Ålesund is restricted to the scientific community, I had to secure a letter of invitation from a scientist whose research would coincide with my visit. After several months, Vittorio Pasquali from the National Research Council of Italy wrote a letter on my behalf to the Norwegian government. Vittorio was studying the effects of light on the behavior of the Lepidurus arcticus—a small crustacean that only lives in Arctic ponds. This letter gave me access to interview the other research scientists who were stationed there.

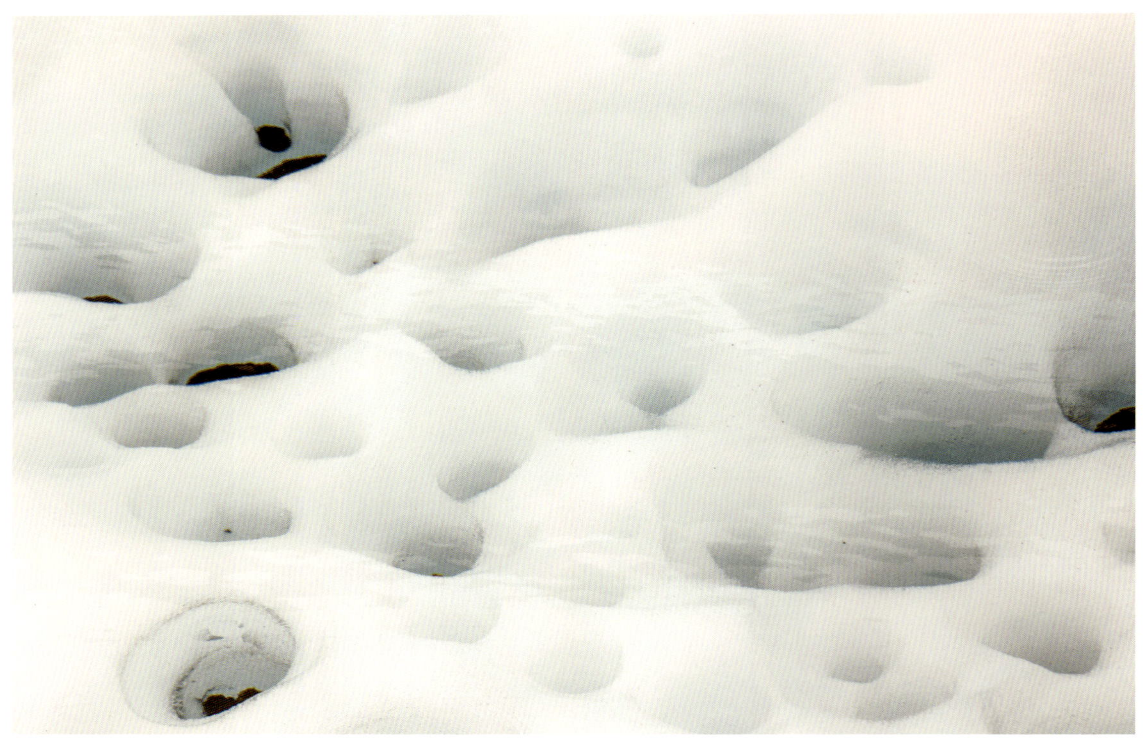

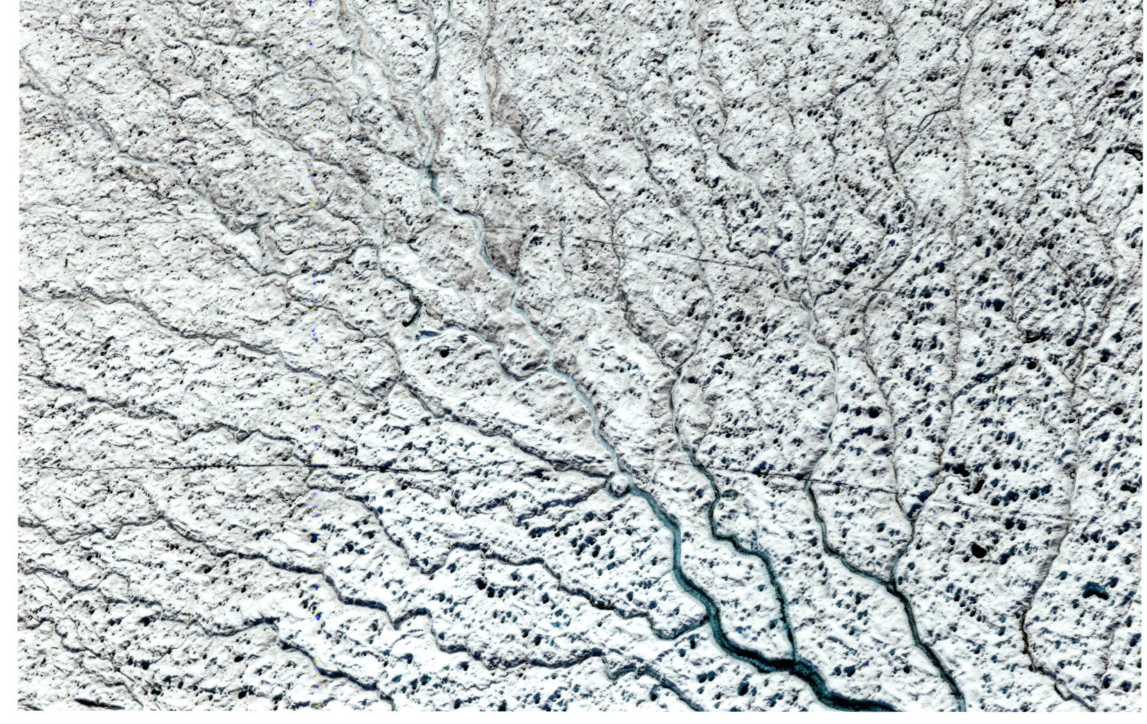

top THE GREENLAND ICE SHEET, JULY 20, 2007.
bottom THE GREENLAND ICE SHEET, JULY 16, 2016.

These scientists were studying a range of subjects including: the effect of climate change on the ocean's kelp population and on Arctic greenhouse gases, pollution's effect on the DNA of Arctic birds, and the effect of increased radiation on phytoplankton.

While at Ny-Ålesund, I was fortunate to spend an afternoon in the Kongsfjorden inlet, boating through small icebergs while watching thousands of Arctic birds, including glaucous gulls and fulmars, nesting on steep rocks jutting out of the water. In the background I could hear the thunder of calving glaciers releasing chunks of ice into the sea.

I knew that the majesty of Svalbard would change, but I wondered if its mountain glaciers would *exist* by the end of the century.

I continued my journey on June 16 by traveling through the Arctic Ocean to the North Pole, where I would be able to experience the Arctic's sea ice. In order to reach the North Pole, I had to travel on a Russian nuclear-powered icebreaker leaving from Murmansk, Russia.

Once again, I was mesmerized by the Arctic's splendor. The vast frozen fields were absolutely breathtaking. My senses were stimulated as I watched, listened, and felt the ship break its way through the endless white expanse. Large blue-green blocks of ice lifted out of the ocean and fell back on themselves. Signs of melt were everywhere. Areas of open water were studded with ice paddies that would be used as stepping-stones for the occasional polar bear. When I embarked on my journey, I thought that I would see several polar bears, but during my two-week trip, I encountered only three adults and three cubs.

The sporadic snow paddies were a clue to the difficulty the bears have in living and navigating the Arctic waters.

For thousands of years, the sea ice during the Arctic winters through the month of June was always too thick for surface vessels to access the North Pole. But now, because of climate change, our vessel was the third earliest to ever reach the Pole, and the only vessel to arrive during summer solstice. With a balmy temperature of 32 degrees Fahrenheit, the ice at the North Pole was too thin to disembark. It took several hours to find an ice floe that could support the weight of our group.

While this was an amazing experience, it disturbed me to know that my trip through the Arctic Ocean was only possible because of the Arctic melt.

In 2007, I had photographed icebergs, glaciers, and the ice sheet in Ilulissat, Greenland. Nearly a decade later, I decided to return so that I could visually record the difference in the landscape and document the impact climate change has had on the area. I was also afforded the opportunity to visit the northern part of Greenland's ice sheet and observe ice-core drilling.

During my first visit to Ilulissat, the temperature was 30 degrees Fahrenheit, and Disko Bay was spotted with colossal snow-covered icebergs that had calved from the Jakobshavn and surrounding glaciers. The ice sheet was blanketed with fluffy snow studded with cryoconite holes—cylindrical depressions caused by solar radiation being absorbed by sediment that has landed on the ice surface. When I returned to Ilulissat in 2016, the Jakobshavn glacier was calving at such a rapid rate that the entire inlet was filled with small icebergs that continually emptied into Disko Bay. They were in a constant state of melt: waterfalls tumbling from their tops and rivulets raining from their interiors. Icebergs cracked, split, and fell into the bay daily.

The majestic Eqi glacier, which I had photographed in 2007, had retreated so much that it was now almost entirely on bedrock. The constant calving no longer produced icebergs; instead, it released small sediment-colored pieces of snow. Taking the same aerial flight over the ice sheet that I took in 2007, I now saw rough peaks of snow and silt that were studded with hundreds of meltwater ponds, some so large that they could be considered lakes. The meltwater ponds would eventually empty into deep moulins, which became streams that drained into the waters surrounding Greenland.
The temperature in Ilulissat just nine years later was a temperate 65 degrees Fahrenheit.

Since 1955, Greenland's ice sheet has served as a unique research database with the introduction of ice-core drilling. Scientists analyze the data derived from ice-core segments to determine what the atmospheric conditions, temperature, and sea level were during a specific time period. This information is used to predict future climates under similar past atmospheric conditions.
Alan Stoga, the chairman of the Tällberg Foundation, invited me to watch the first ice cores being drilled at the East Greenland Ice Core Project (EGRIP), located at 76 degrees North. Tällberg's mission is to encourage global conversation about issues critical to the evolution of our societies, including climate change.
Our seven-member delegation met on July 16 in the town of Kangerlussuaq and flew in an LC-13C Hercules plane to the campsite, located directly over the North-East Greenland Ice Stream.

The Greenland ice sheet stretches for miles, providing an endless white vista with hints of ultraviolet blue. The horizon undulates in conjunction with the levels of underground streams. For four days we camped at EGRIP, learning the importance of the data that will eventually come from ice-core research. It would take three years to extract cores from the final depth of twenty-six hundred meters, equivalent to one hundred thousand years ago.

Scientists predict that the sea level could rise three to six feet or more by the end of the century, inundating coastal area worldwide and displacing tens of millions of people. The melting of mountain glaciers and Greenland and Antarctica's ice sheet will be significant factors to sea level rise.
Will the Arctic ice become a "new wonder" of the world—a natural phenomenon that existed for a short period of time and then finally disappeared?

I think about the different forms of ice within the Arctic Ocean.
I think about the soft, subtle folds in the snow within the Svalbard glaciers.
I think about the towering icebergs that I saw in 2007 that are now half the size.
I think about the glistening blue meltwater ponds now studding the glaciers.

This book is a visual testimony to the fragile and shifting landscape of the Arctic, which is now melting at an unprecedented rate. The photographs that follow serve as documentation of the expansive beauty of the Arctic now and the dire situation that it continues to face if we do not provide a sustainable environment for the future of our planet.

RUSSELL GLACIER, KANGERLUSSUAQ, GREENLAND, JULY 16, 2016.

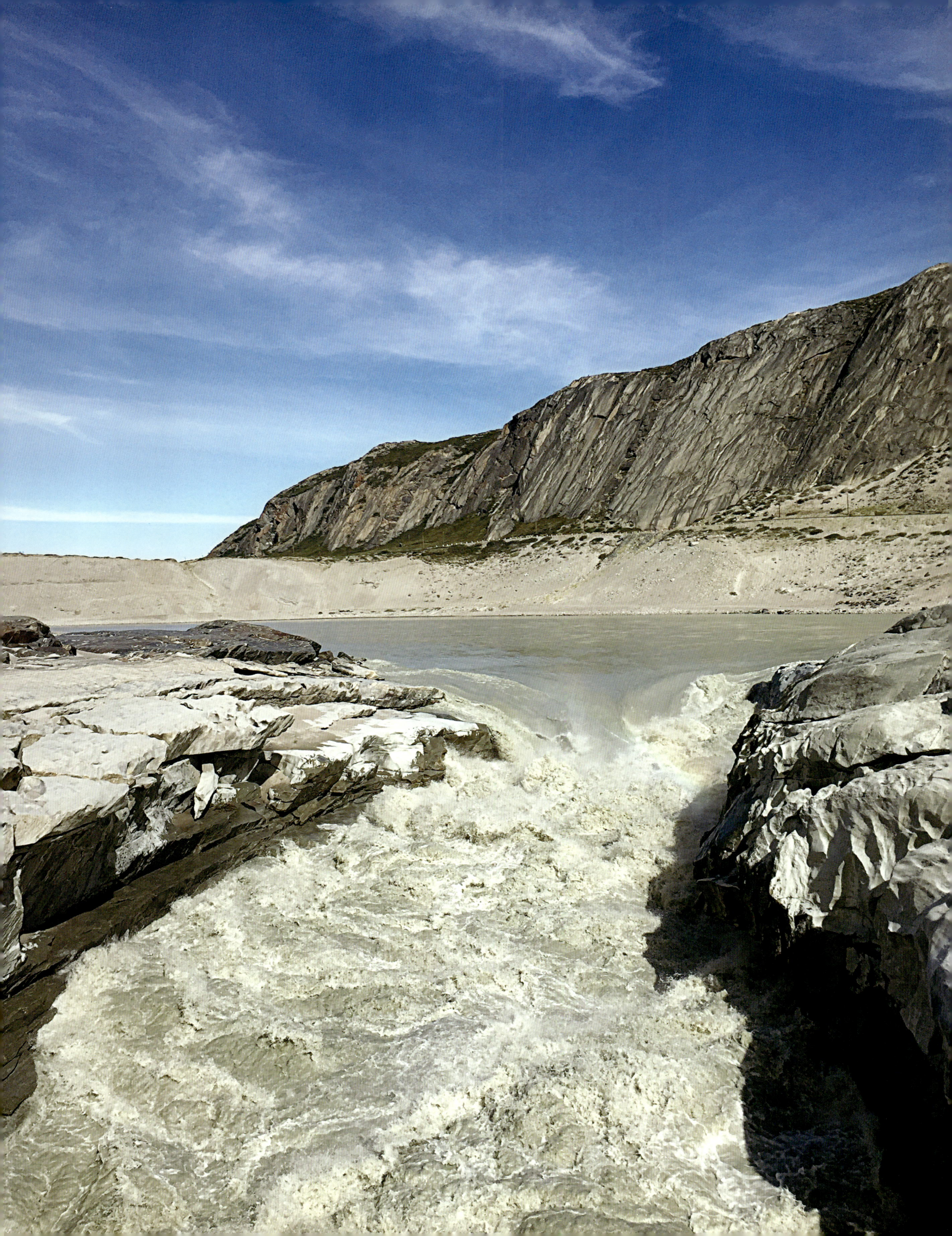

INTRODUCTION
BY JOE ROMM

Some say the world will end in fire,
Some say in ice.
From what I've tasted of desire
I hold with those who favor fire.
But if it had to perish twice,
I think I know enough of hate
To say that for destruction ice
Is also great
And would suffice.

ROBERT FROST

Modern civilization depends on the Earth having just the right amount of ice. And that in turn depends on humans using just the right amount of fire.

Too much fire, too much burning of coal and oil and natural gas, leads to too much warming, which in turn melts ice everywhere. At the poles, especially in the Arctic, that melting process replaces highly reflective white ice and snow with dark blue sea or dark land, both of which absorb more solar energy and lead to more ice melting. That amplifying feedback, a vicious cycle, causes the Arctic to warm twice as fast as the planet as a whole, and it inexorably links fire and ice to the fate of humanity.

We are in a world of too much melting ice and headed toward a world of no ice at all, a world where sea levels keep rising and rising until every coastal city in the world is a new Atlantis.

It is vital to tell this story, to document it, and that is Diane Tuft's passion and talent—visually recording a landscape that is disappearing. Since 1998, she has been tracking the effects of global warming on the landscape. Capturing both infrared and ultraviolet light waves through her photography, she has said, "I am able to record what the naked eye cannot see."

It is vital to tell this story because the most important ice on the planet is far away from where most people live so they can not see what is happening to it firsthand. It is important because it is not too late to save most of that ice and because failing to do so would destroy civilization as we have come to know it.

For most of human evolution, there was too much ice. During the great Ice Ages of the past million years, thick glaciers covered large swaths of the Earth. During the short interglacial periods, the ice retreated. These cycles were driven by slow changes in the Earth's orbit, which in turn changed how the sun's fire warmed the planet.

Modern human civilization—the emergence of cities, large-scale agriculture, and an economy that could sustain billions of people—was enabled by the stable climate we've had for some eleven thousand years in the current interglacial. During this time, millions and then tens of millions and then hundreds of millions and ultimately billions of people settled where the climate was most suited for living and farming. Again and again, many of the settlements that turned into megacities were along the coasts, where natural ports could become major trading hubs and rich agricultural deltas could sustain a growing population.

Ironically, before humans harnessed hydrocarbon-fueled fire on a massive scale and released billions of tons of heat-trapping carbon dioxide into the atmosphere, the Earth was cooling again. We were headed back into another Ice Age very, very slowly. During the past five thousand years, the Earth on average cooled about 1.3 degrees Fahrenheit—until the last one hundred years, when it has warmed that amount and more.

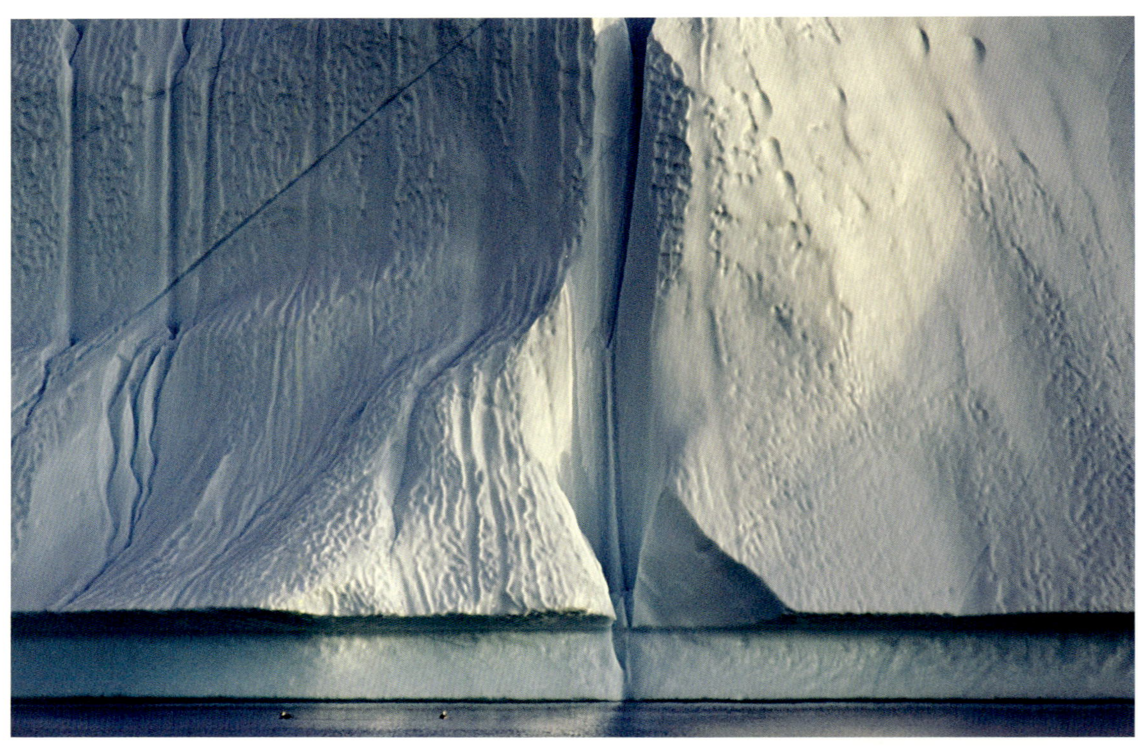

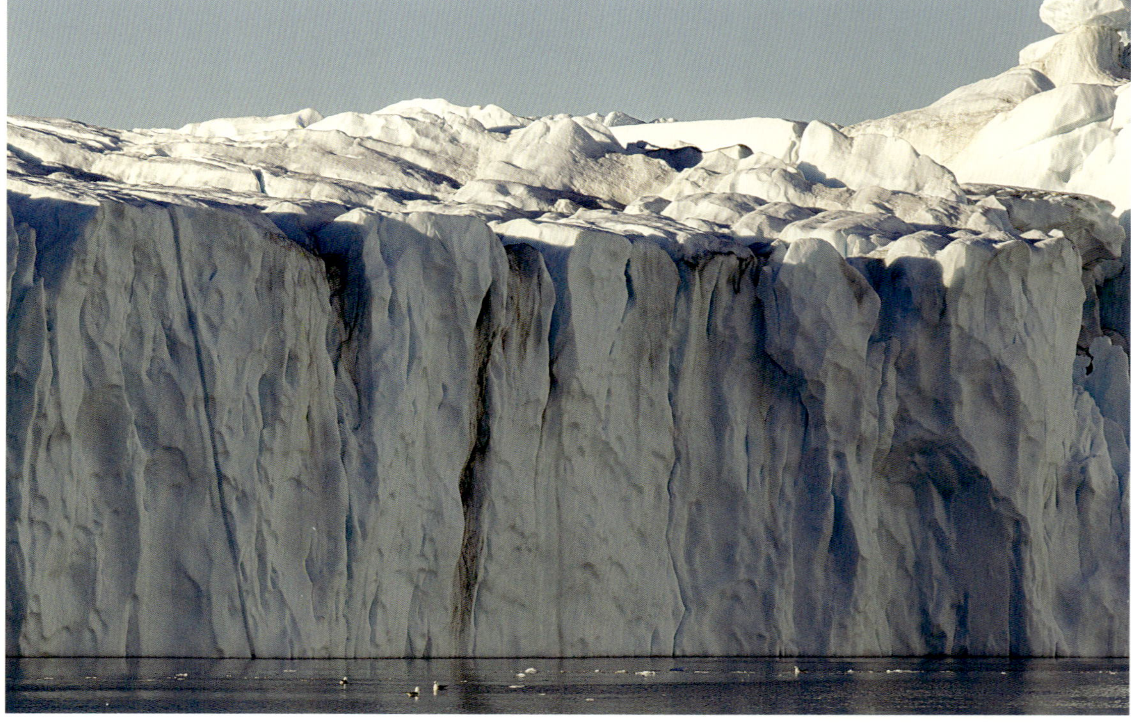

top ICEBERGS IN DISKO BAY, GREENLAND, JULY 22, 2007.
bottom ICEBERGS IN DISKO BAY, GREENLAND, JULY 14, 2016.

Whatever benefit we've had from holding off the next Ice Age, however, has been overwhelmed by the unprecedented global warming driven by our out-of-control use of hydrocarbon fire. Indeed, the rate of warming since 1900 is fifty times greater than the rate of cooling in that previous five thousand years! And we are on track to speed up the warming rate fivefold this century. This is far beyond the rate of warming modern humans, animals, and plants have ever experienced. Two decades ago, climatologist Wallace Broecker, who popularized the term "global warming," fatefully said, "The climate system is an angry beast, and we are poking at it with sticks."

Thanks to hydrocarbon fire, by the second half of this century the Earth will have more than nine billion people, a large fraction of whom will be living in places that simply can not sustain them—either because it is too hot and/or dry, the land is no longer arable, their glacially fed rivers have dried up, or the seas have risen too much.

This brings us back to ice and the Arctic. Because the Arctic is warming so much faster than the rest of the Earth, it is the place where the biggest symptoms of catastrophic climate change appear first. Unfortunately, what happens in the Arctic doesn't stay in the Arctic.

First, rapid Arctic warming is speeding up the melt of the great Greenland ice sheet—an area almost the size of Mexico covered in a sheet of ice up to two miles thick. If we melt all of its ice, sea levels would be some twenty feet higher. That might take centuries, but the melt rate has increased fivefold in recent years thanks to global warming. Coupled with the accelerated melting of the even vaster Antarctic ice sheet, scientists now project we will push sea level rise higher than previously estimated, upwards of six feet this century. No coastal city will escape this inundation. No rich agricultural delta will escape being ruined by intruding salt water.

Second, rapid Arctic warming is hastening the disintegration of the permafrost—a locker of frozen vegetation and soil so large that it contains twice as much carbon as the atmosphere does today. Starting as early as next decade, the permafrost is expected to start releasing into the air vast amounts of carbon in the form of carbon dioxide along with methane, which is an even more potent heat-trapping gas. This will lead to more global warming and more permafrost melt. The perma-melt is another dangerous amplifying carbon cycle, one that could add as much as an extra 1.5°F in total warming by century's end.

Third, rapid Arctic warming is speeding up the already staggering rate of loss of Arctic sea ice. Considerable recent research suggests that sea ice loss and the amplified Arctic warming has already contributed to the recent jump in extreme weather in the northern hemisphere, potentially amplifying such epic disasters as the California drought and superstorm Sandy. It appears that we are weakening the overall jet stream, which normally keeps weather patterns moving along like the wind keeps a sailboat moving. The result is weather that gets "stuck"—becalmed in the doldrums—with heat waves, droughts, and deluges sticking around much longer than they once did.

Fourth, recent research has implicated accelerated Greenland ice melt in the slowdown of the Gulf Stream system that powers the Atlantic Ocean's circulation. And that slowdown in turn appears to be one reason "ocean temperatures off the U.S. east coast are warming faster than global average temperatures," as climatologist Stefan Rahmstorf has explained, which in turn supercharges Atlantic hurricanes and other superstorms. Also, that slowdown may be why sea levels are rising much faster on the U.S. East Coast than in most other places in the world.

So what is happening to the ice in the Arctic—both to the sea ice and to the land-locked ice in Greenland—could not be more important to the fate of humanity. And that is why it is so important to document.

Diane Tuft has dedicated her life to documenting and exposing climate impacts using photography. Her first trip to the Arctic was in 2001. By 2012, she won a National Science Foundation grant to take part in its Antarctic Artists & Writers Program. She spent forty days living at McMurdo Station in Antarctica, where the wind speed averages forty miles per hour, and the temperature averages -32°F. This is the land of the "30-30-30" rule: At -30°F, with winds over thirty mph, human flesh freezes solid in thirty seconds. Her remarkable photographs of this hostile, beautiful, otherworldly place can be found in her previous monograph, *Gondwana: Images of an Ancient Land*.

In the past two years, Tuft has continued her polar-warming work by photographing the Arctic sea ice and Greenland ice sheet—both of which are melting far faster than scientists had feared just a decade ago. Few things have more stark beauty than the meltwater, icebergs, Arctic Ocean, and Greenland glaciers, as you can see in the stunning images that Tuft has captured for this new book.

Yet underneath the breathtaking beauty of the images of dissolving sea ice and melting glaciers is a warning. The melting of the ice is poised to take away from us much more than a momentary breath. Indeed, we are fast approaching tipping points of ice loss that will lead to changes in sea level, ocean circulation, and weather patterns, which scientists have warned will be irreversible for the next fifty generations. We are leaving very deep and dangerous footprints in our short walk on this planet.

Meltwater ponds add a turquoise beauty to any scene of ice. Yet, as the Alfred Wegener Institute for Polar and Marine Research reported a few years ago, "in places where melt water collects on the ice, far more sunlight and therefore energy is able to penetrate the ice than is the case for white ice without ponds. The consequence is that the ice is absorbing more solar heat [and] is melting faster"—the very vicious cycle that causes the Arctic to warm up so much faster than the rest of the planet.

Icebergs, of course, literally have nine-tenths of their body beneath the seas, so they are a defining metaphor for unseen danger. These mostly hidden pirates have robbed our ships for centuries, most famously in 1912, when the "unsinkable" *Titanic* ignored warnings of icebergs in the vicinity, maintained a high speed, hit one because it couldn't change course fast enough, and sank. As the BBC has reported, "The ice shelf in Ilulissat [Greenland] is the most likely birthplace of the *Titanic* iceberg."

Now, hydrocarbon fire has brought us another danger from Greenland that so many choose to ignore while we blindly keep our hydrocarbon economy burning full steam ahead. "There was this big machine, this human system, that was pushing forward with so much momentum that it couldn't turn, it couldn't stop in time to avert a disaster. And that's what we have right now," said Academy award-winning director James Cameron on the hundredth anniversary of the disaster that he immortalized in a blockbuster movie. "You've got the starving millions who are going to be the ones most affected by the next iceberg that we hit, which is going to be climate change," he added, "We can see that iceberg ahead of us right now, but we can't turn."

One last piece of the *Titanic* story—the disaster was foretold fourteen years in advance. In 1898, a novel told the story of "the largest craft afloat and the greatest of the works of men.... Unsinkable—indestructible." That ocean liner also carried more than two thousand passengers, had a shortage of lifeboats, struck an iceberg in the North Atlantic, and lost more than half her passengers. Incredibly, the title of this ominously prescient book was *Futility, or the Wreck of the Titan*.

In the case of climate change, it's not a fictional novel that is foretelling what will happen, it is science. The very scientific method that allowed humanity to tame hydrocarbon fire on such a massive scale that we are terraforming the planet—literally changing the world—now warns that we are headed on a collision course with catastrophe.

In this vital book, Diane Tuft shows us stunning images in the part of the world seeing the greatest warming-driven change. She is not just documenting how hydrocarbon fire is rapidly transforming the northern ice-scape—she is also foretelling the future of what will happen if we don't reverse course rapidly. The world will end in fire and no ice, unless we stop that from happening.

Joe Romm

Founding Editor, ClimateProgress.org

following pages FAST ICE, ARCTIC OCEAN, 87 DEGREES N, -2 DEGREES C.

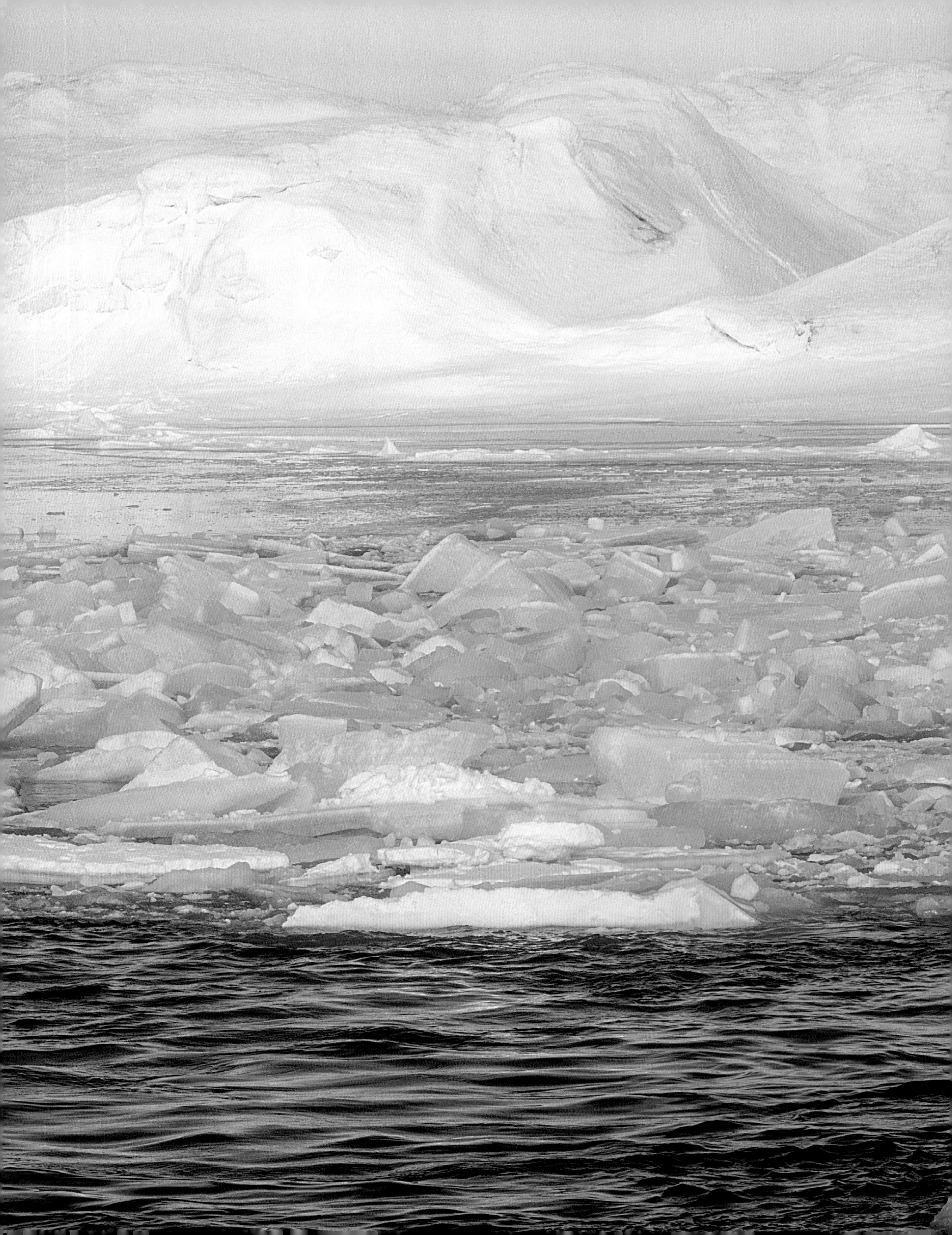

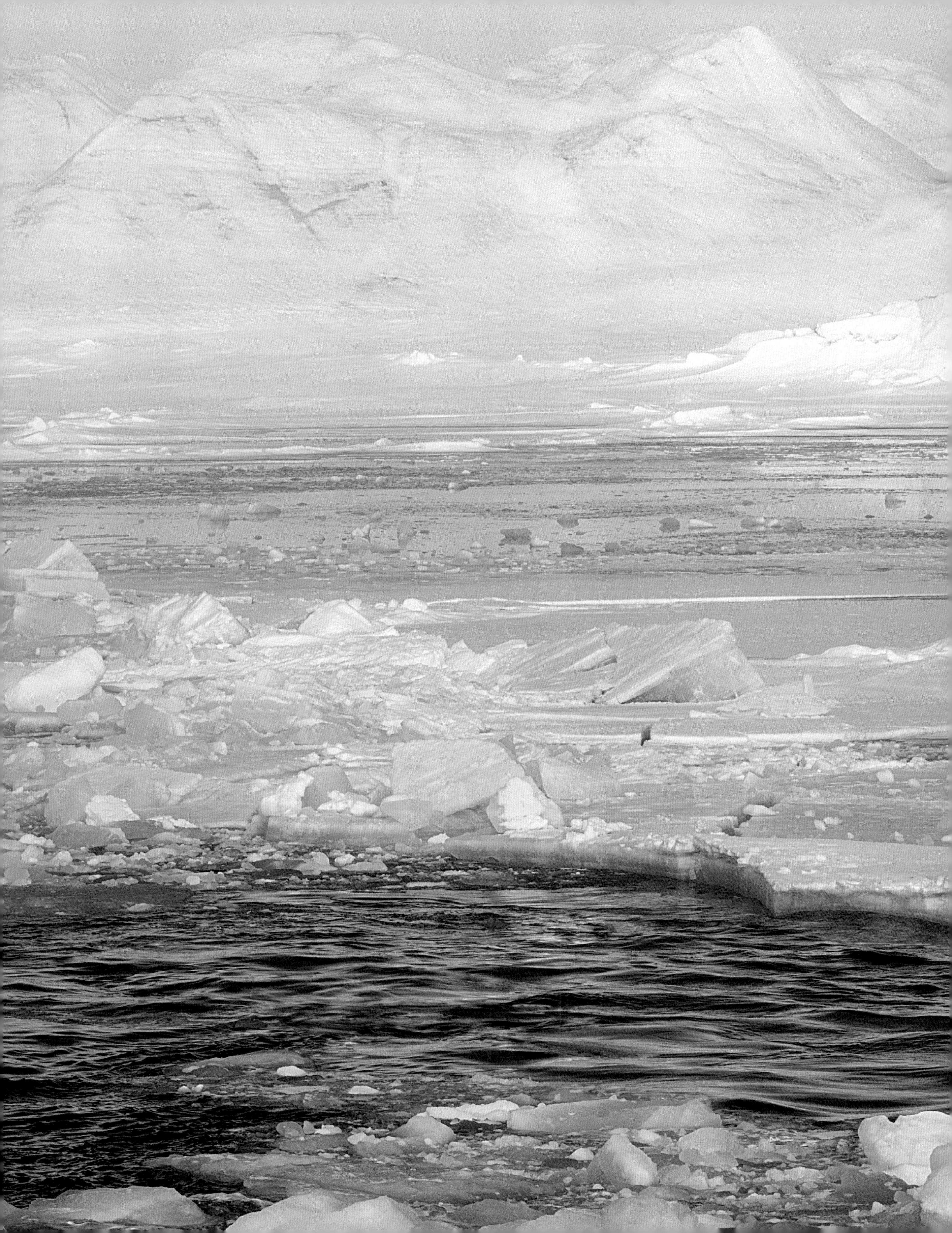

GLACIER

glacial migration
powerful yet delicate
conquered by the sun

in constant unrest
labyrinth sloping towards sea
surging waters creep

roar of dark thunder
escapes as relics of ice
breaking from the mass

jagged blue peaks laced
with colors of sediment
crevasses cut ice

ponds of meltwater
flow between the pyramids
red river valleys

wind sweeping across
snow covered mountain ranges
patterns created

fallen sediment
disperse tangles of webs
over the surface

purple blue shadows
of ultraviolet light
drift across ridges

striations in ice
mapping years of atmosphere
predicting future

frozen water's edge
retreating and receding
glacier's final breath

ICE FOLD, RECHERCHEBREEN, WEDEL JARLSBERG LAND, SVALBARD, NORWAY.

ULTRAVIOLET LUMINESCENCE, RECHERCHEBREEN, WEDEL JARLSBERG LAND, SVALBARD, NORWAY.
previous pages SHADOW'S EDGE, RECHERCHEBREEN, WEDEL JARLSBERG LAND, SVALBARD, NORWAY.
following pages SNOW PATTERNS, SVALBARD, NORWAY.
pages 34-35 WITHIN KONGSBREEN, SPITSBERGEN, NORWAY.

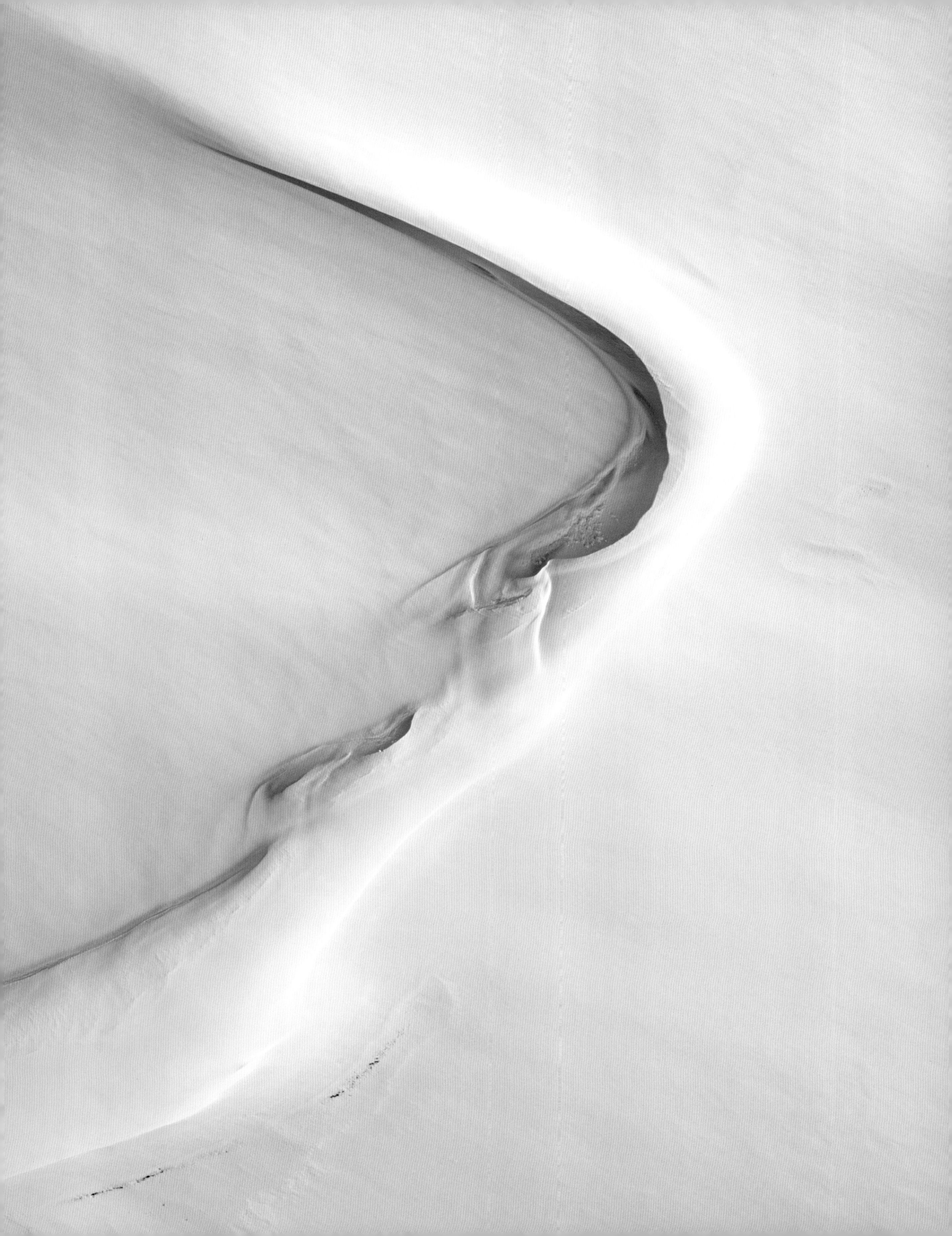

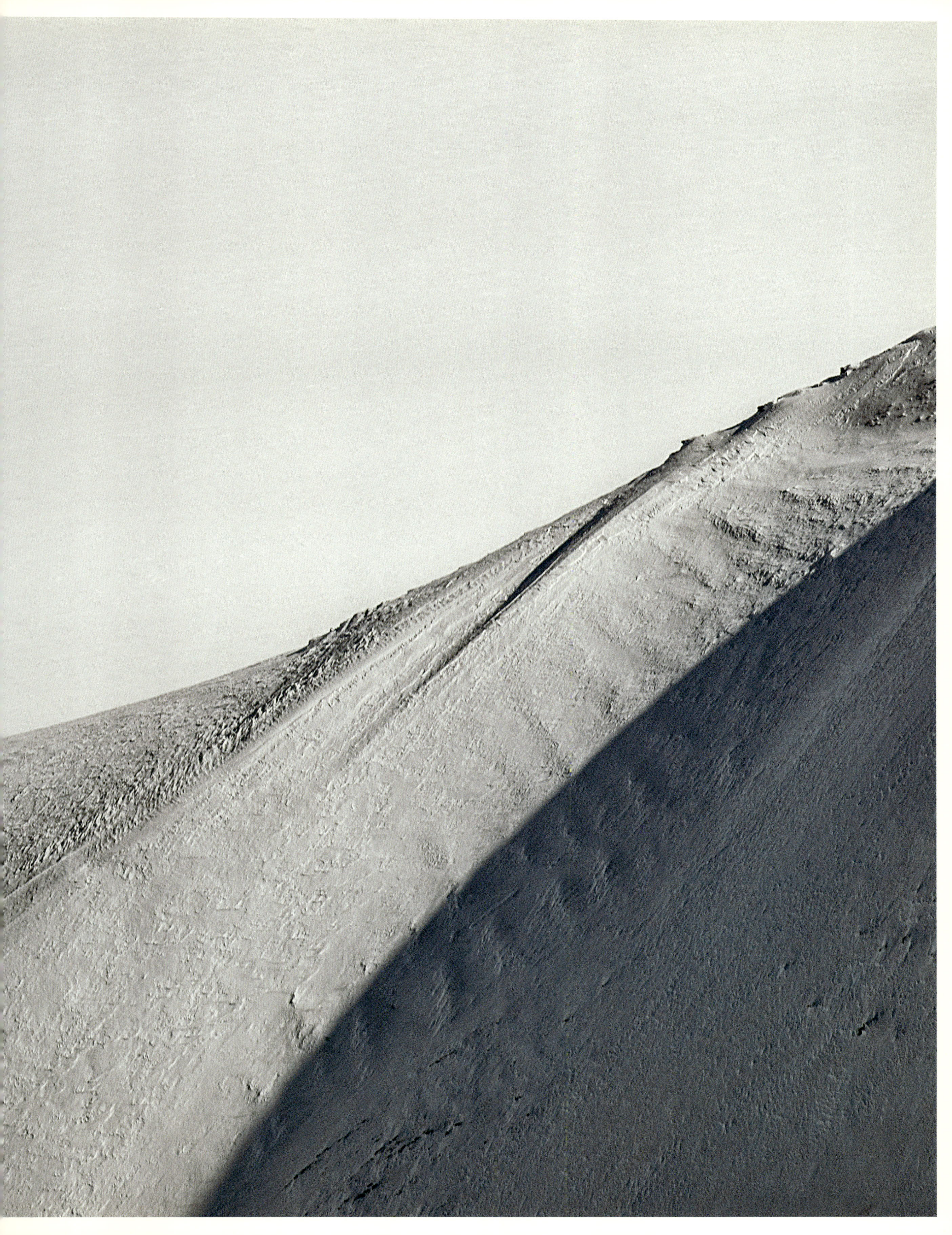

“What’s the use of having developed a science well enough to make predictions if, in the end, all we’re willing to do is stand around and wait for them to come true?”

ELIZABETH KOLBERT

SASSENDALEN, SVALBARD, NORWAY, 9:03 PM.
previous pages WIND PATTERNS ON KONGSBREEN, SPITSBERGEN, NORWAY.
following pages BLACK PHYLLITE PATTERNS, STEMMEKNAUSANE, SVALBARD, NORWAY.

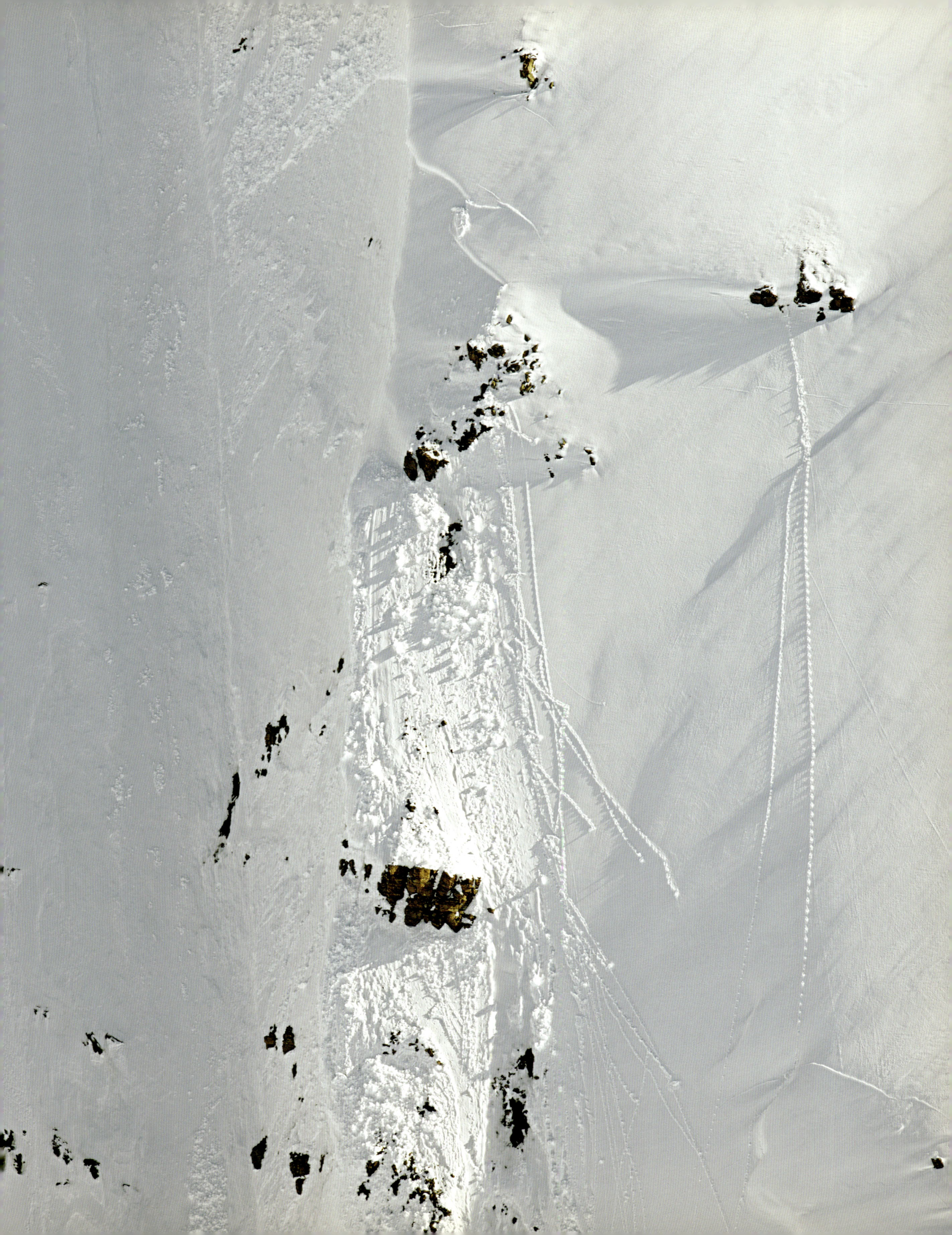

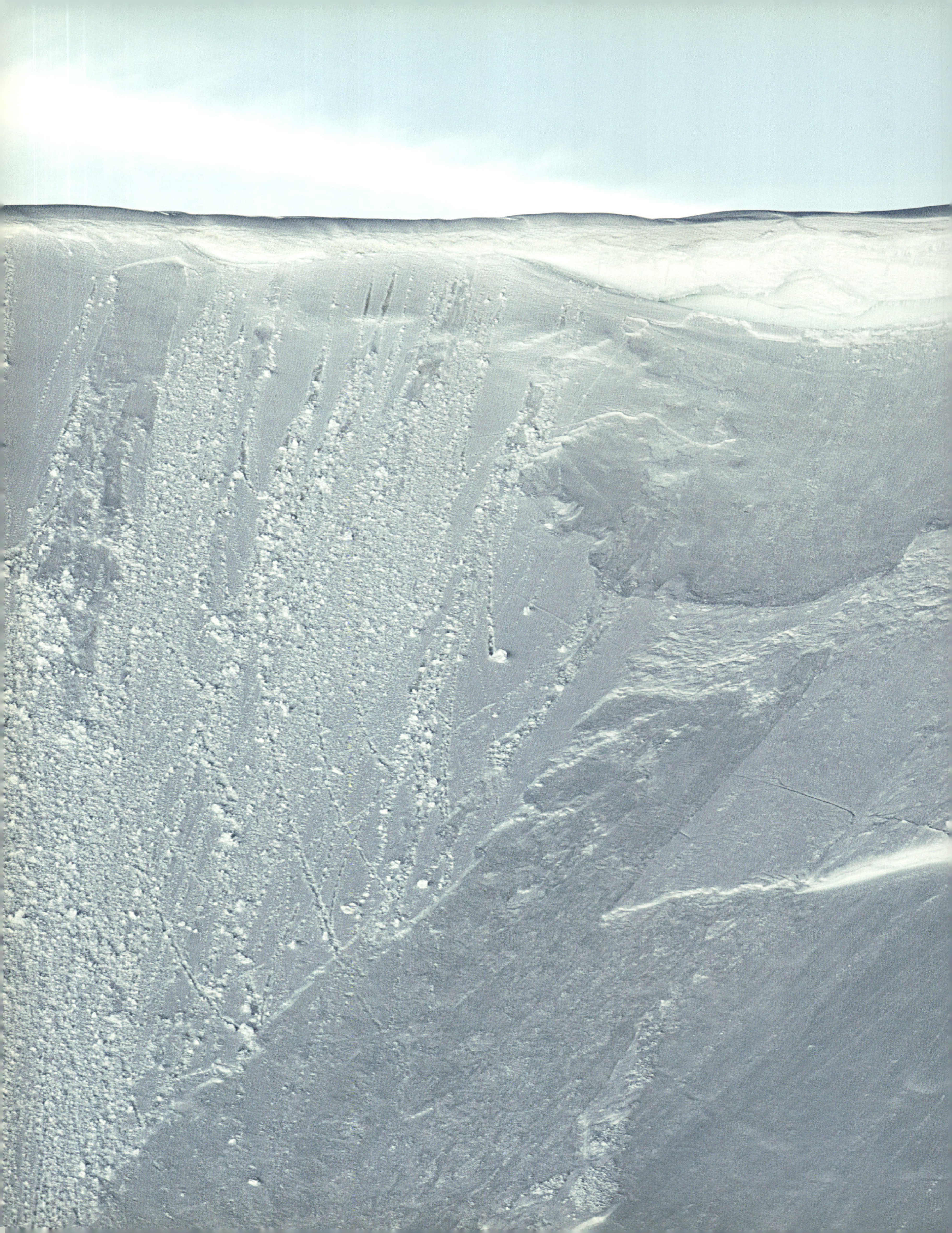

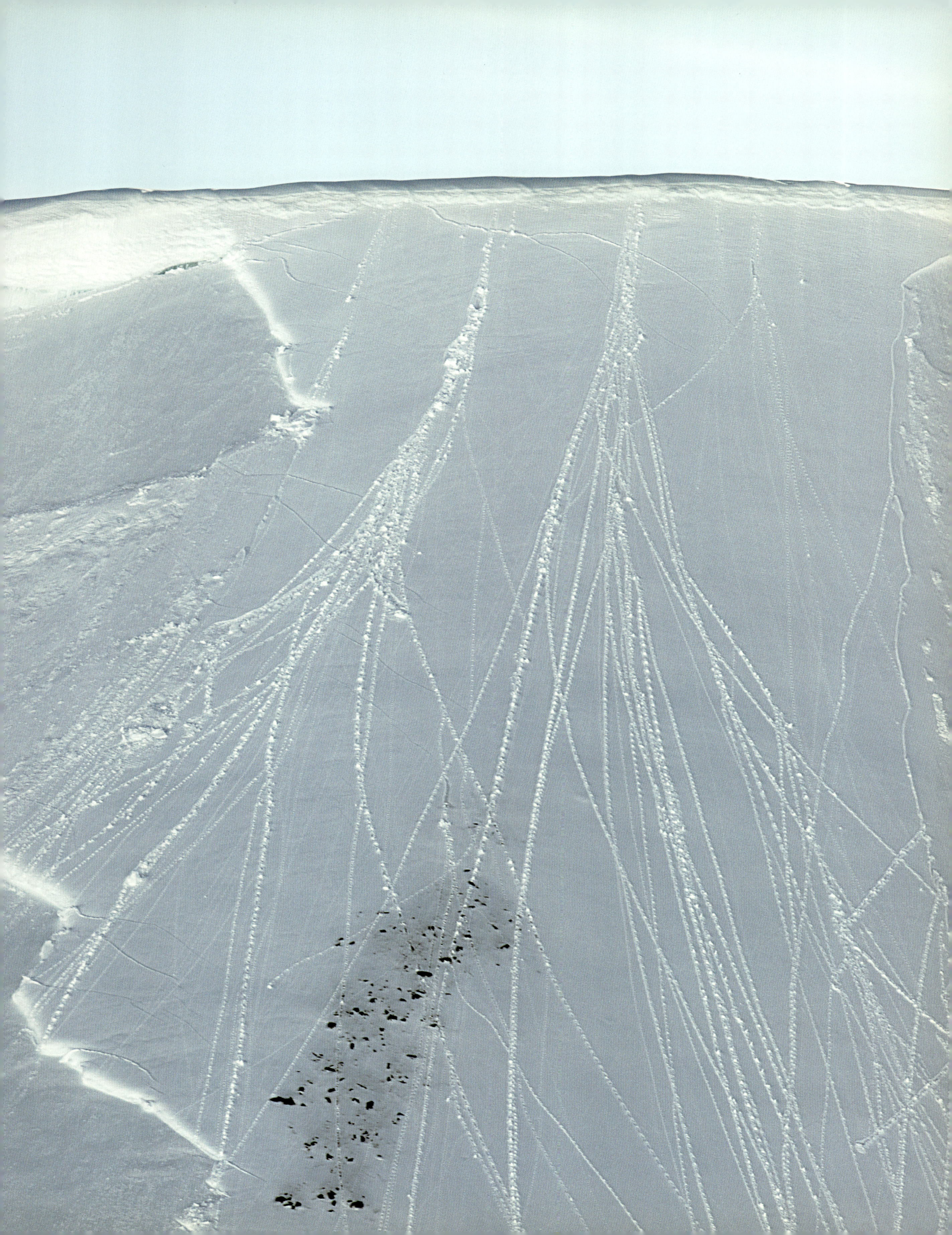

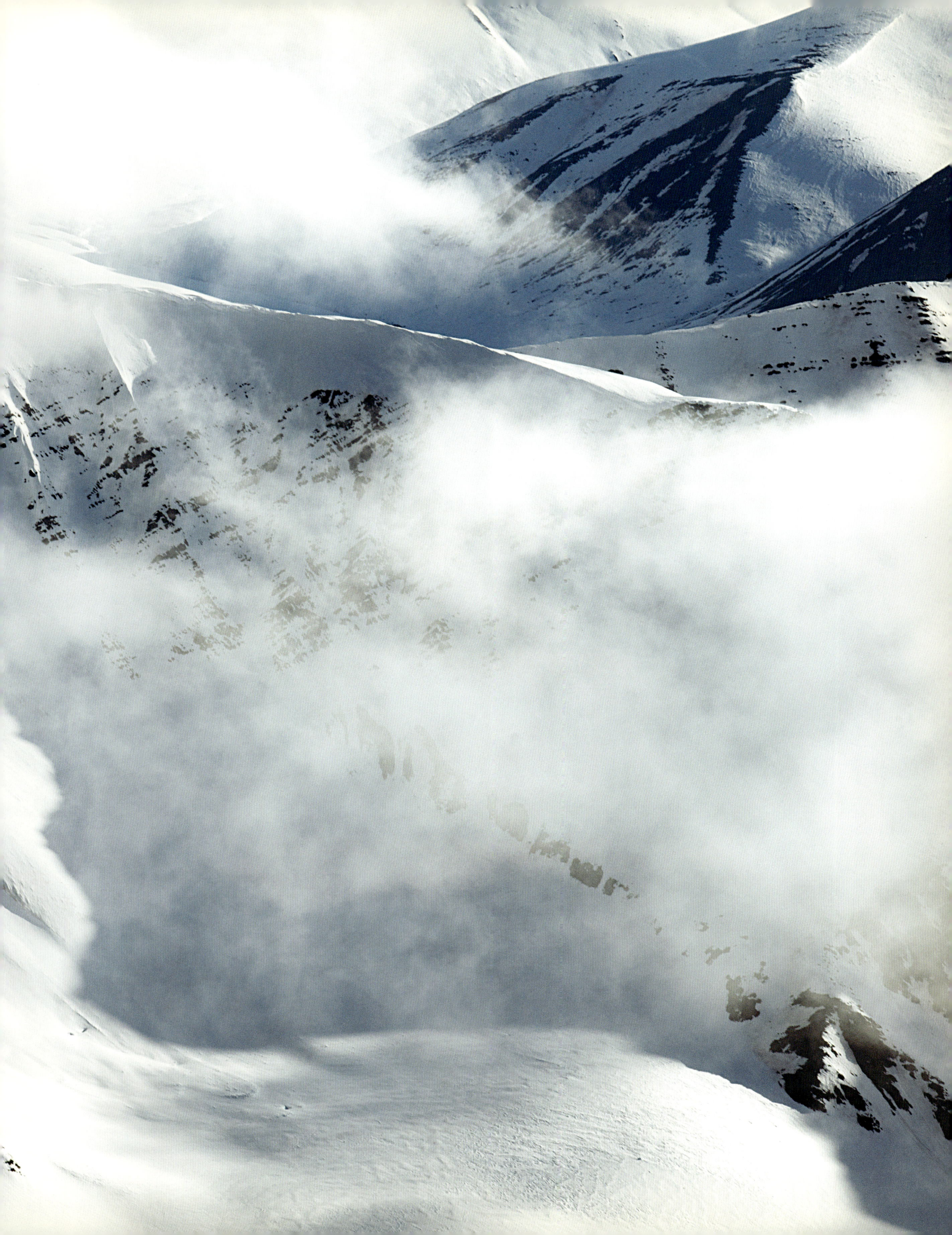

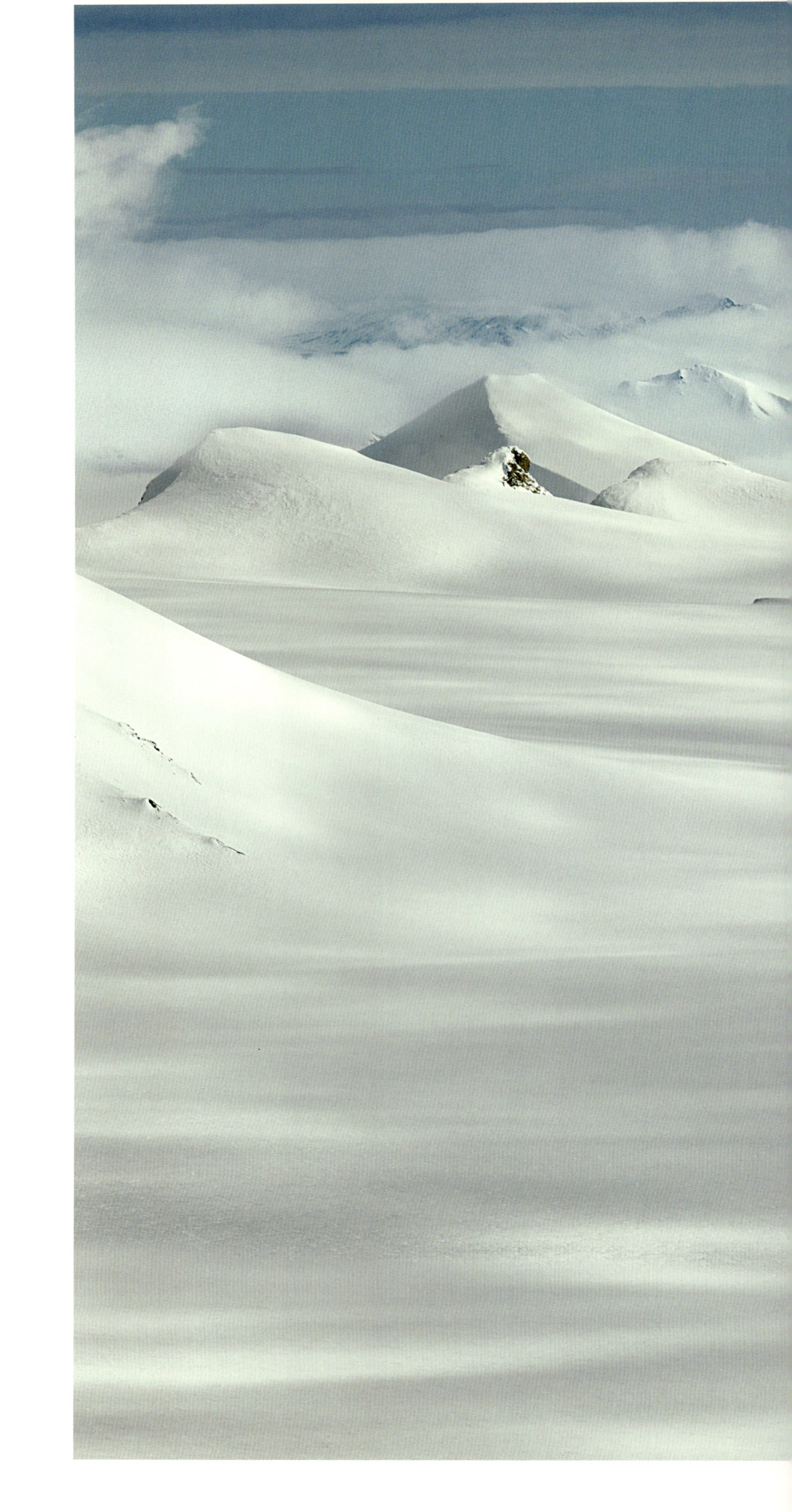

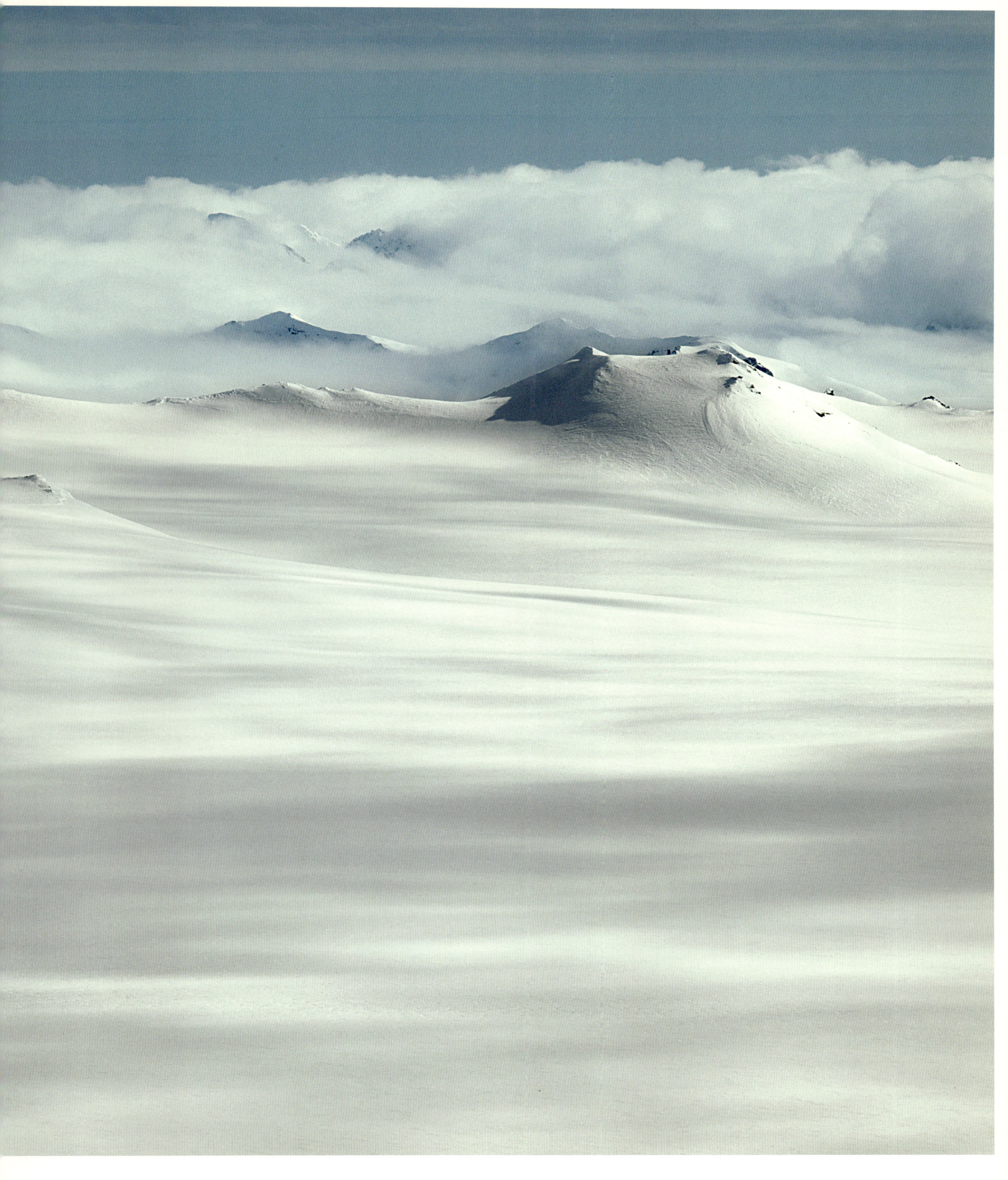

NATHORSTBREEN, WEDEL JARLSBERG LAND.

previous pages SYMPHONY ABOVE STEMMEKNAUSANE SVALBARD, NORWAY.

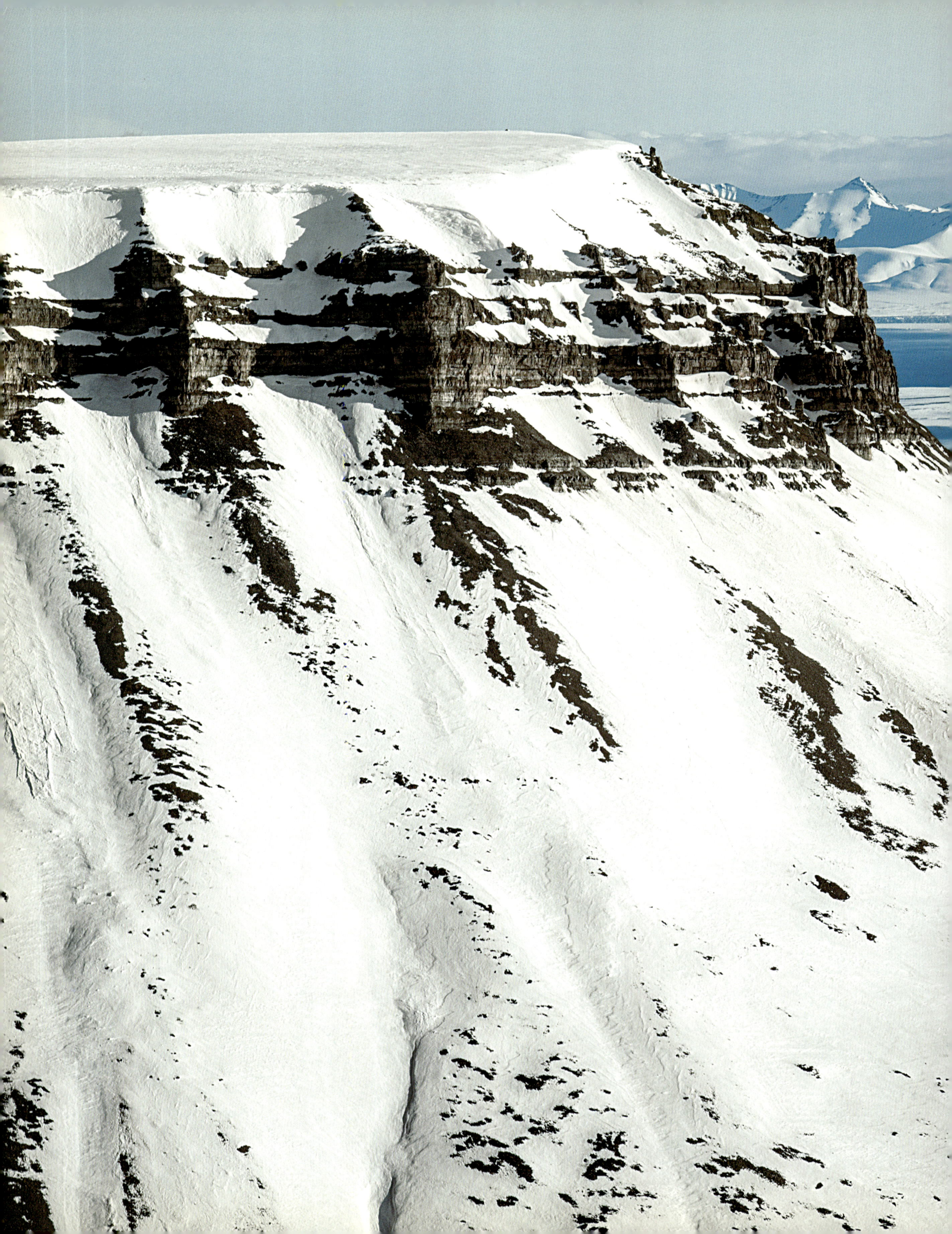

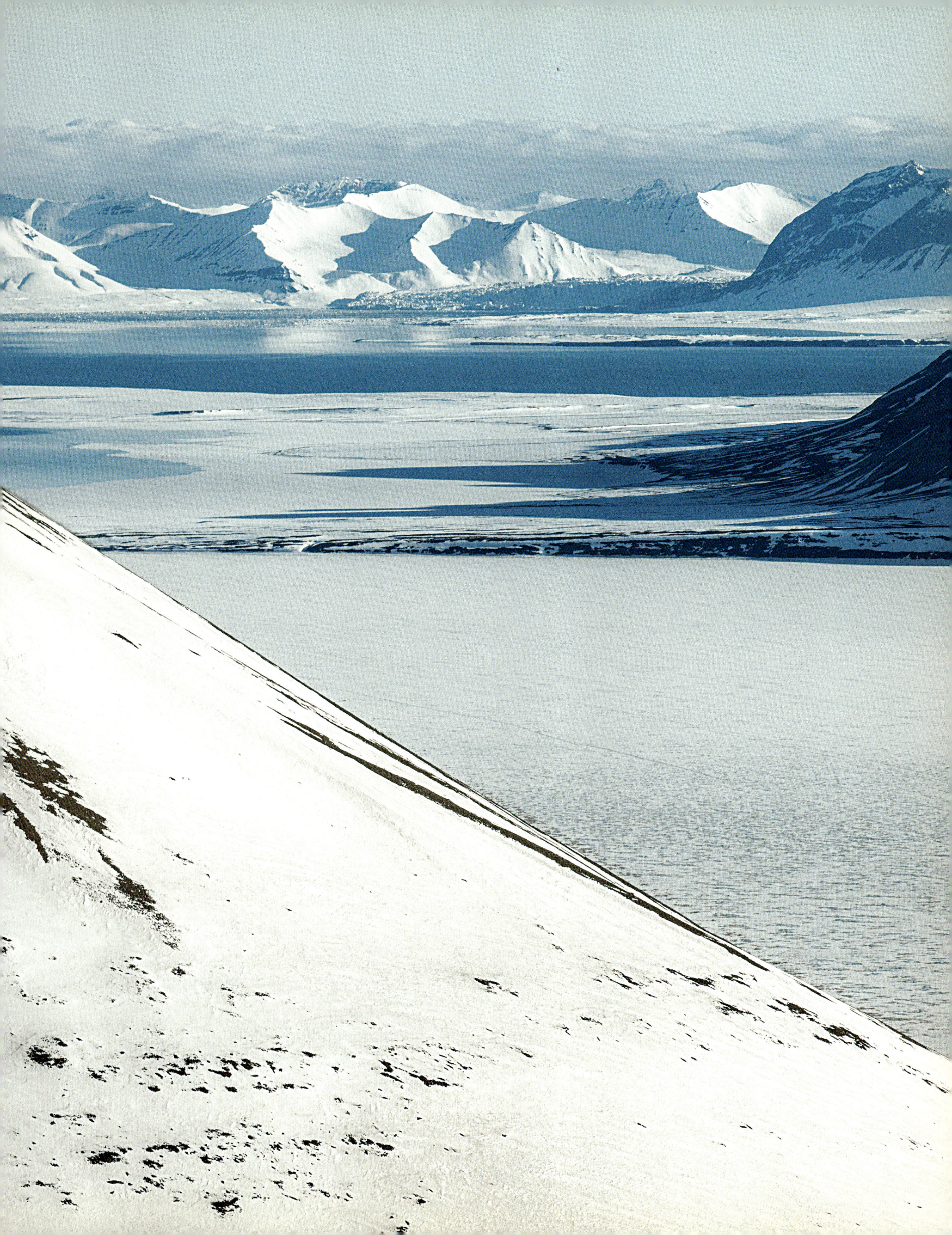

“We never know the worth of water till the well is dry.”

THOMAS FULLER, *GNOMOLOGIA*, 1732

SNAKE ICE RIVER, ABRAHAMSENBREEN, SPITSBERGEN, NORWAY, 79 DEGREES N.
previous pages THREE CROWNS, VIEW TO KONGSFJORDEN, SVALBARD, NORWAY.
following pages EQI GLACIER, DE QUERVAIN HAVN, GREENLAND.

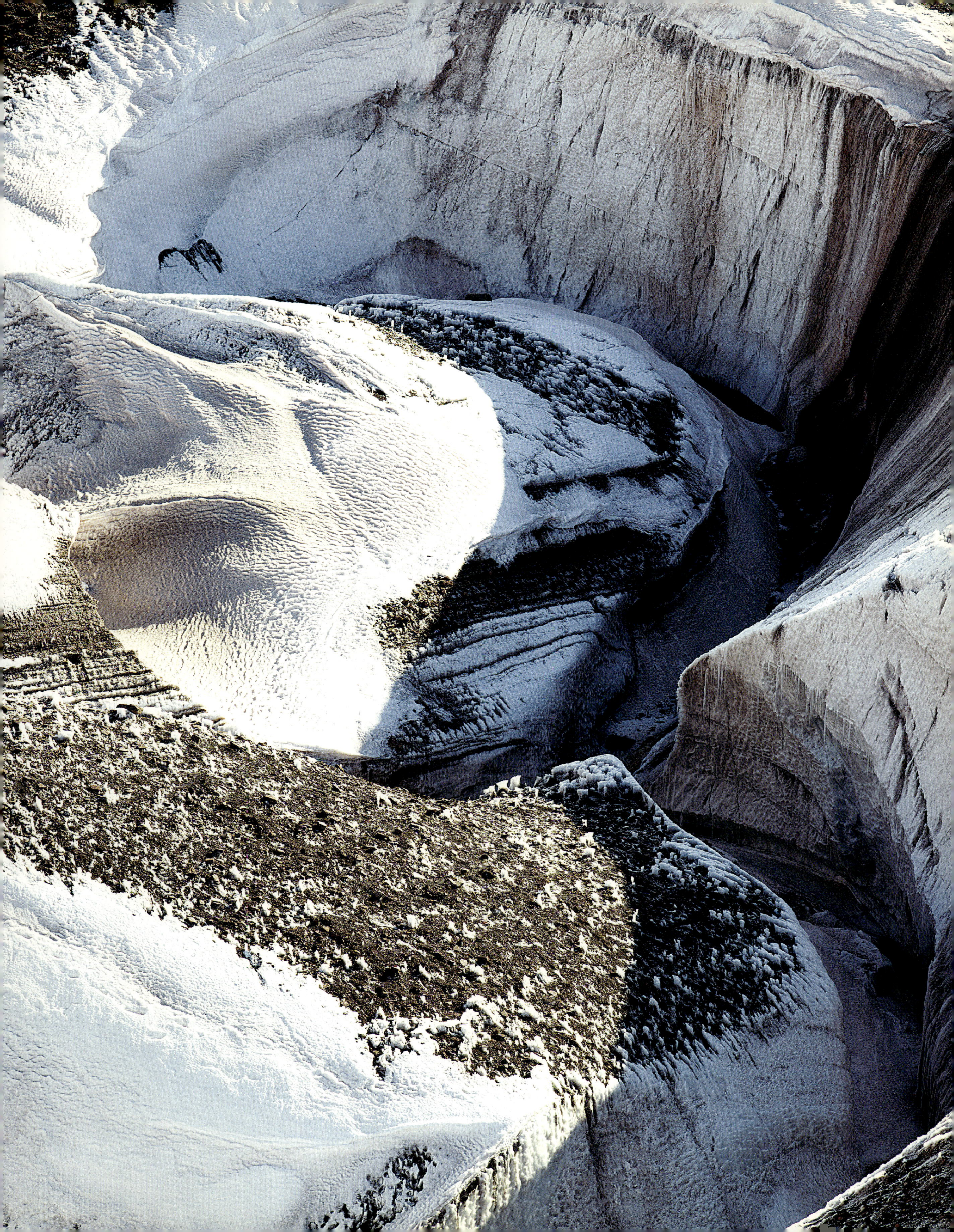

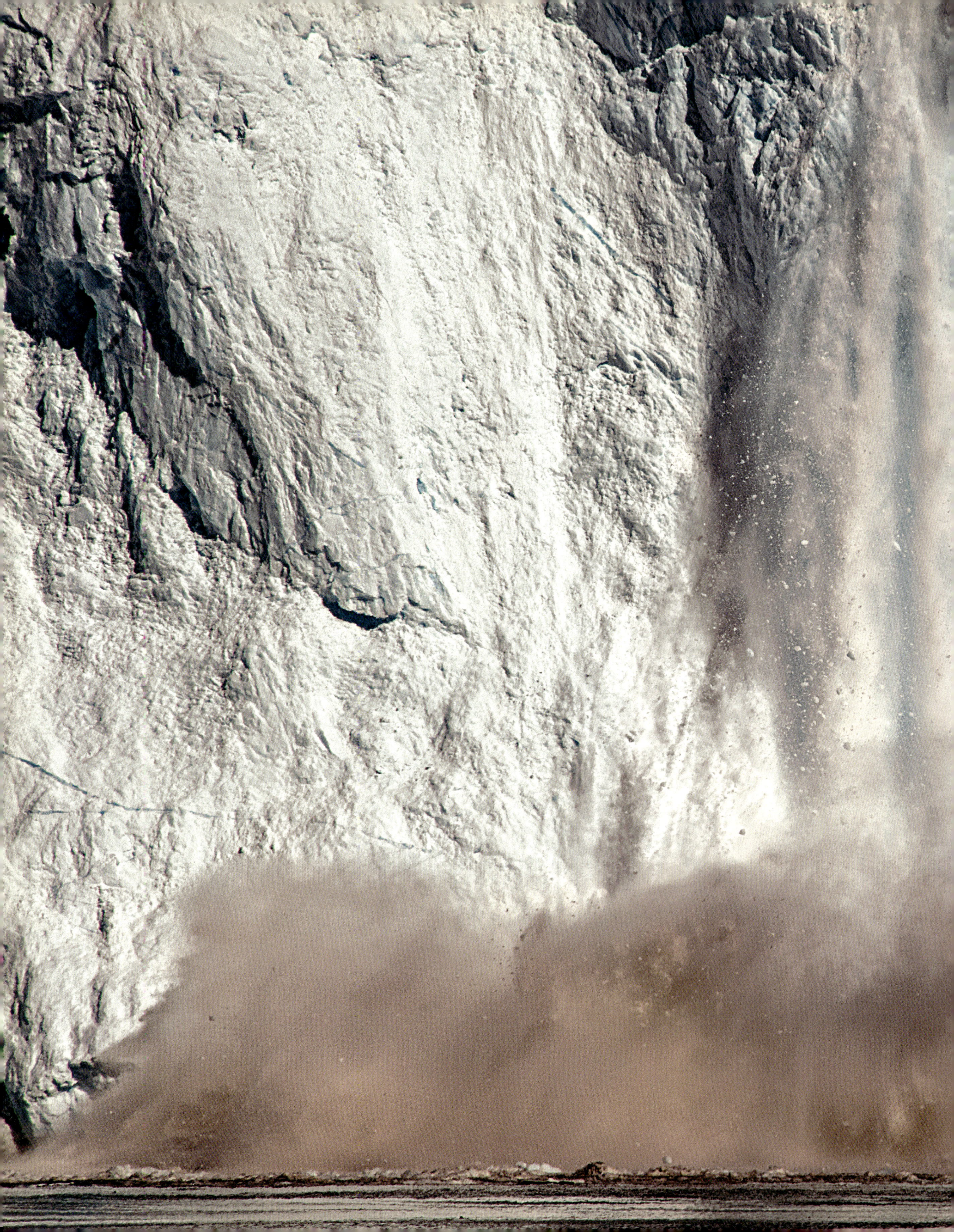

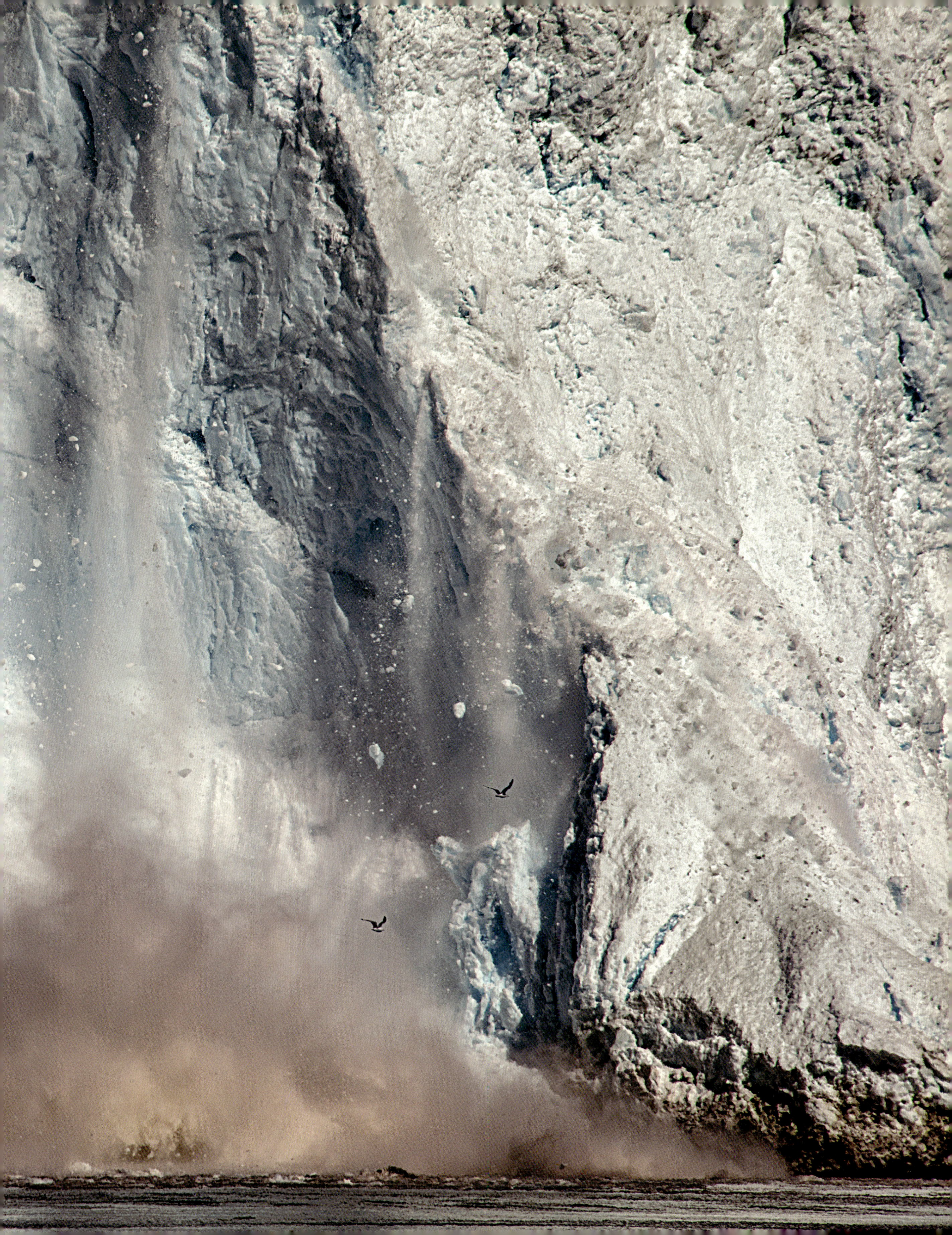

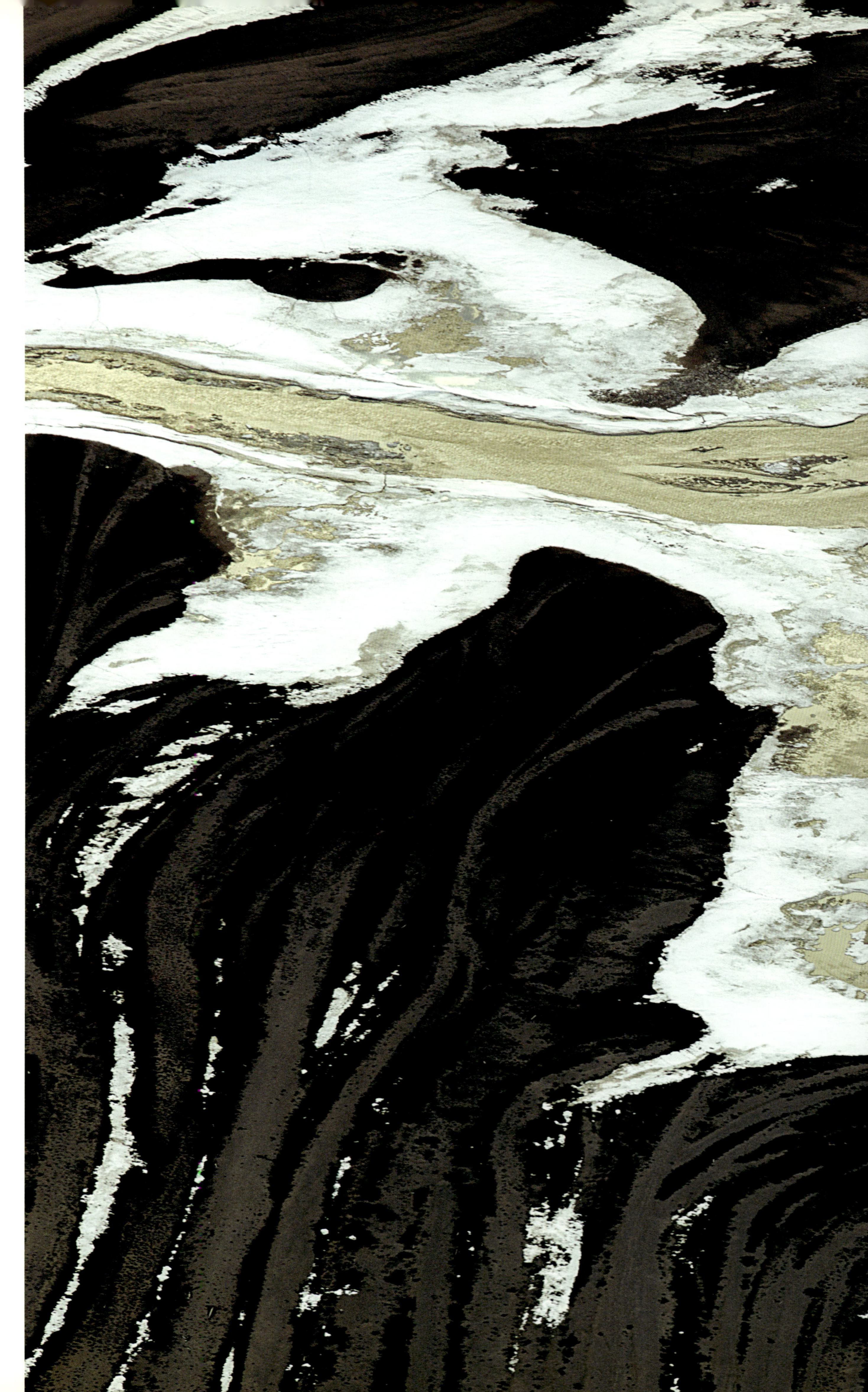

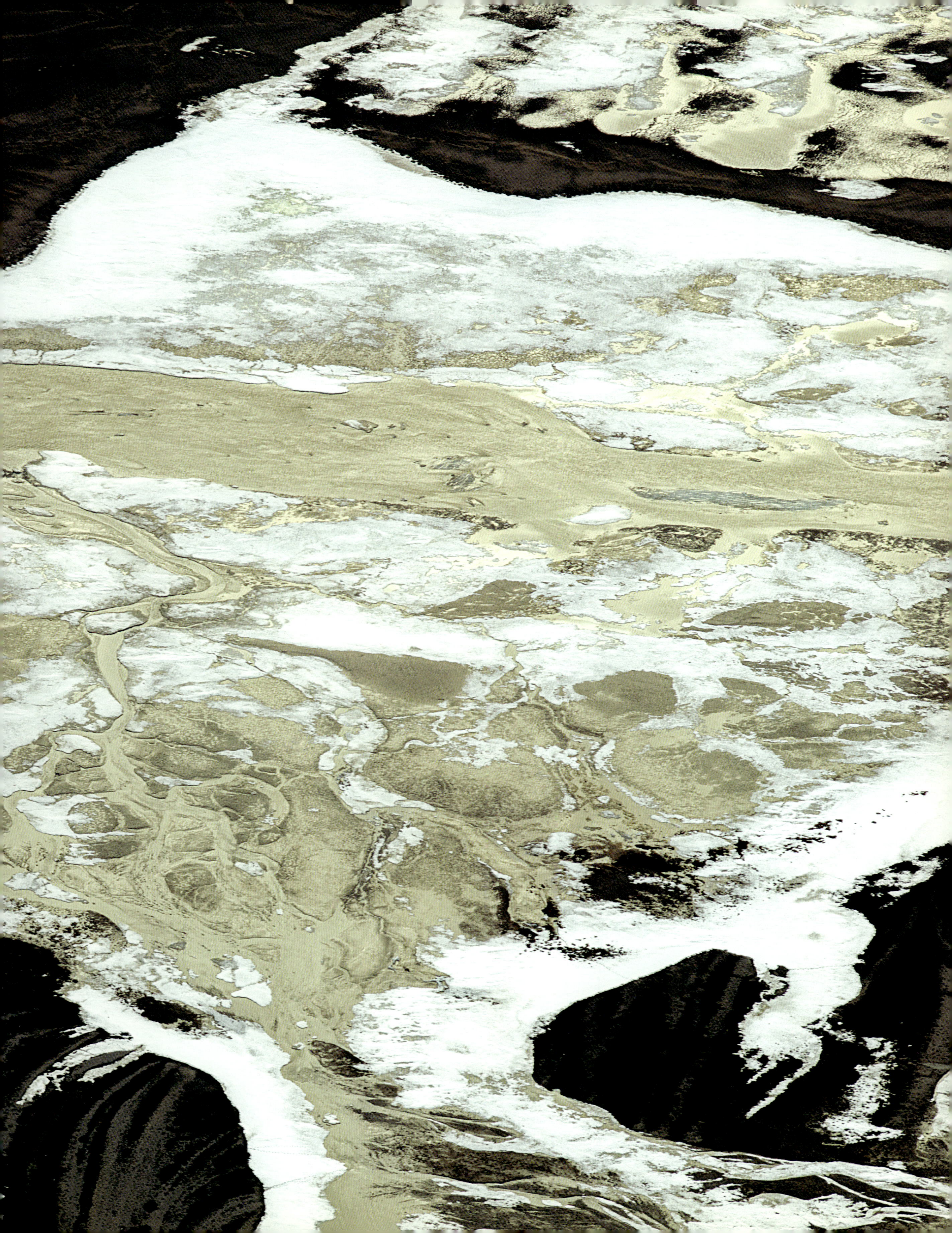

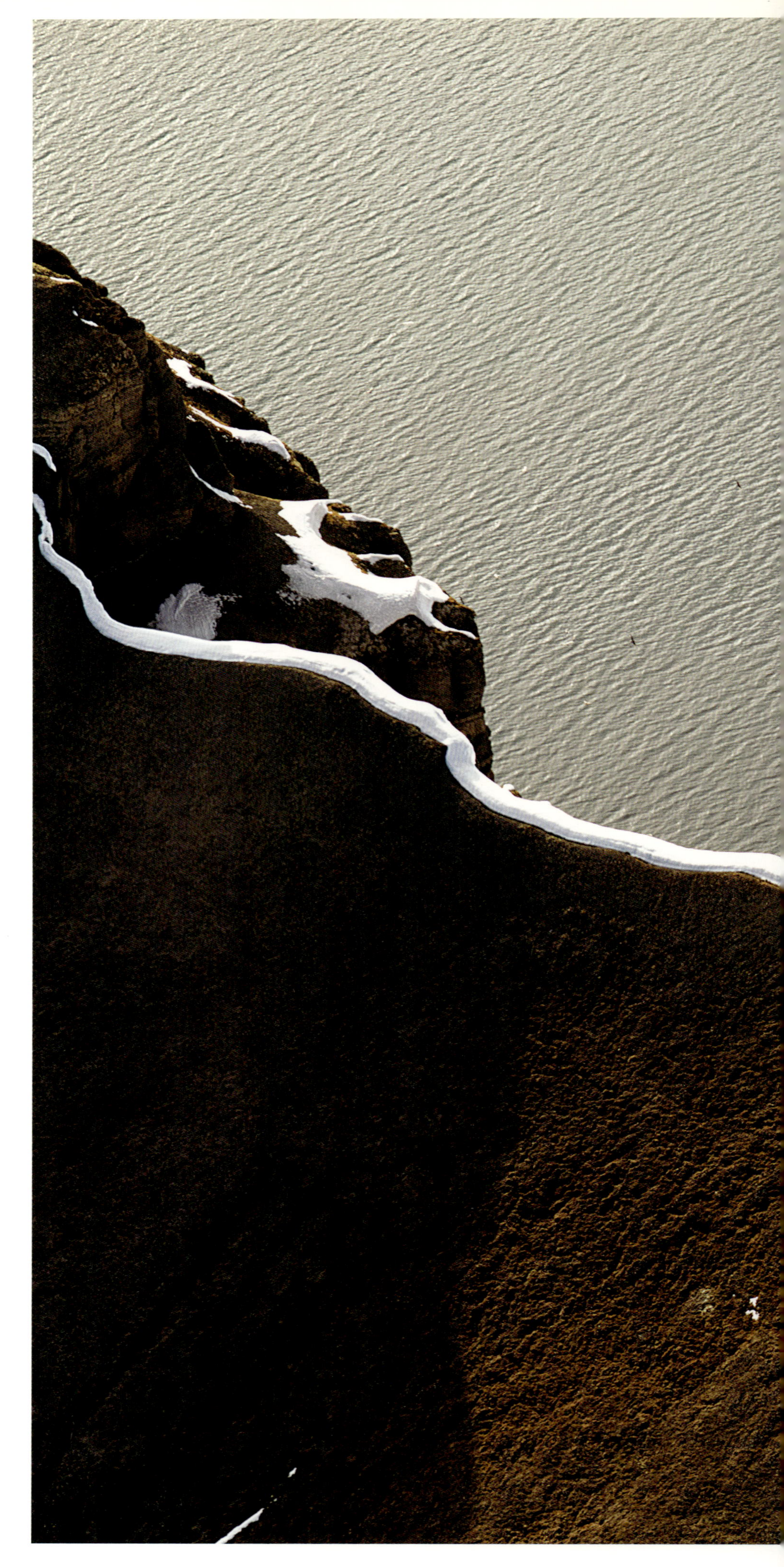

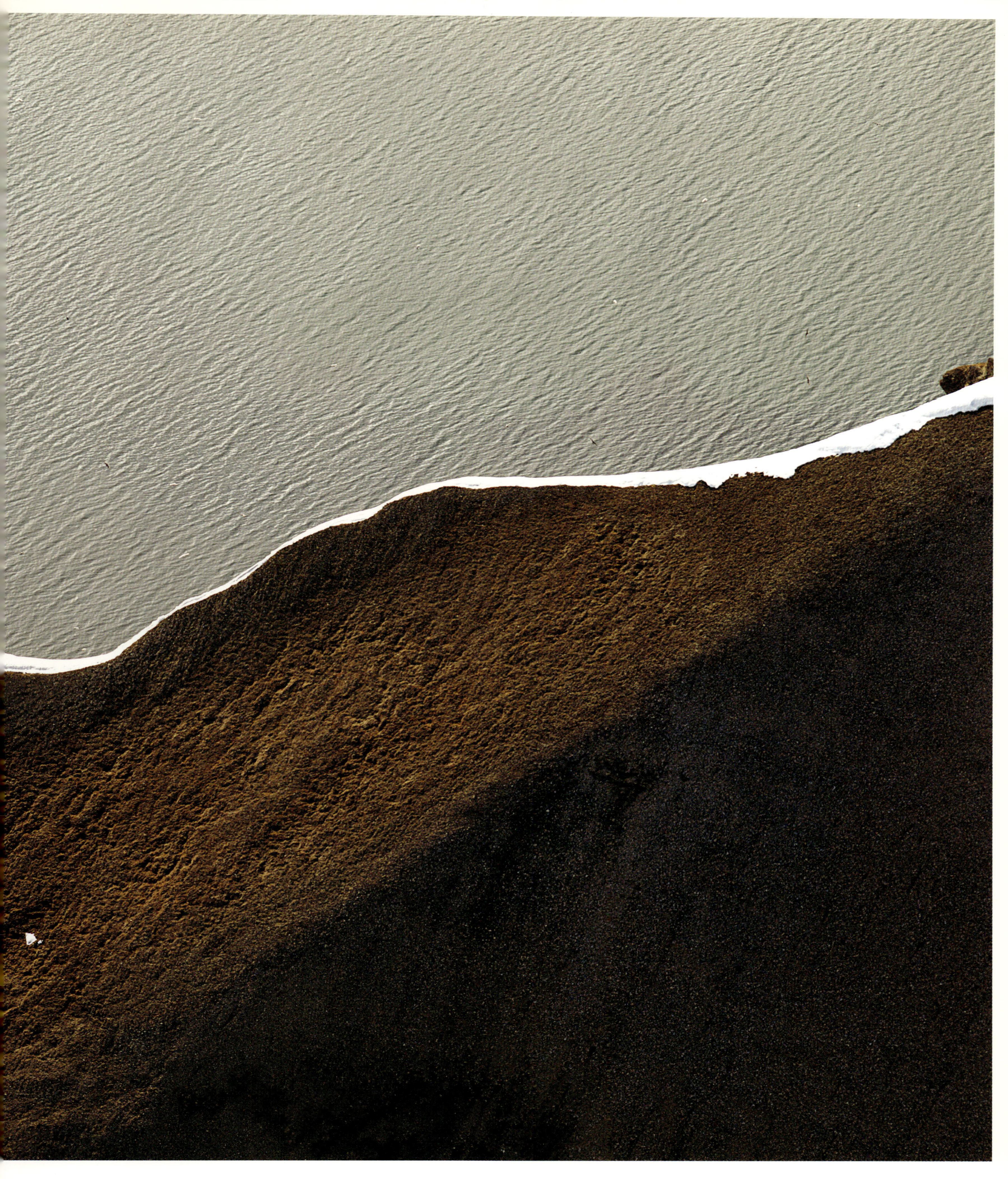

RIDGE OVER ISFJORDEN, NORWAY.
previous pages ICE PATTERNS, WORDIEKAMMEN, SVALBARD, NORWAY.

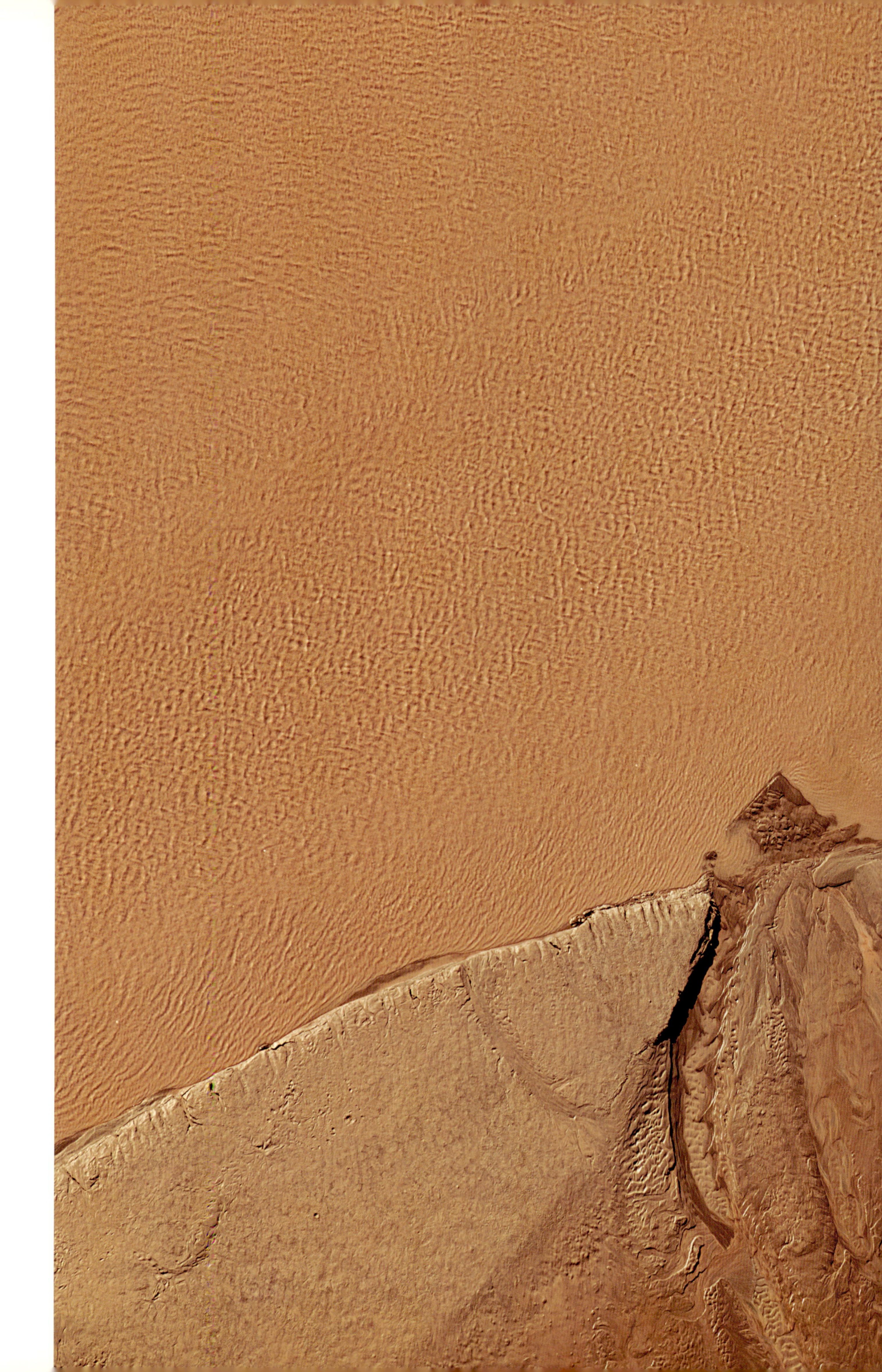

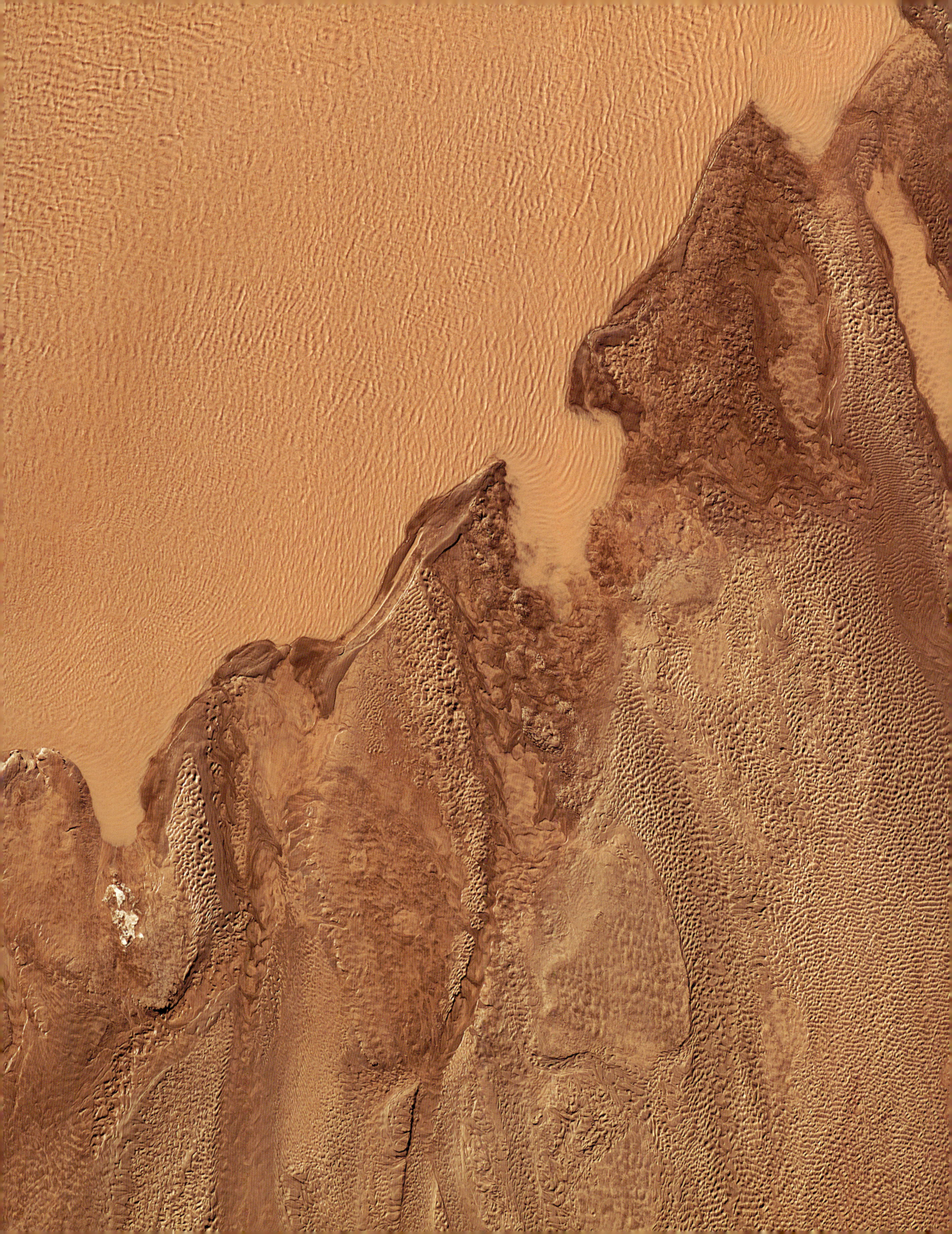

“Let us see how high we can fly before the sun melts the wax in our wings.”

EDWARD O. WILSON

RED SANDSTONE ICE, HOLMSTRÖMØYRA, NORWAY.
previous pages BLOOD RIVER I, WOODFJORDDALEN, SVALBARD, NORWAY.

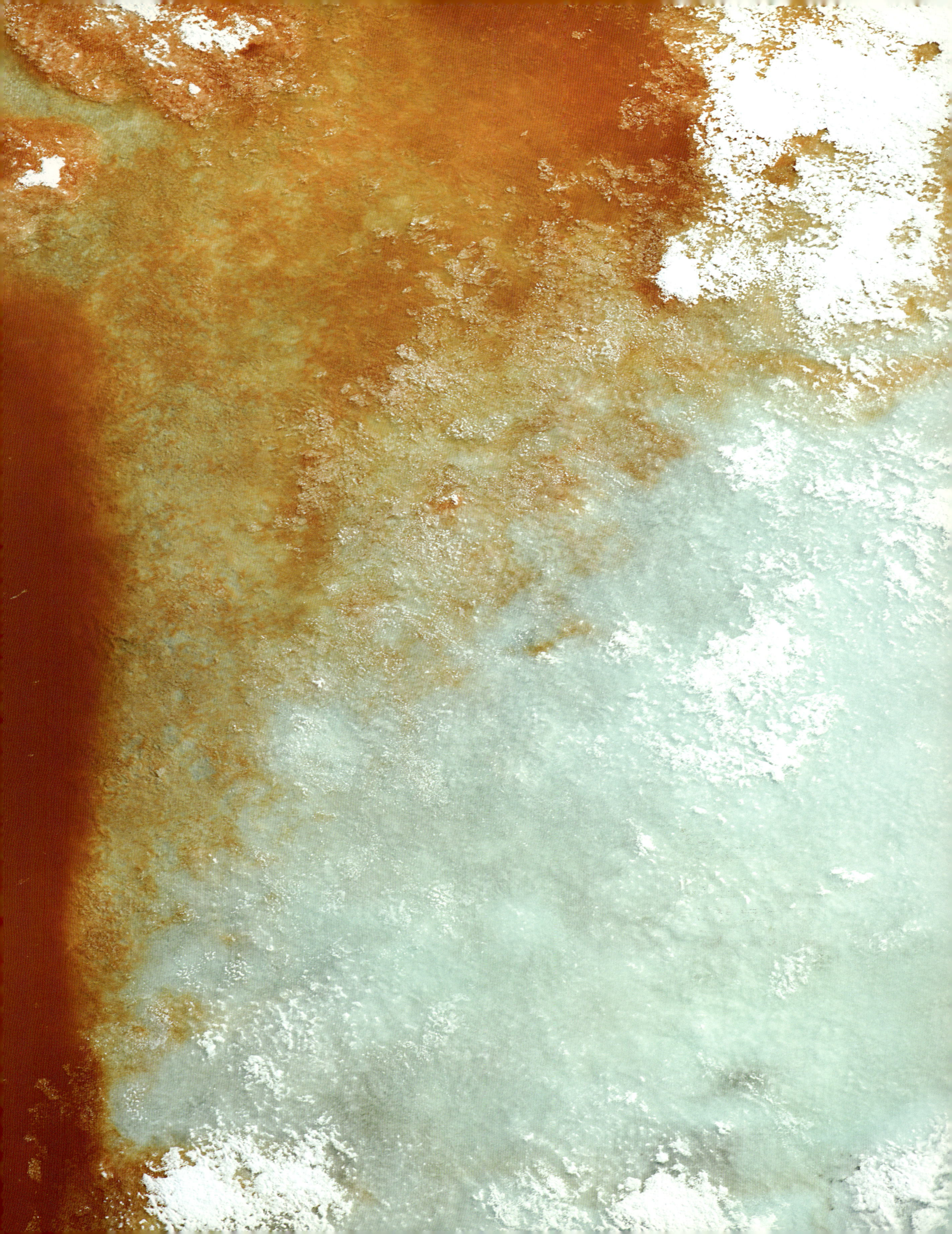

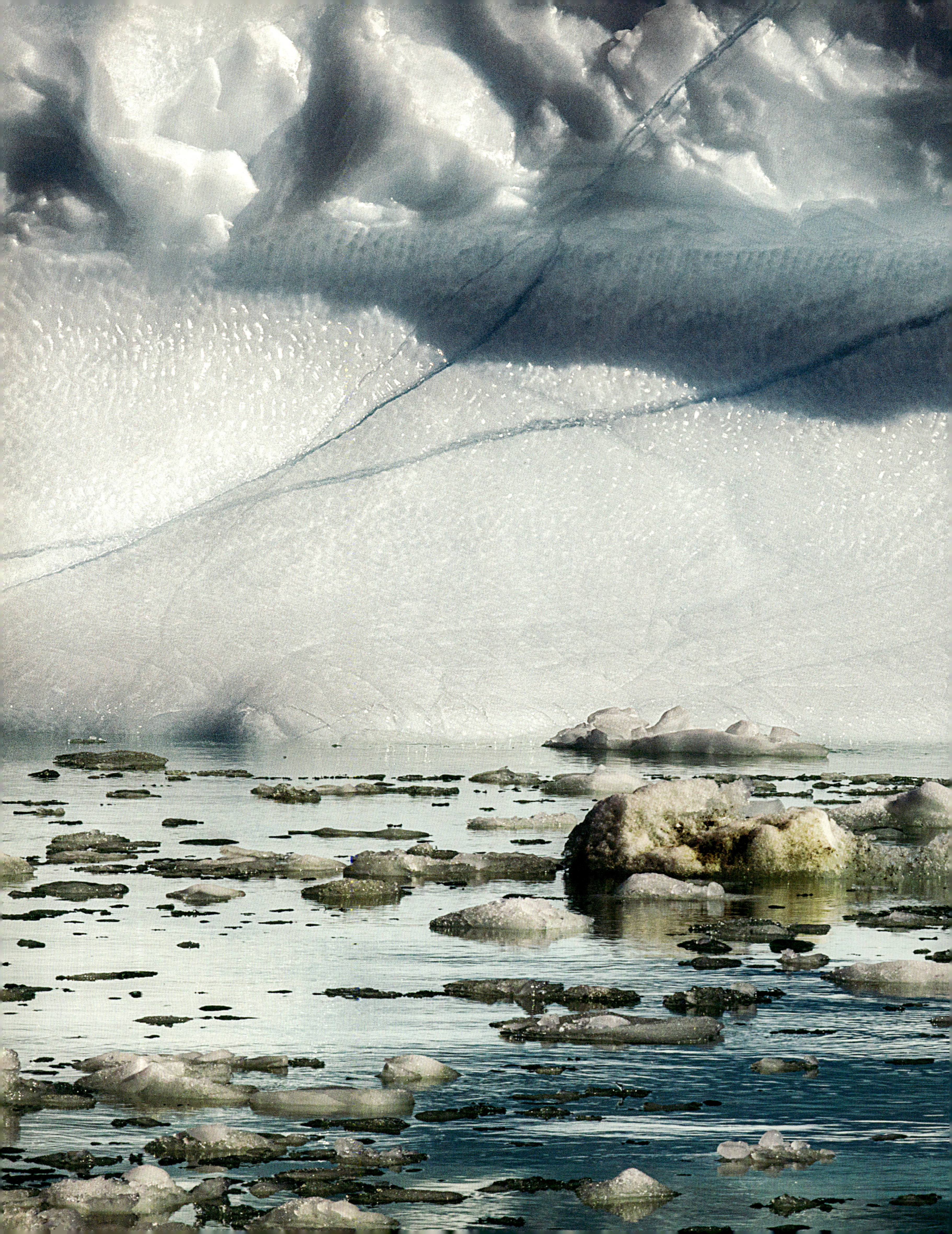

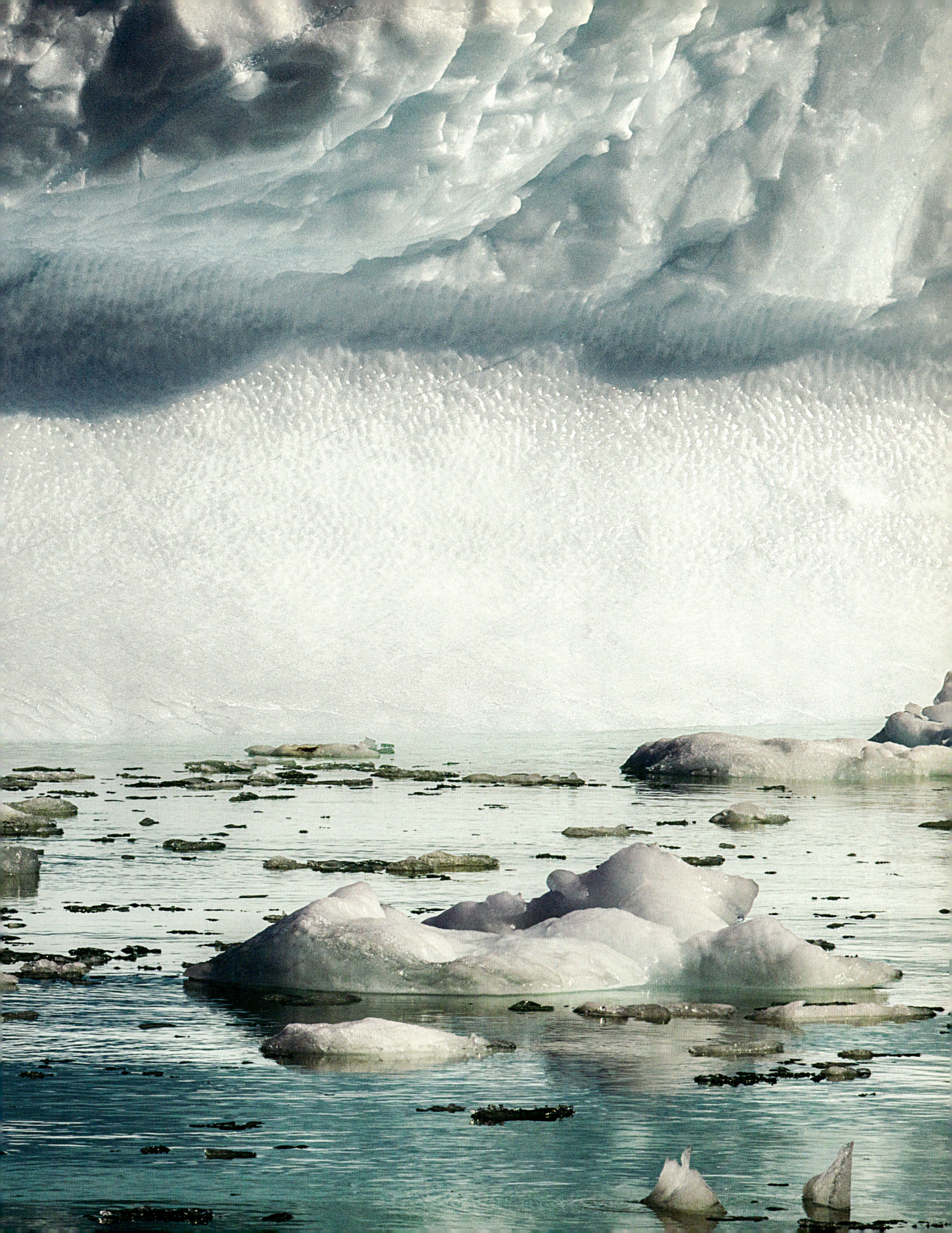

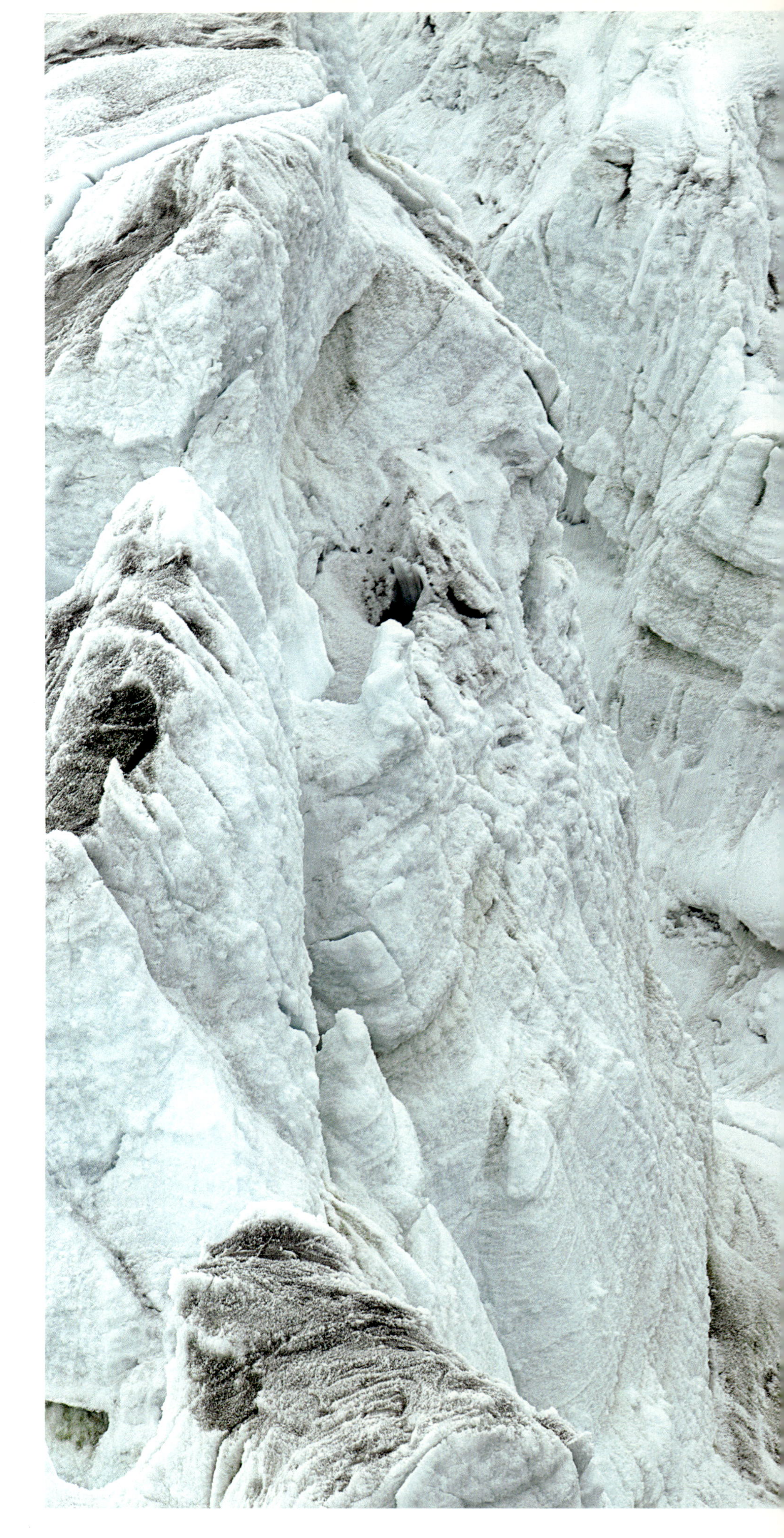

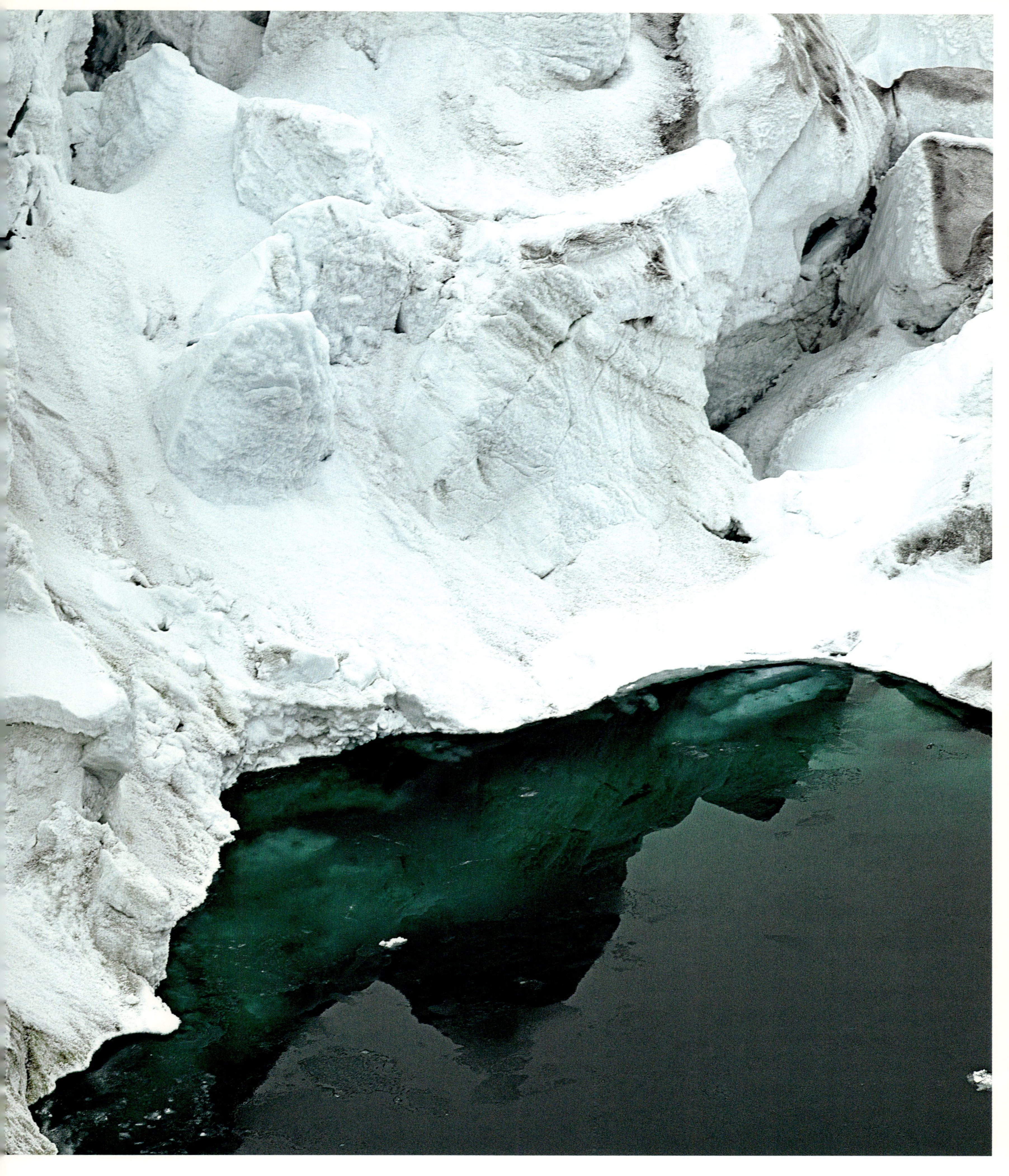

COLLINSON FJORD, FRANZ JOSEPH LAND, NORTHERN BARENTS SEA, 81 DEGREES N, 1 DEGREE C.

previous pages REMNANTS AT 69 DEGREES NORTH, GREENLAND.

following pages LODOWIEC HANS, WEDEL JARLSBERG LAND, SVALBARD, NORWAY.

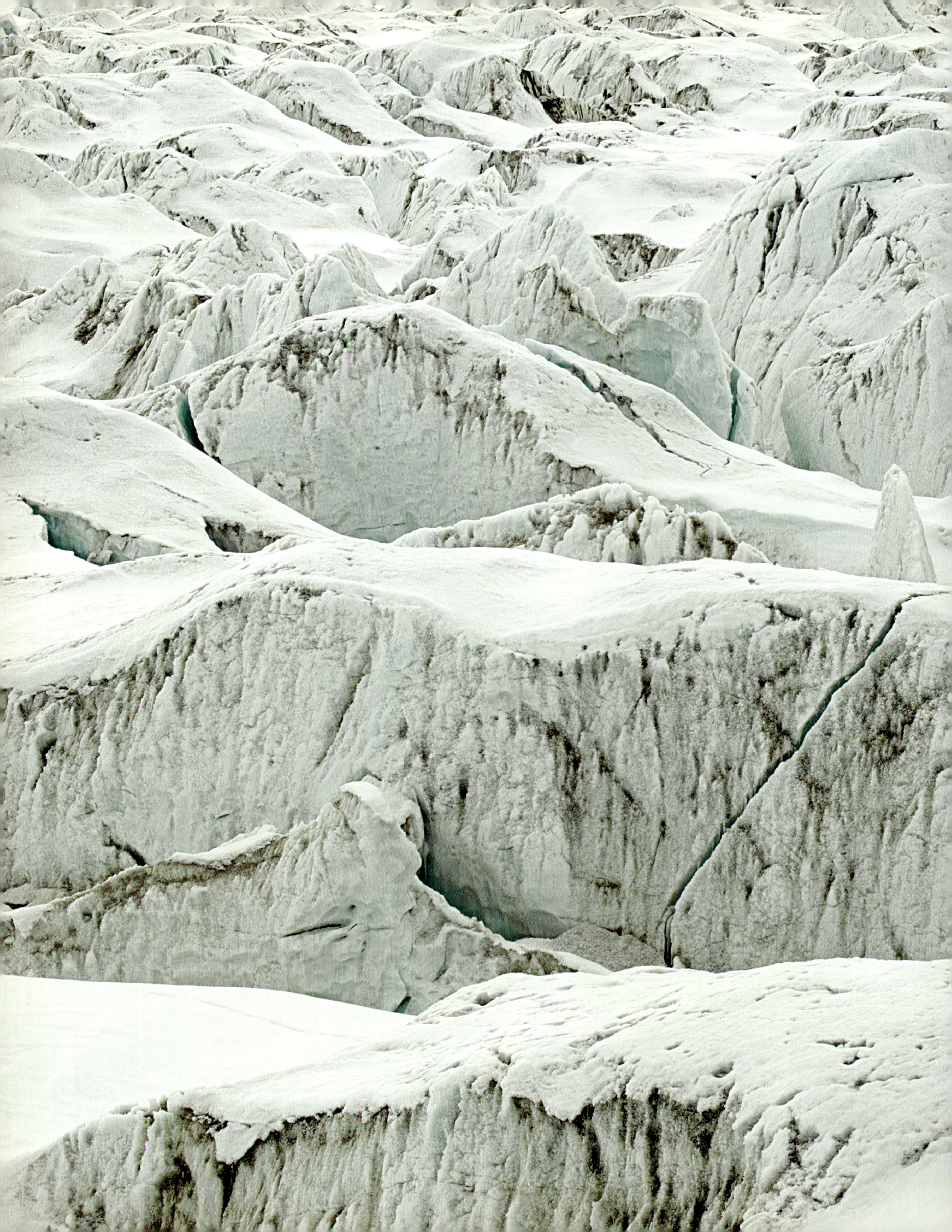

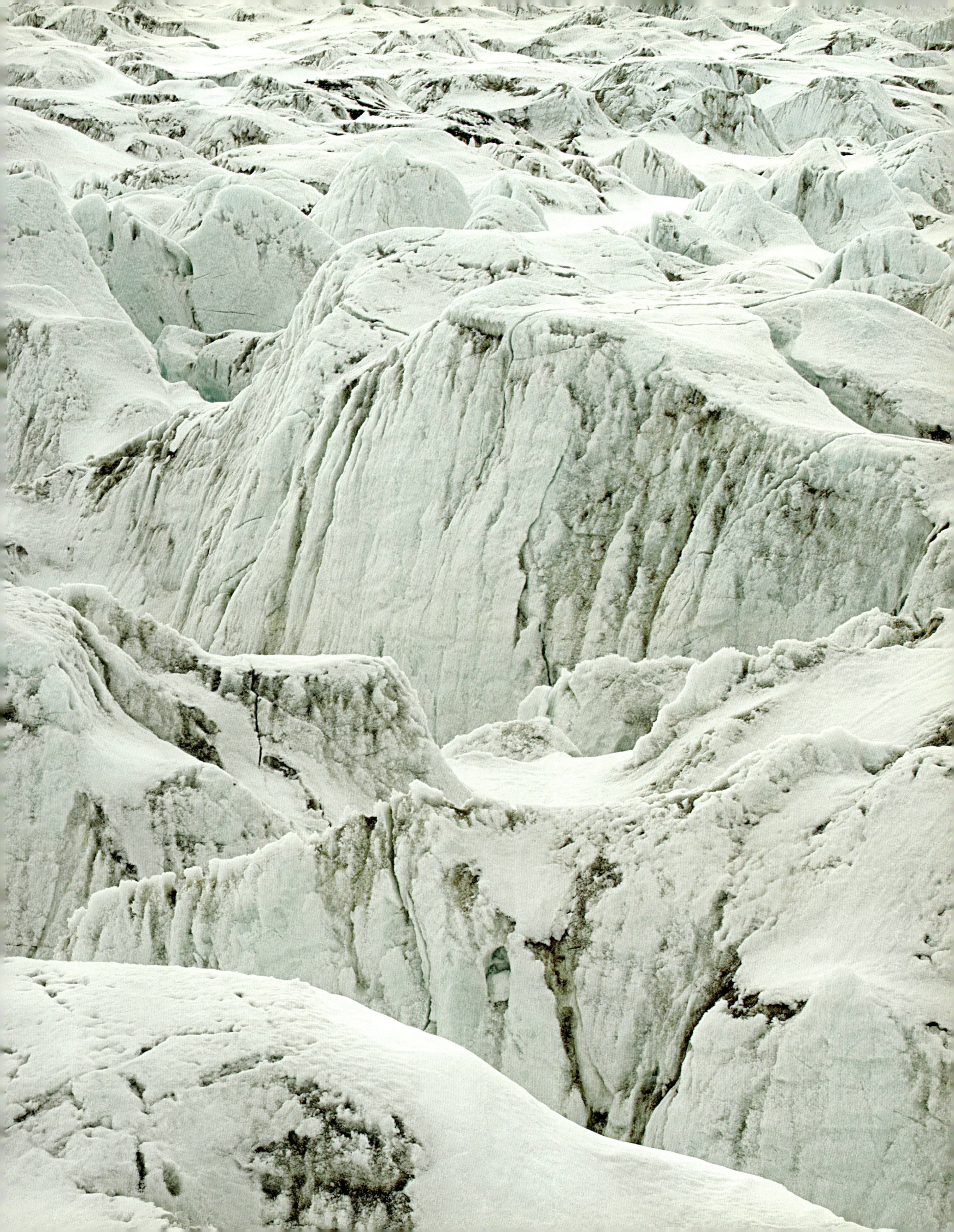

MELTWATER

meltwater ponds carve
silent rising reservoirs
within the ice sheet

transparent lakes drift
resting on changing landscapes
under the low sun

liquid tentacles
crawl throughout hills and valleys
searching for outlets

white quilted pillows
drown in crystal blue water
hoping to escape

pools accumulate
funnel into deep moulins
going out to sea

ice erodes slowly
answers the atmosphere
memories of snow

MELTWATER FLOW, GREENLAND ICE SHEET.

following pages MELTWATER LAKE, NORTHERN GLACIER, GREENLAND.

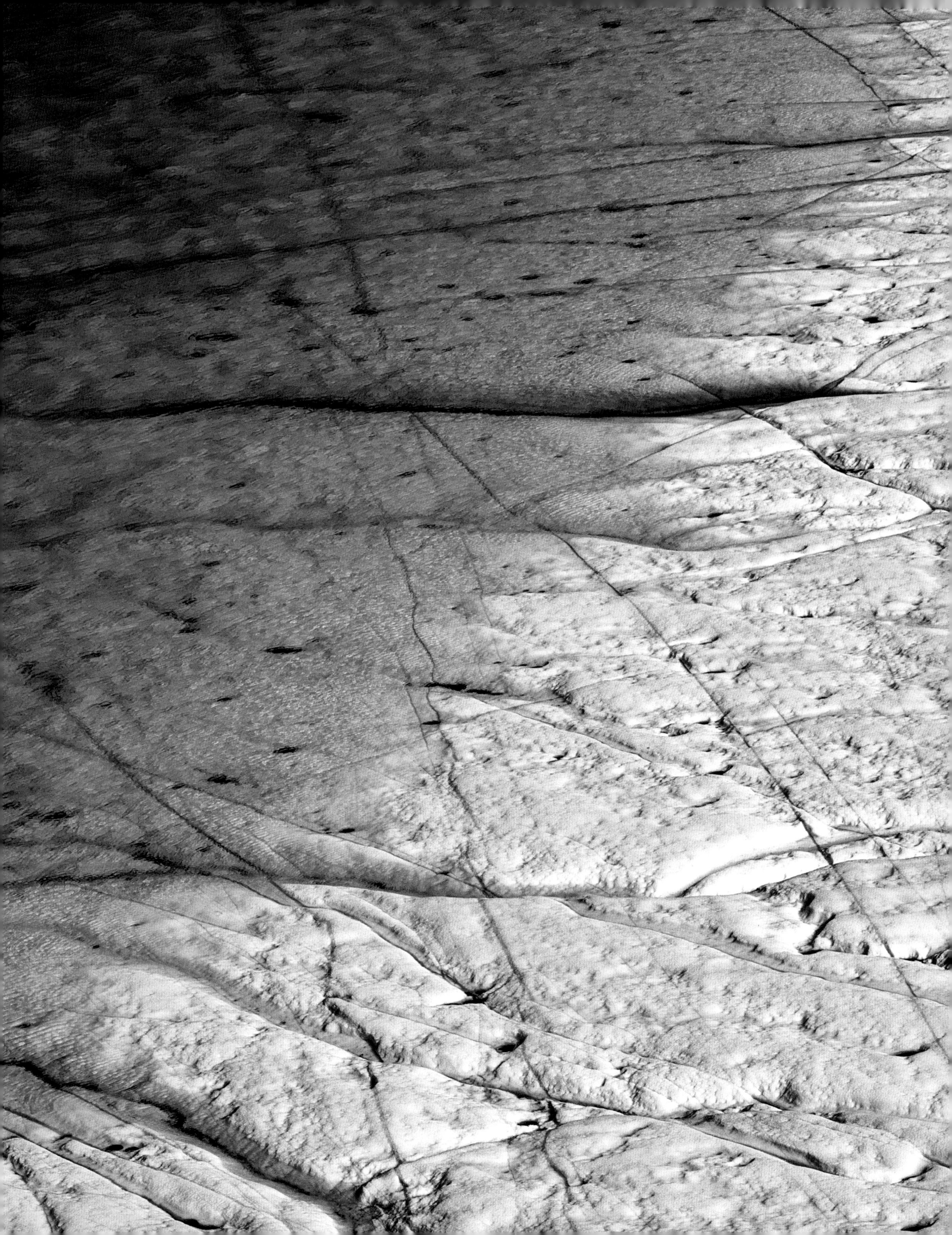

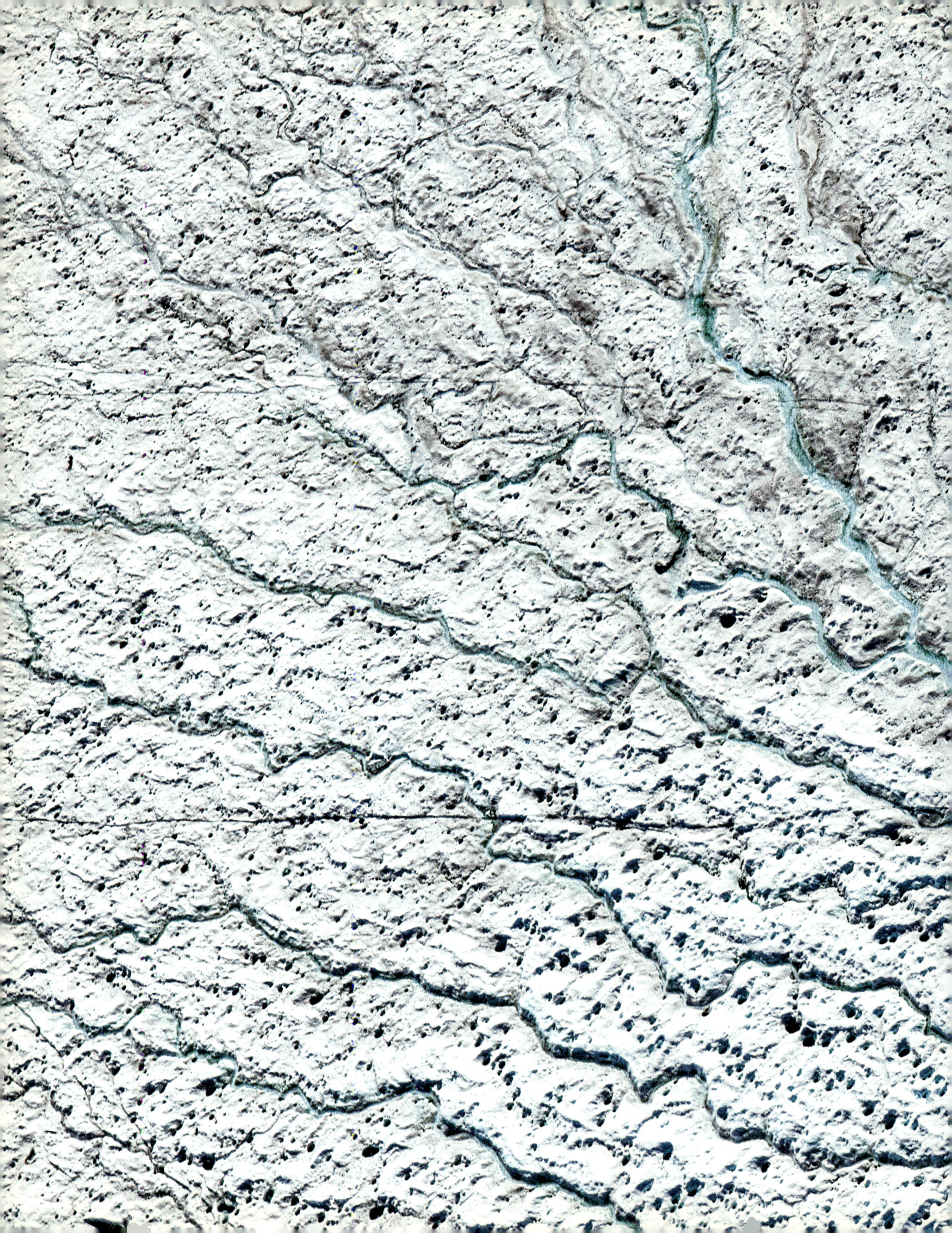

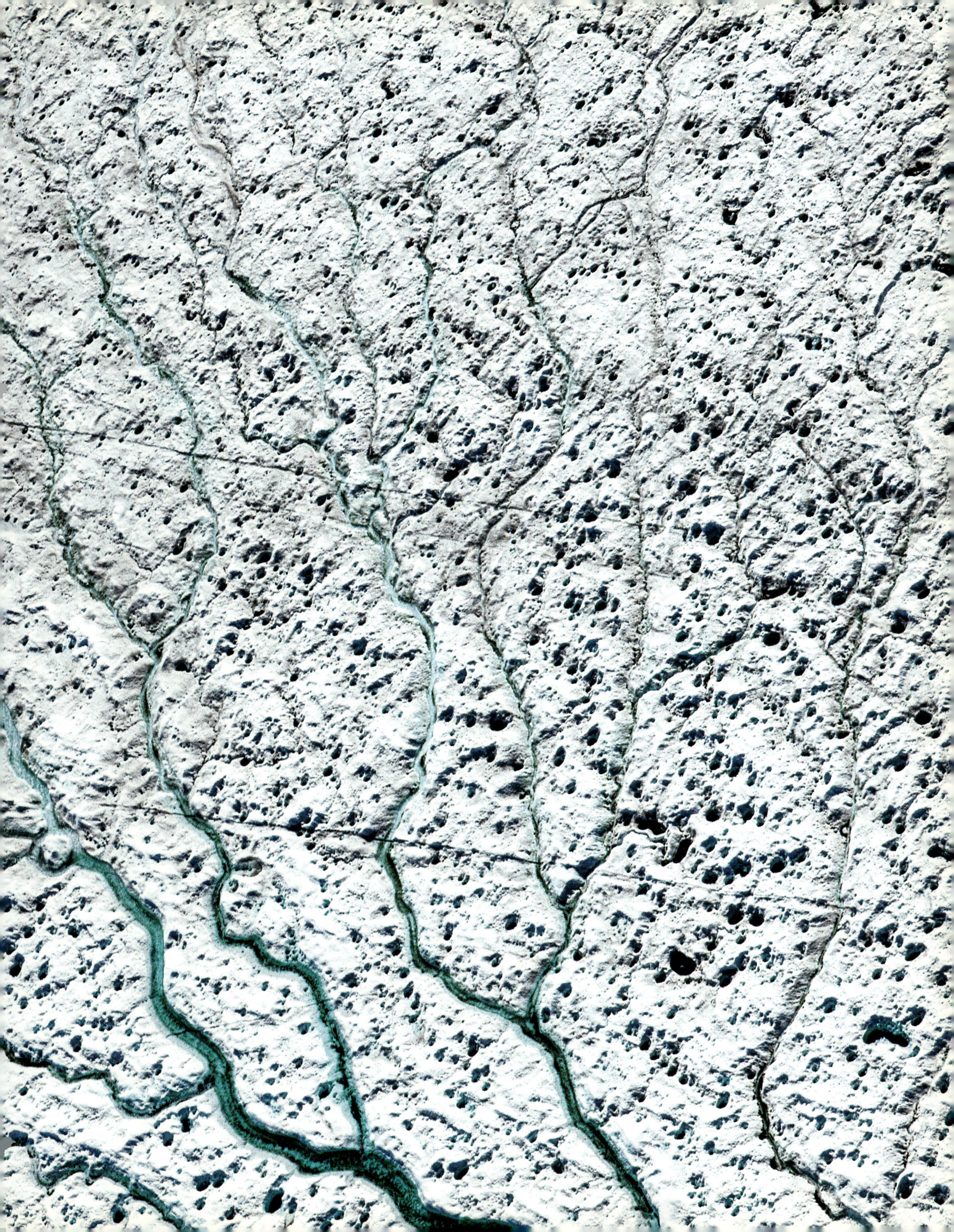

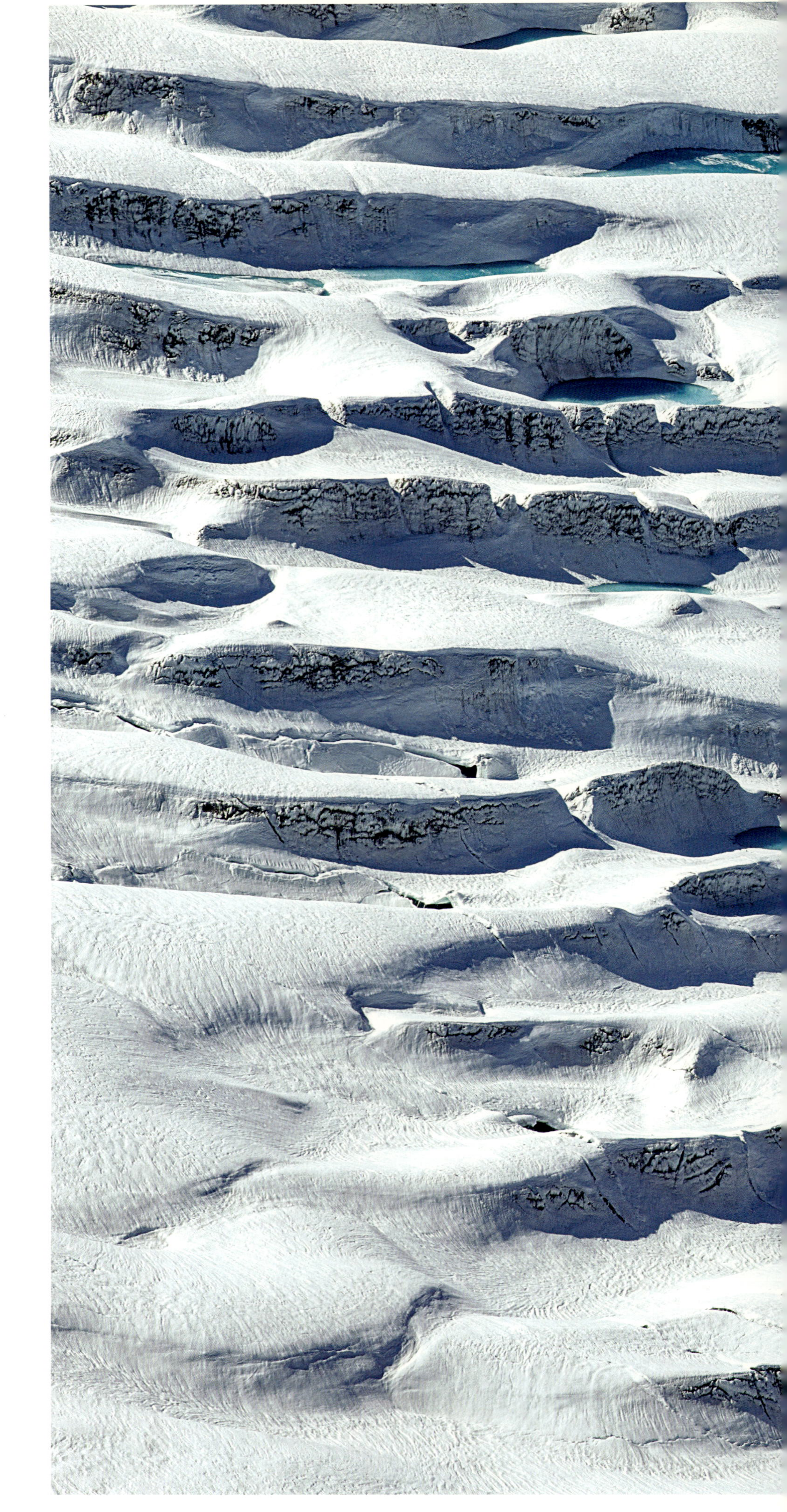

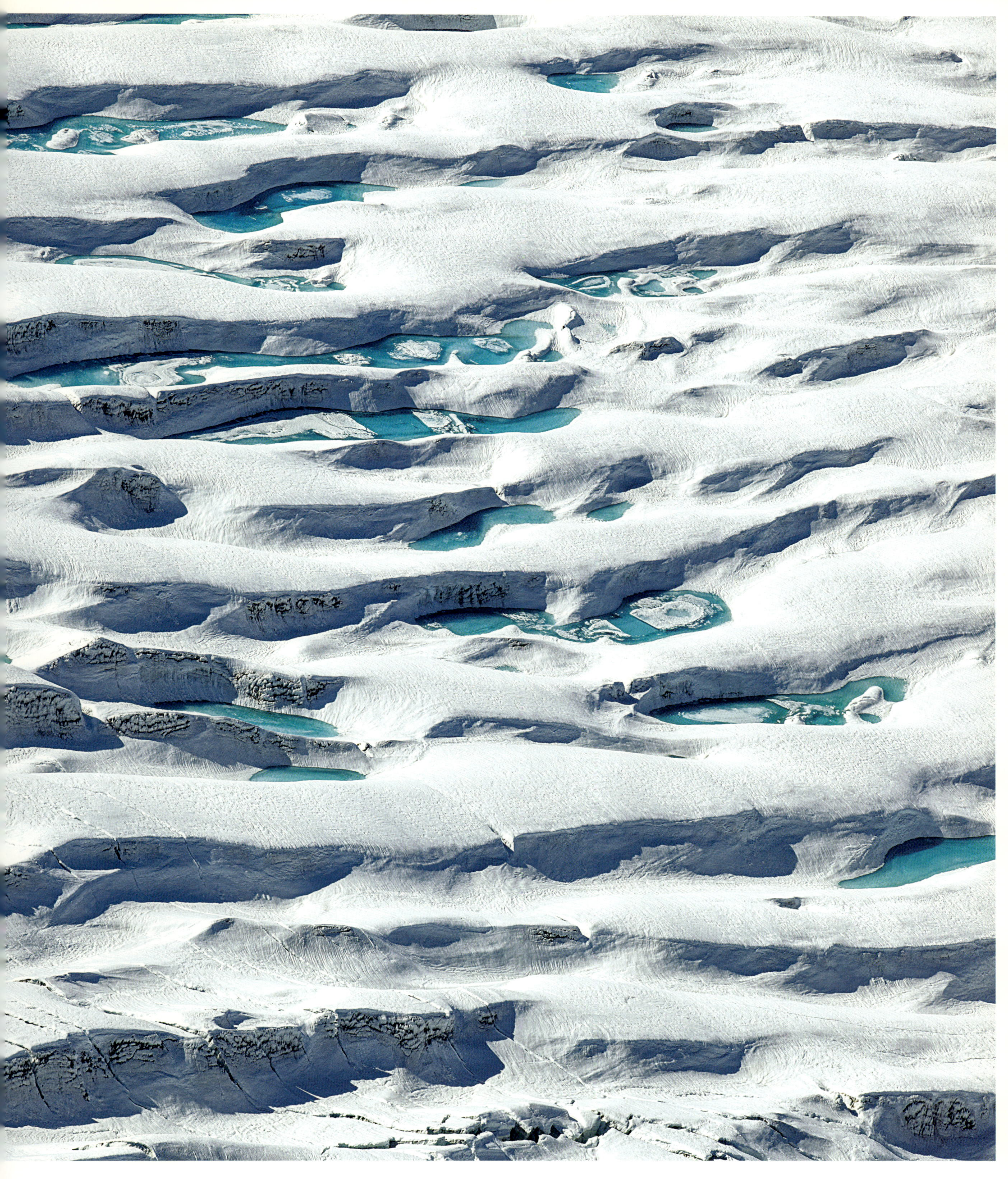

WAHLENBERGBREEN, SPITSBERGEN, NORWAY, 4:27 PM.
previous pages THE GREENLAND ICE SHEET, JULY 16, 2016.

“The Arctic is a camera giving warnings about the health of the planet.”

GRETEL EHRLICH

MELTWATER PONDS, WAHLENBERGBREEN, SPITSBERGEN, NORWAY.

following pages FORMATIONS AT NATHORSTBREEN, SPITSBERGEN, NORWAY.

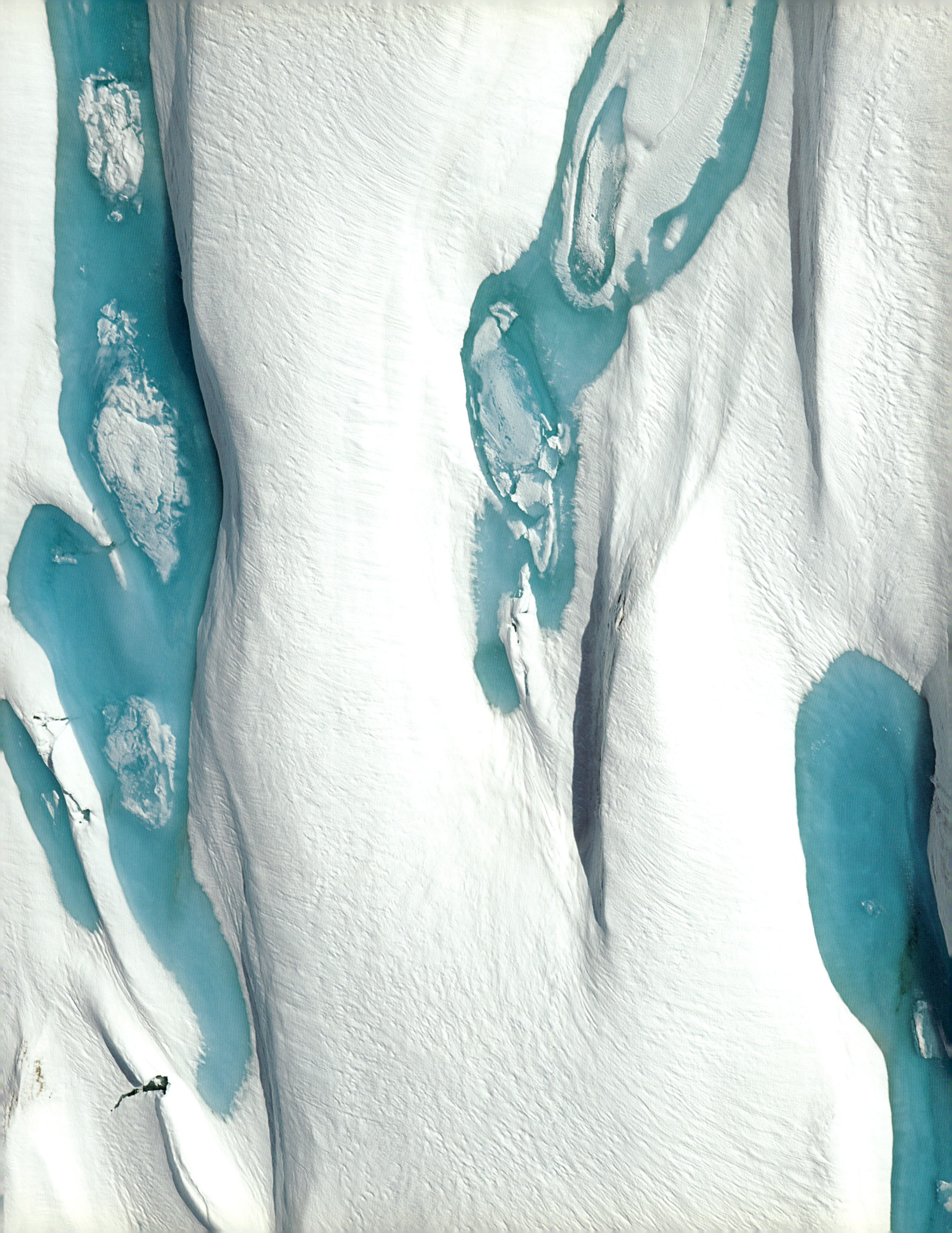

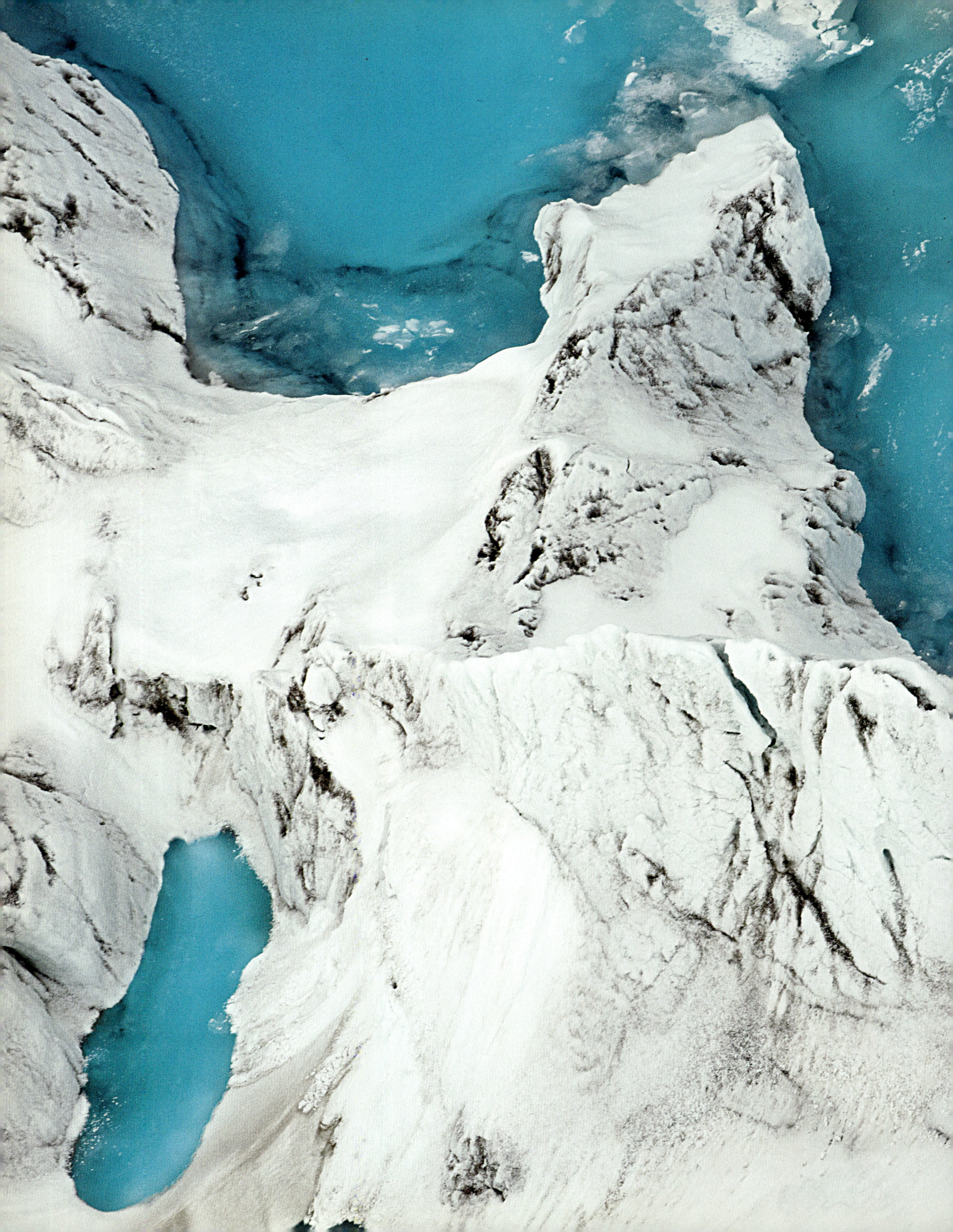

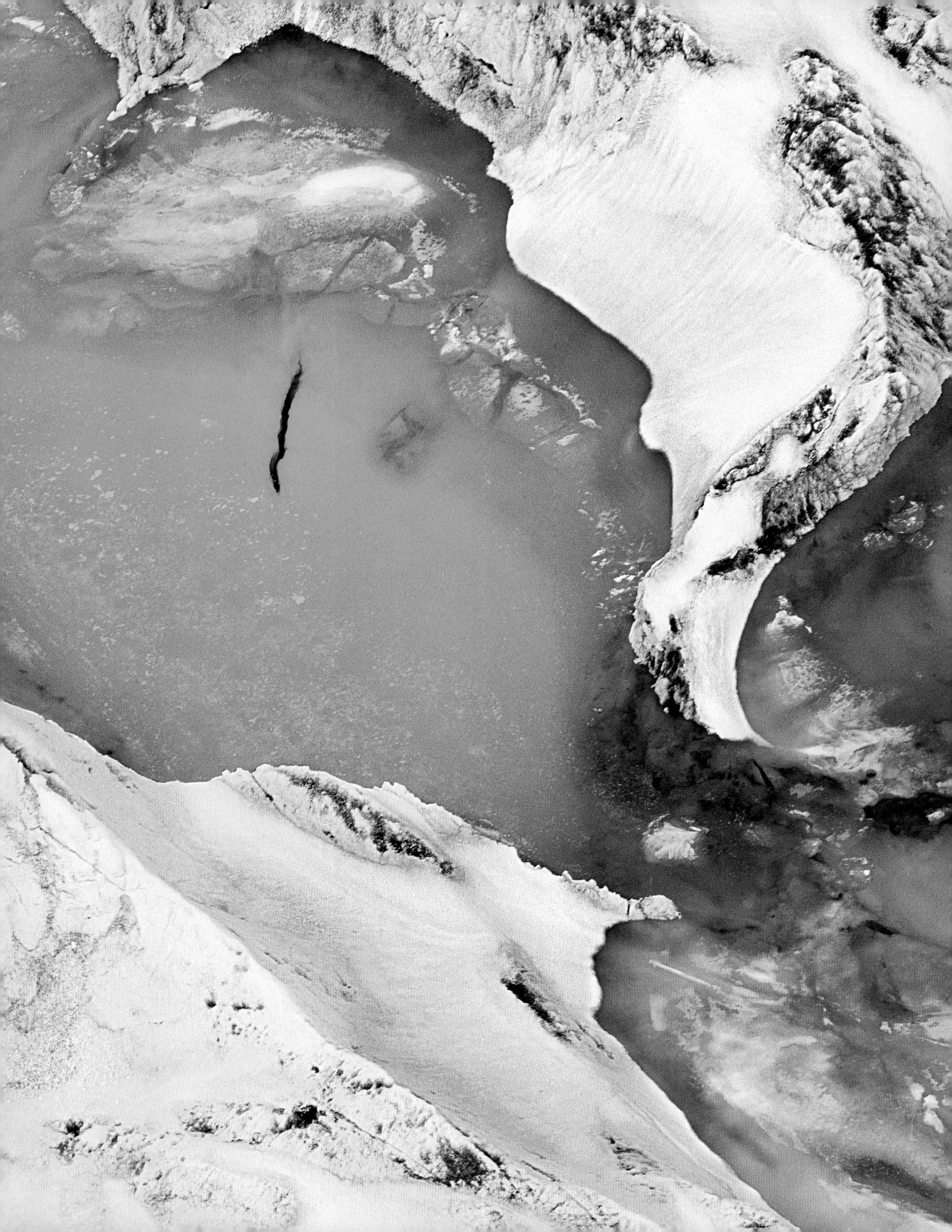

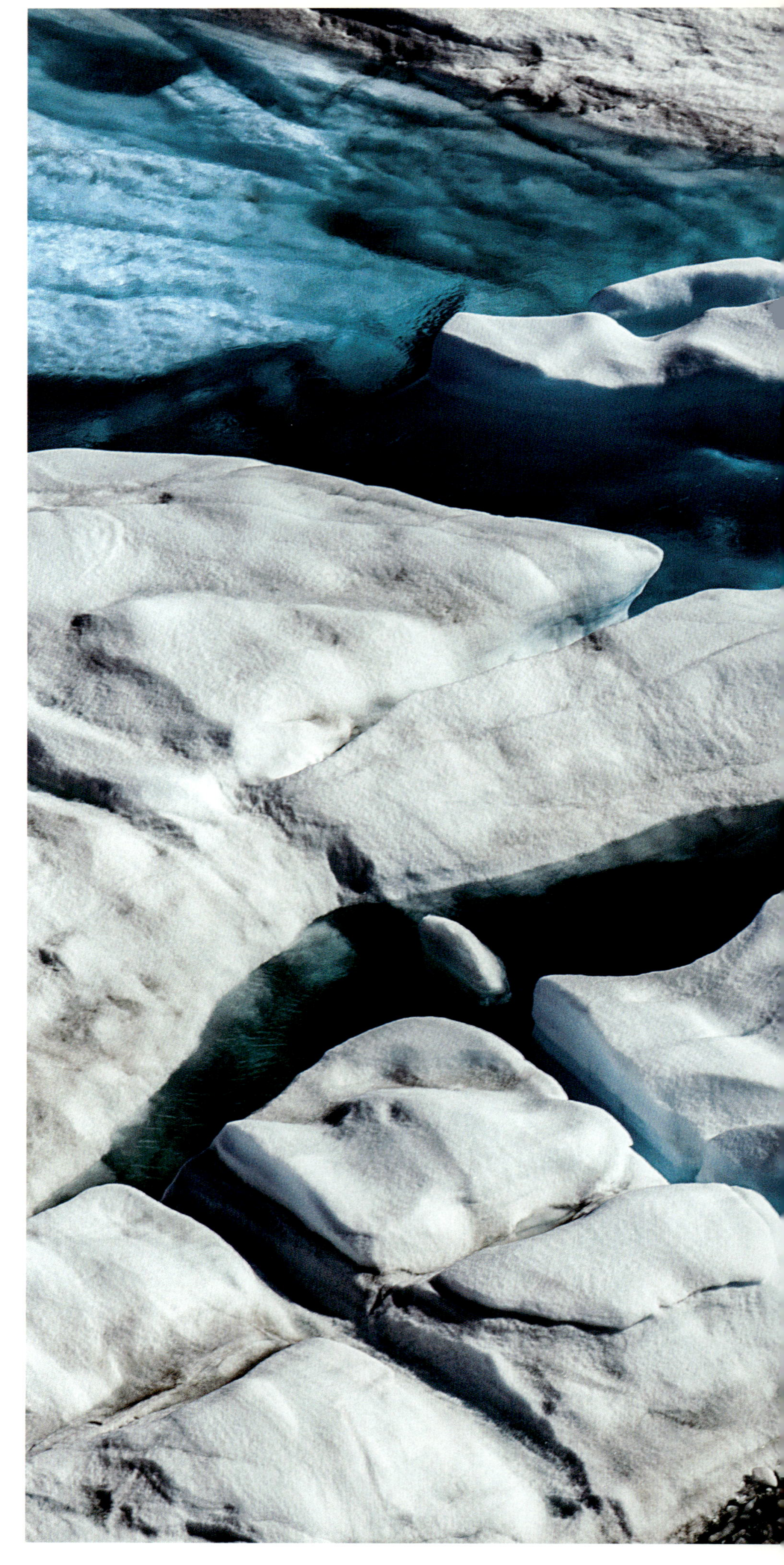

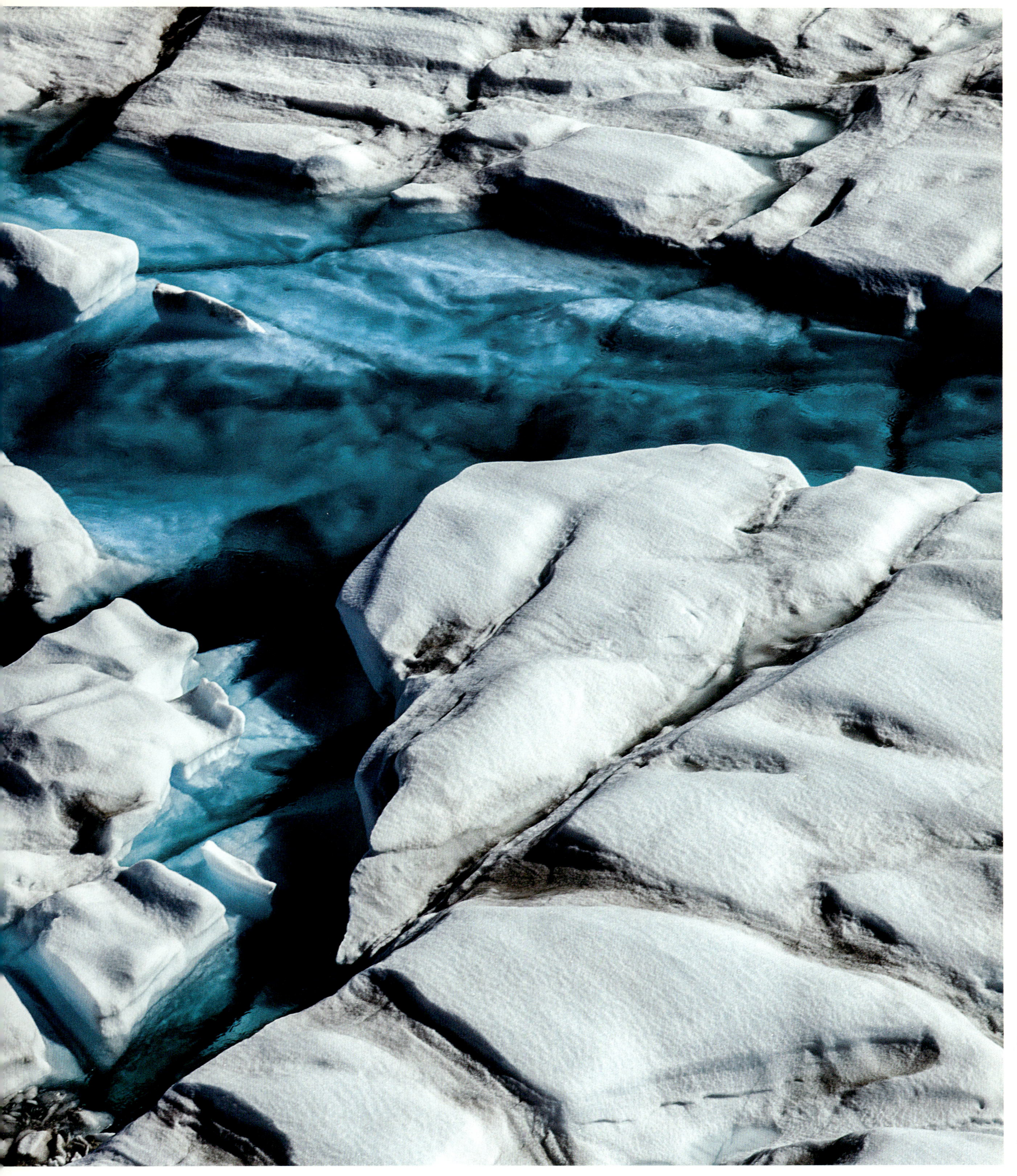

MELTWATER, GREENLAND ICE SHEET.

following pages SEASCAPE, GREENLAND CE SHEET.

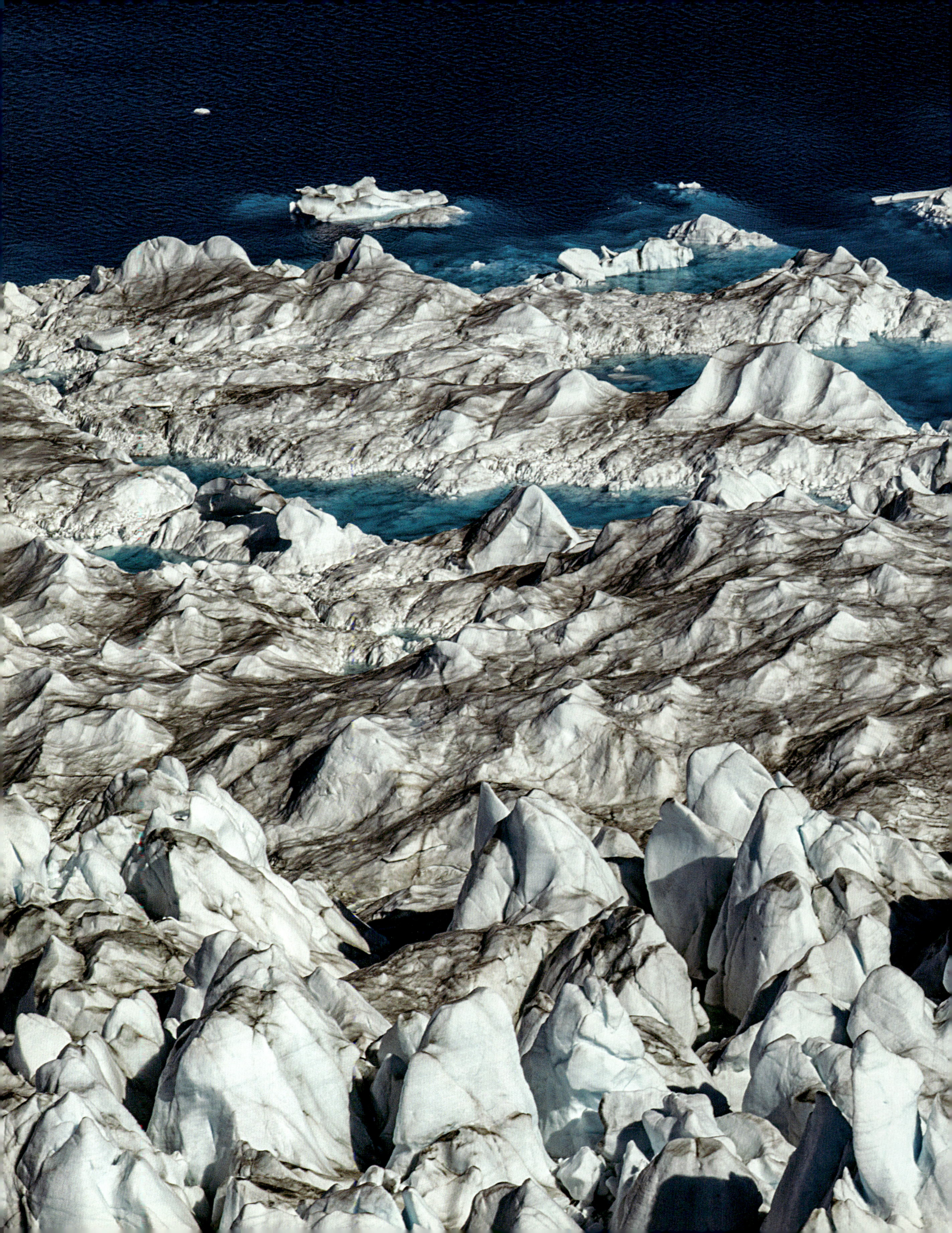

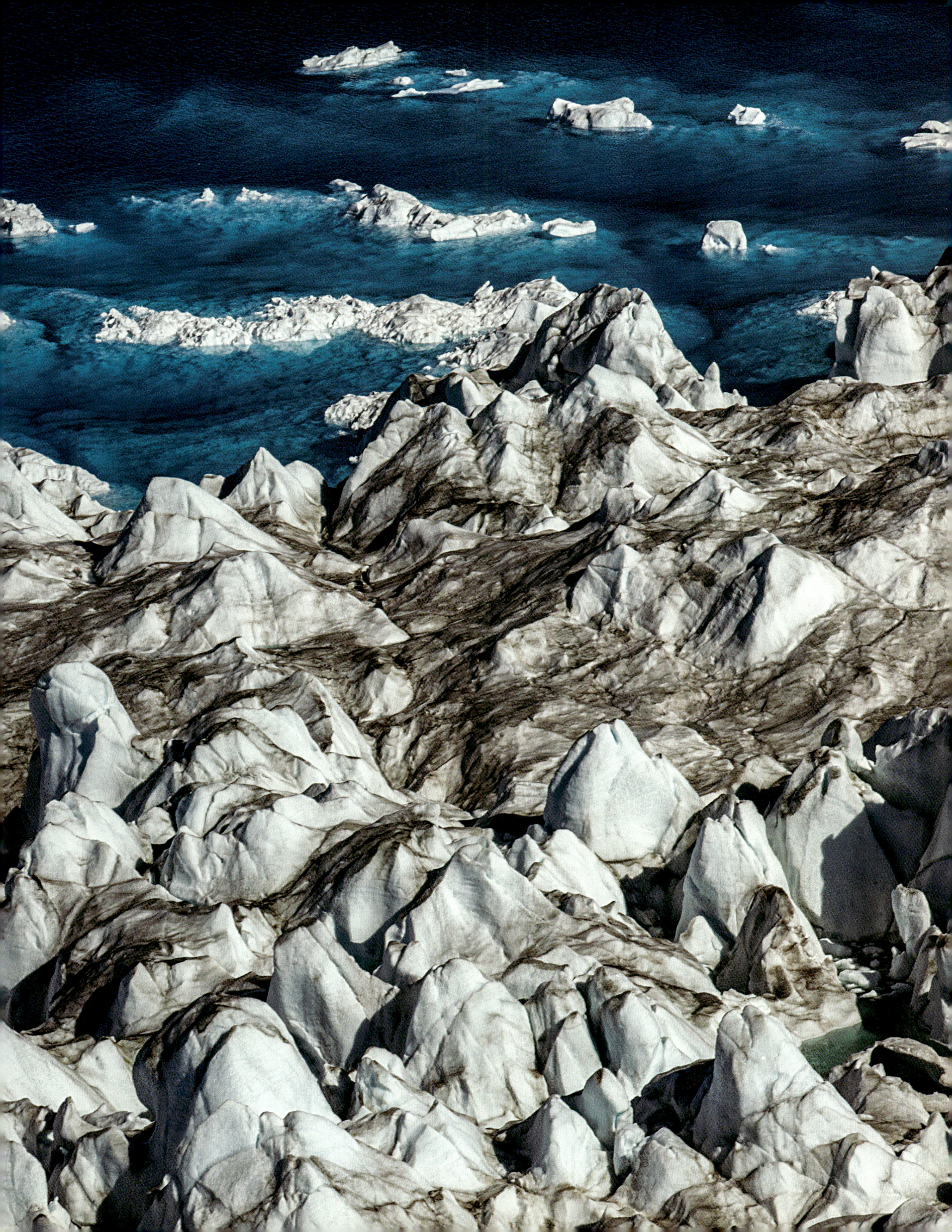

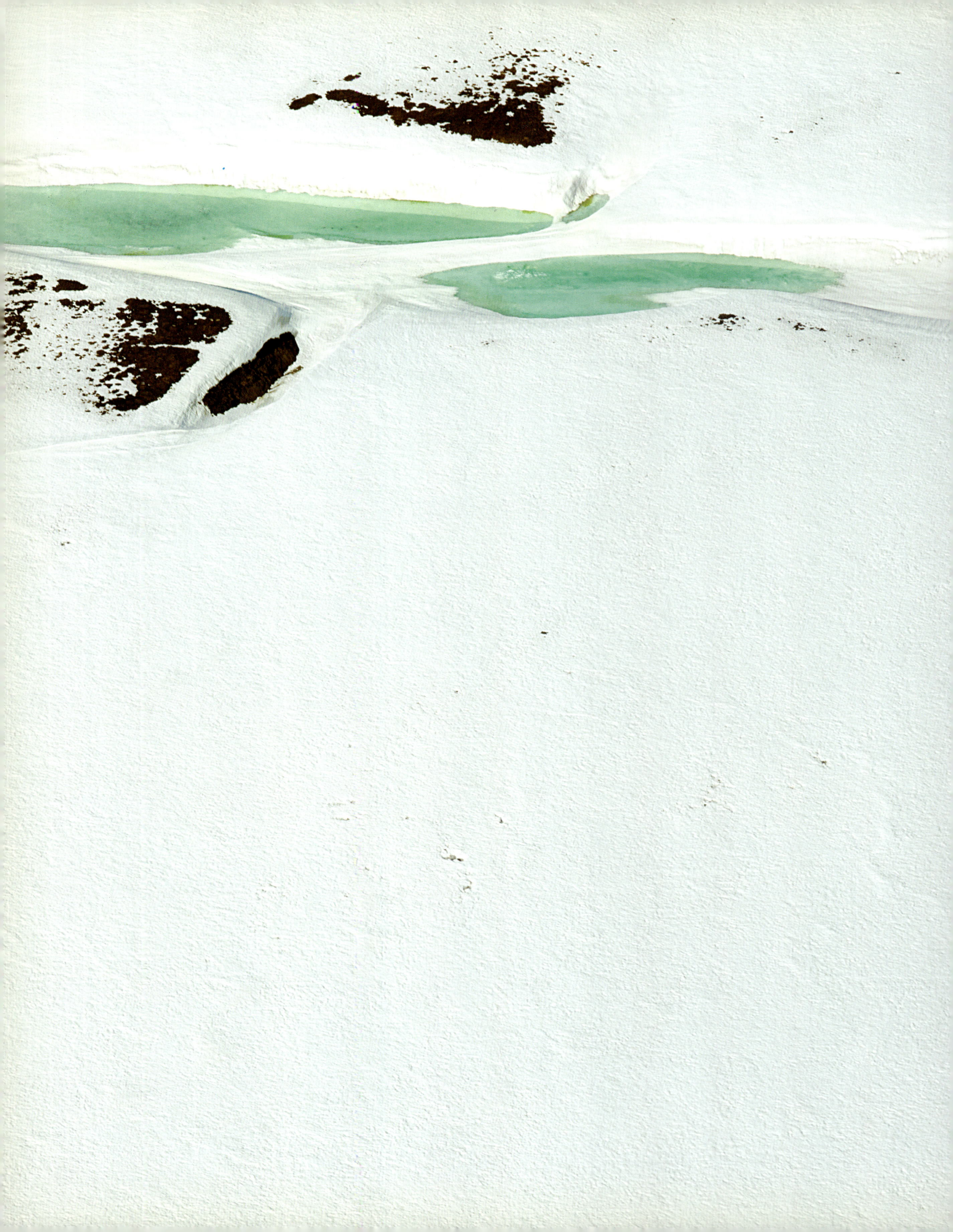

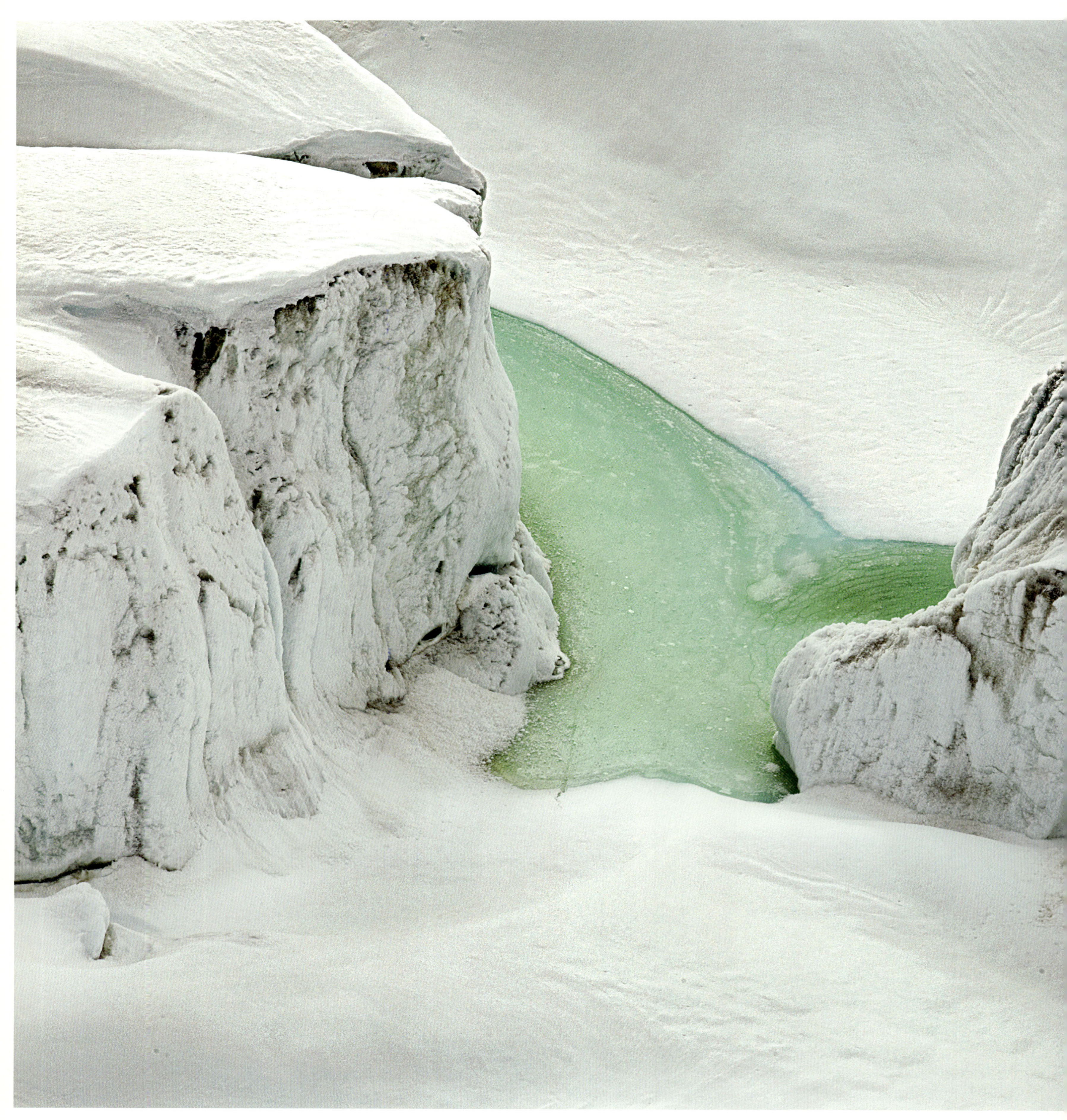

GLACIAL SPLIT AT 79 DEGREES N, WEDEL JARLSBERG LAND, NORWAY.
previous pages THREE ELEMENTS, SPITSBERGEN, NORWAY.
following pages BELOW THE SURFACE, GREENLAND ICE SHEET, 70 DEGREES N.

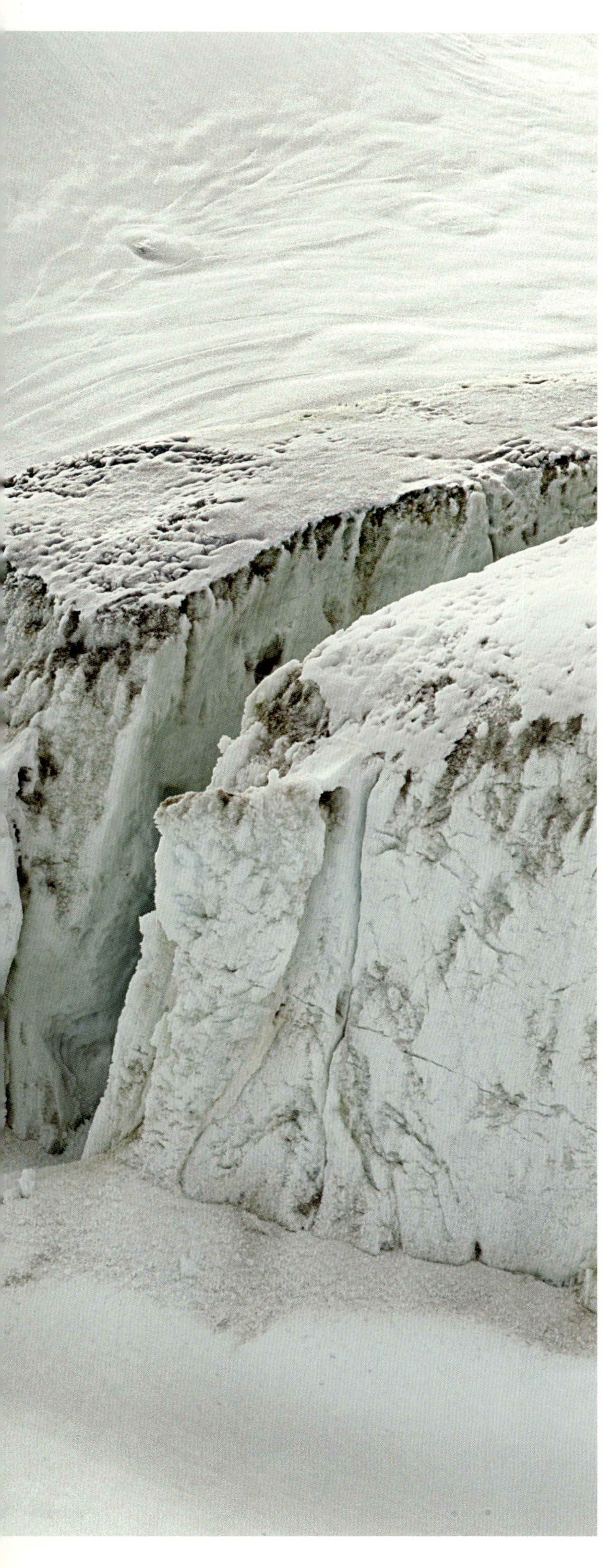

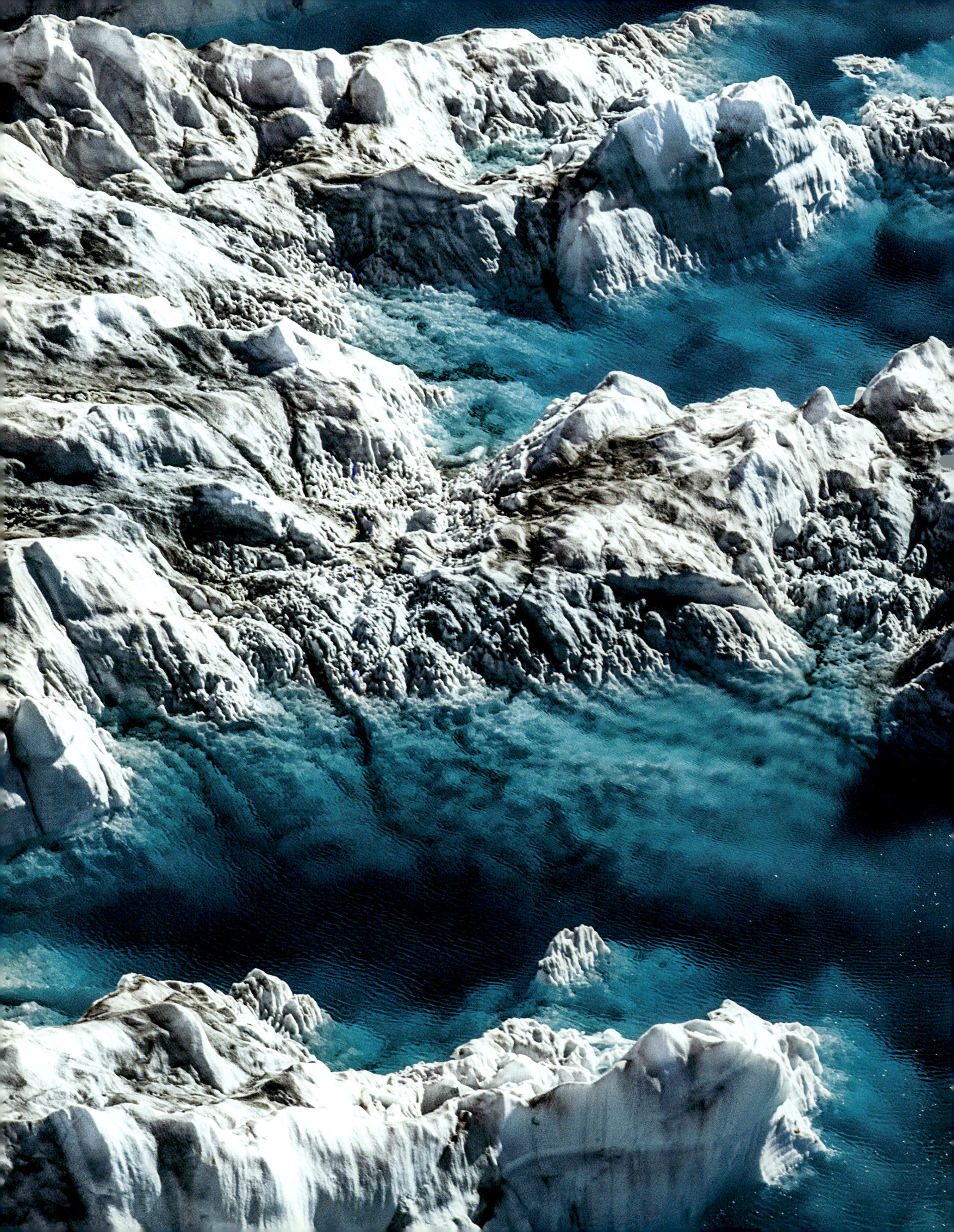

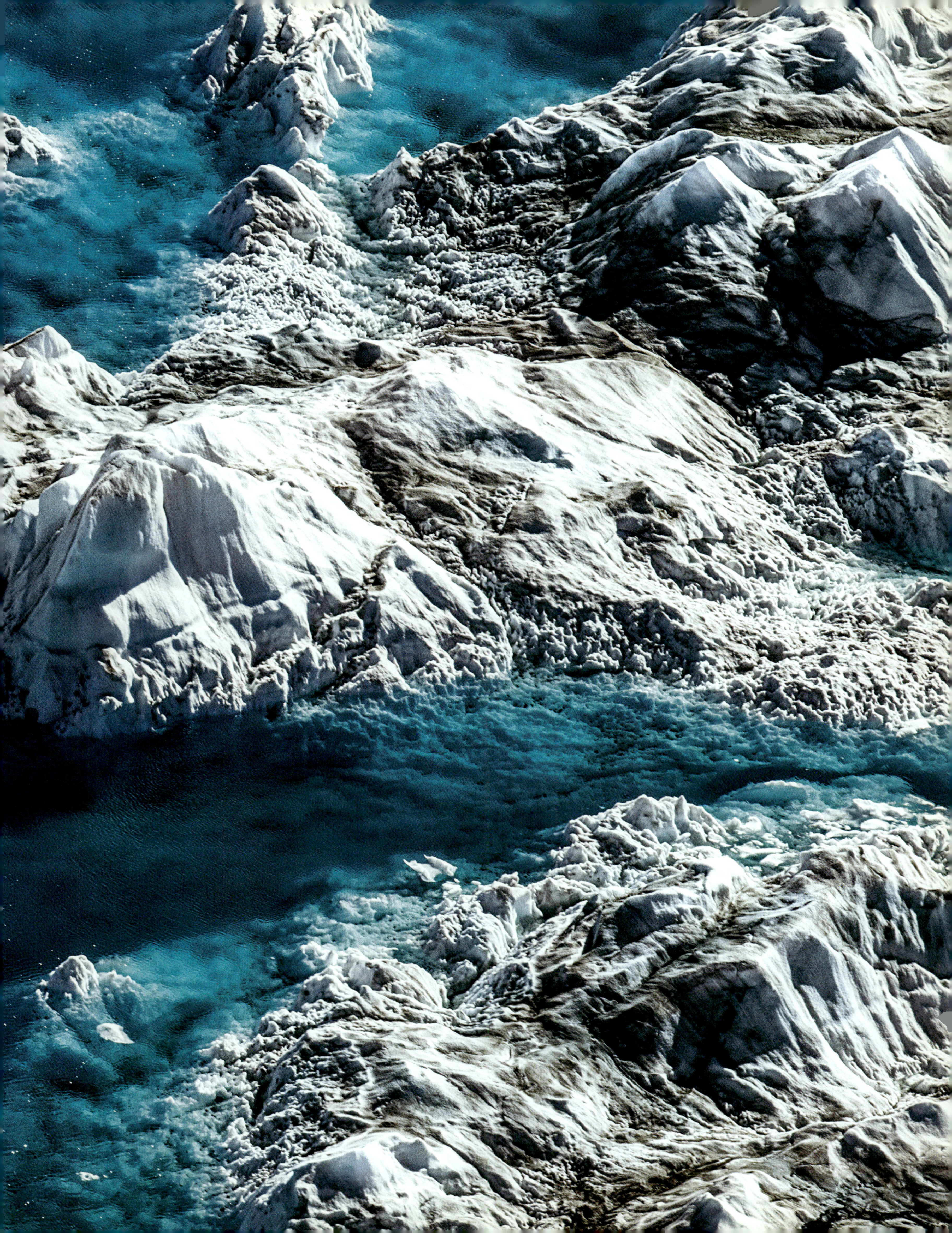

ARCTIC OCEAN

endless ice unweaves
desperate restless paddies
longing to be one

each seeks another
crying to bring unity
ending destruction

ocean memory
recalling frozen waters
protecting itself

ice floes questioning
an uncertain destiny
without boundaries

stepping stones of time
vanish in the horizon
remembering life

the sun overcomes
dismantling the Earth's balance
echoing epitaphs

SPLIT CHORD, ARCTIC OCEAN, 88 DEGREES N, -1 DEGREE C.

following pages ICE PACK AT THE NORTH POLE, 90 DEGREES N, 8:00 PM, 0 DEGREES C.

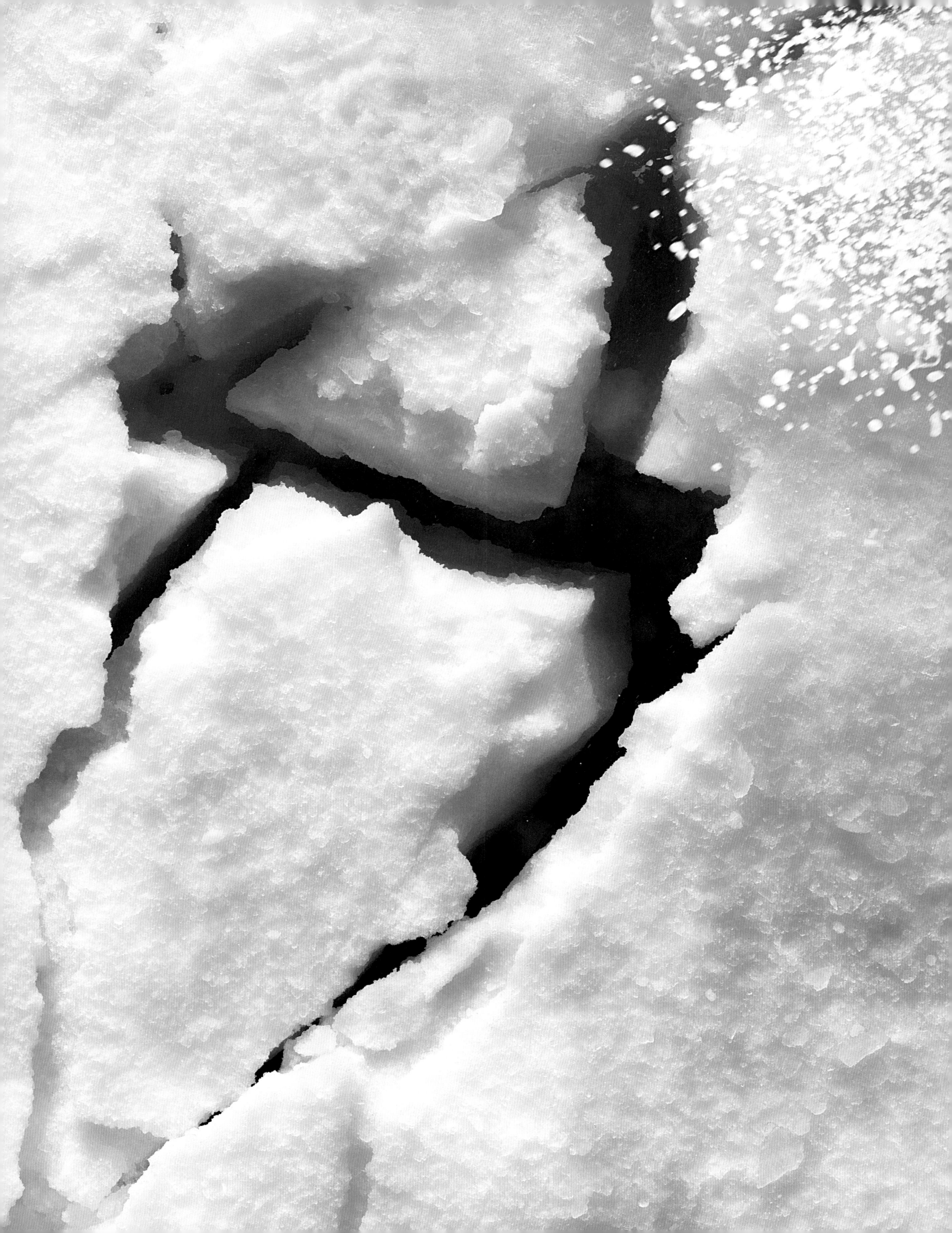

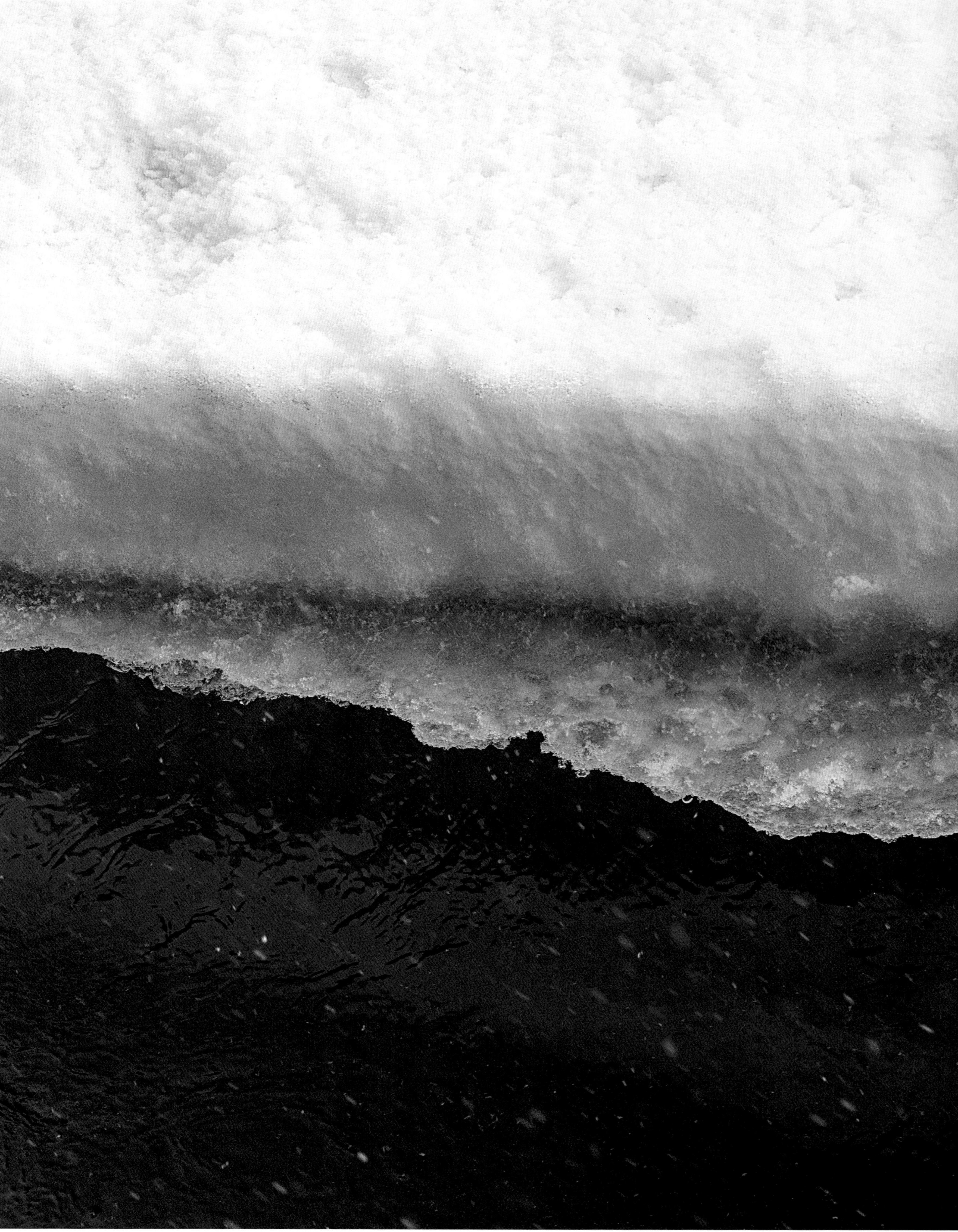

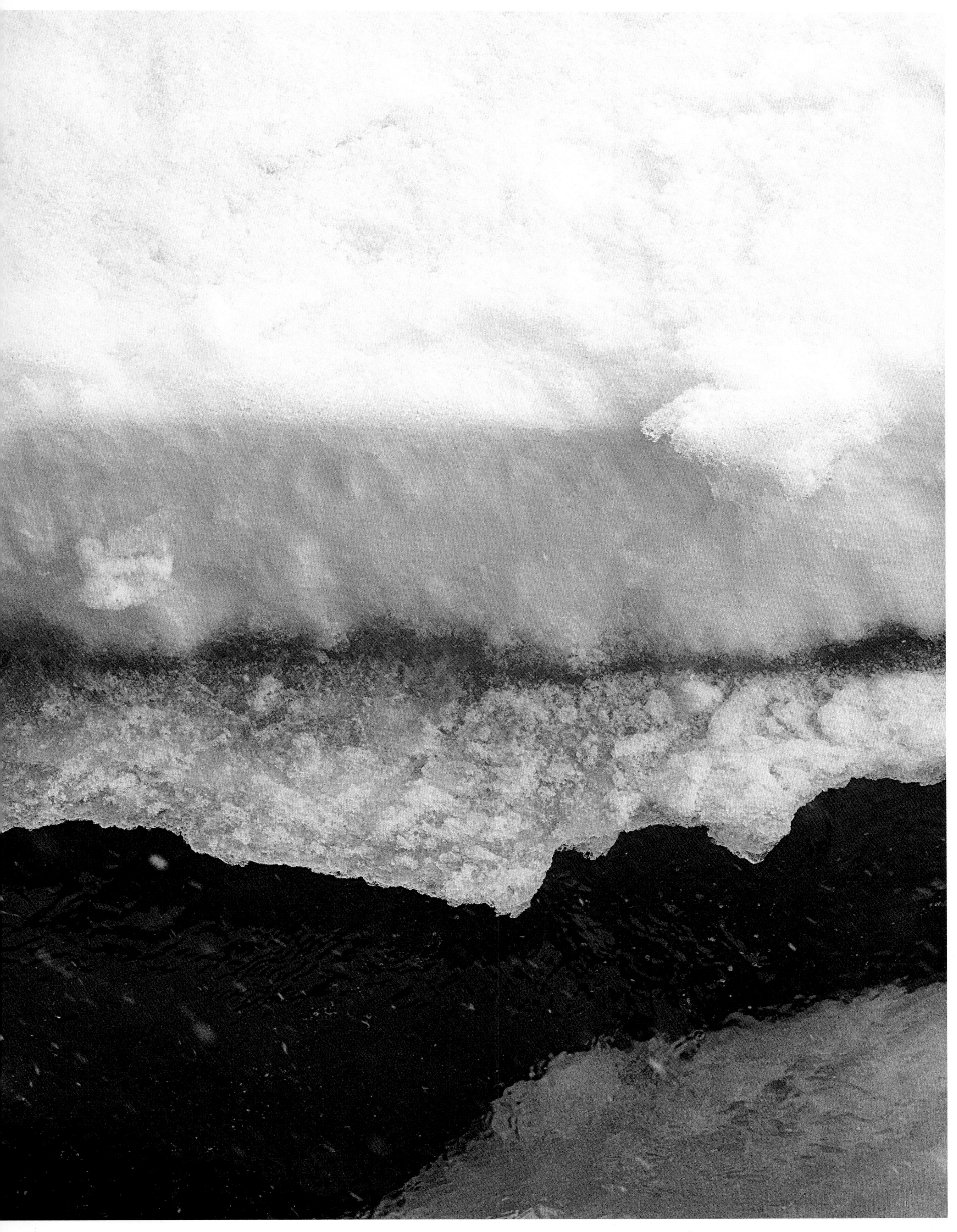

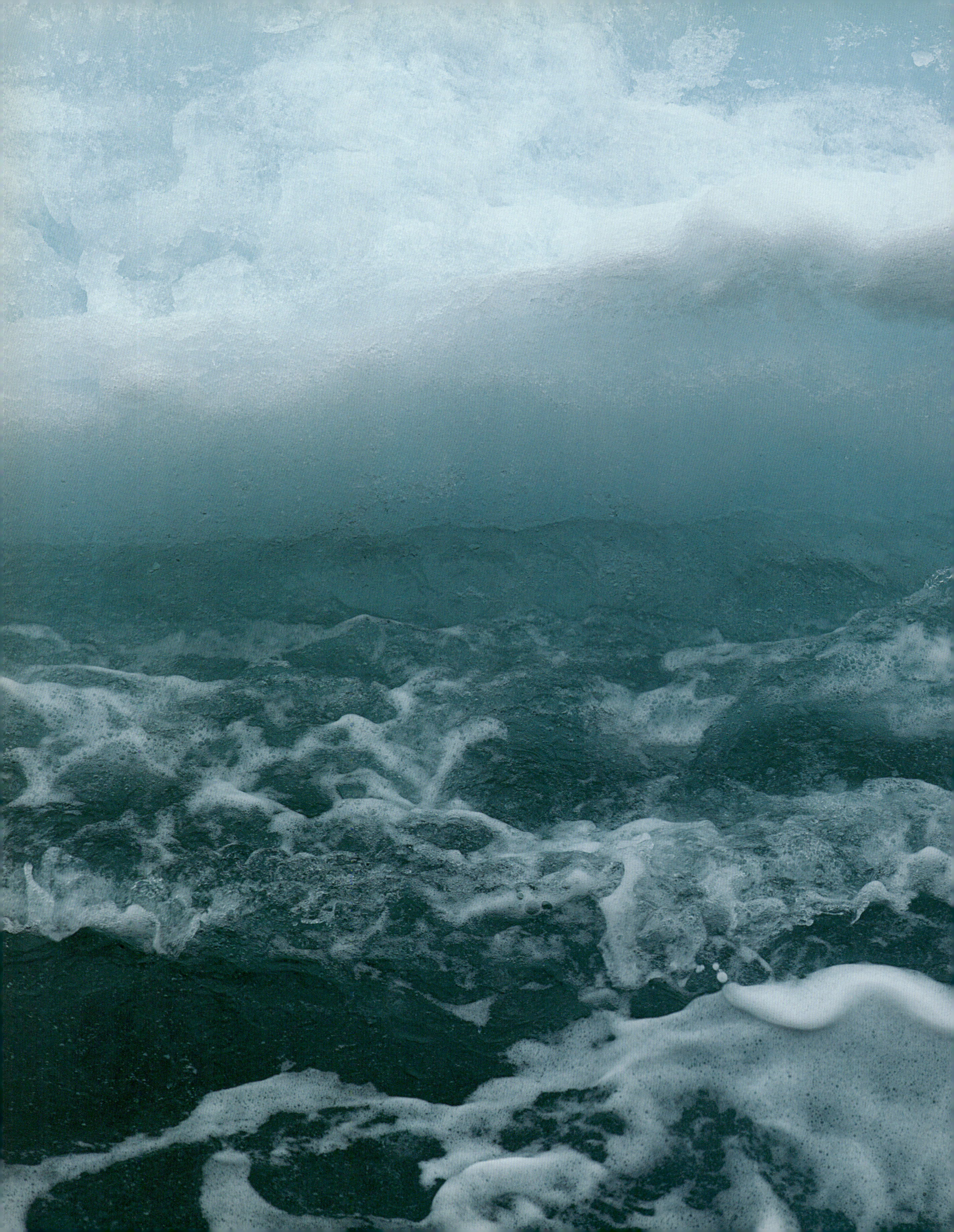

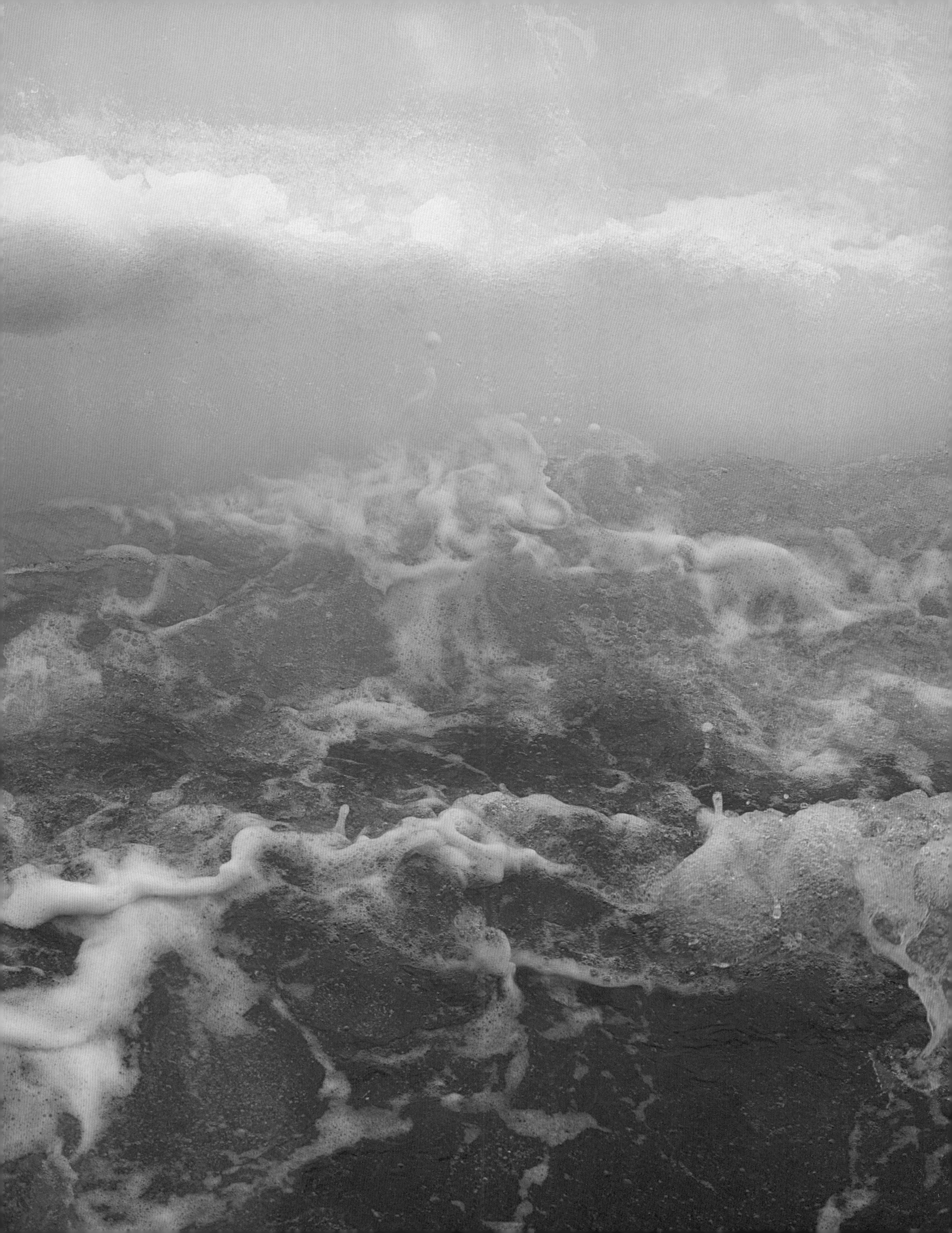

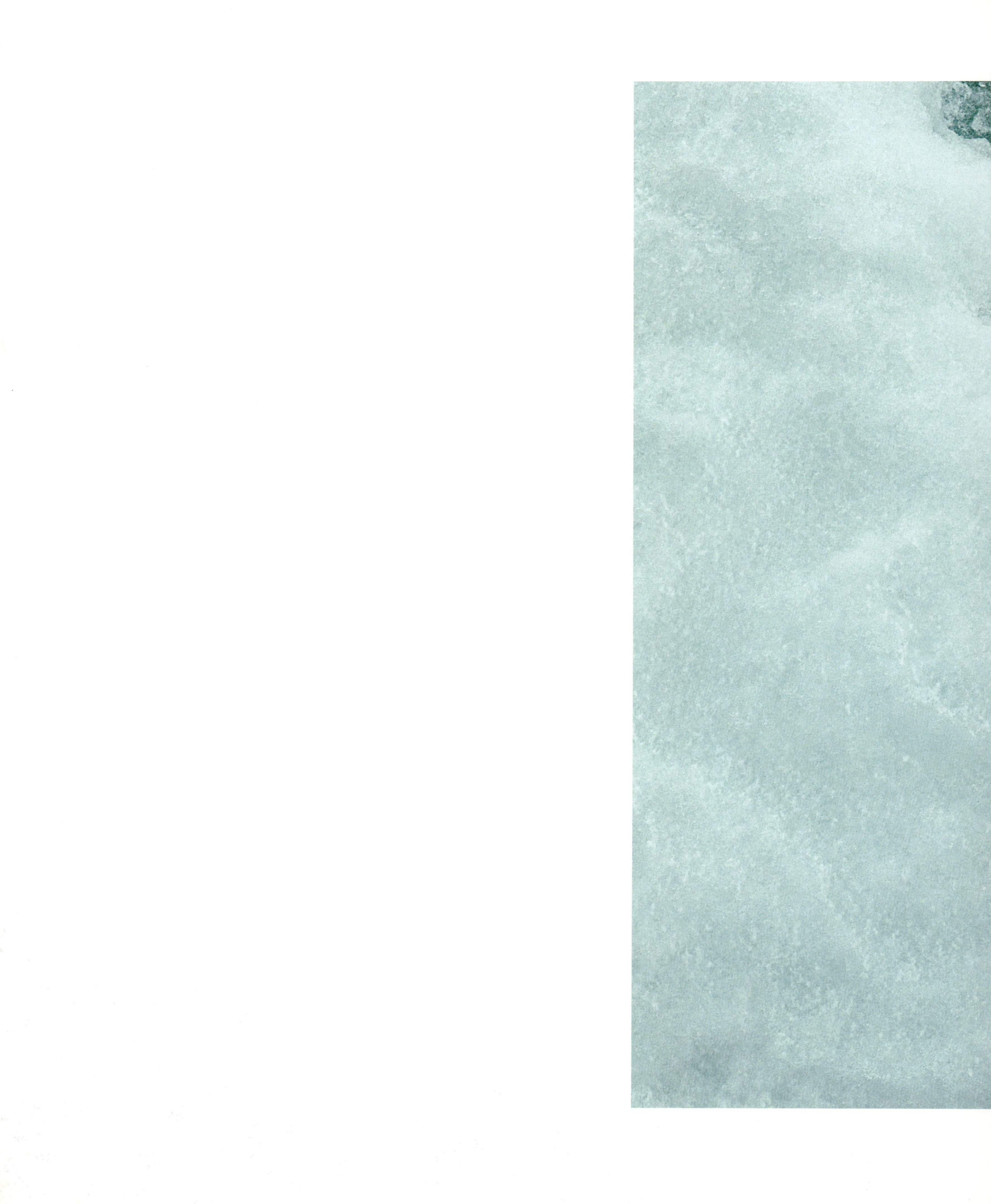

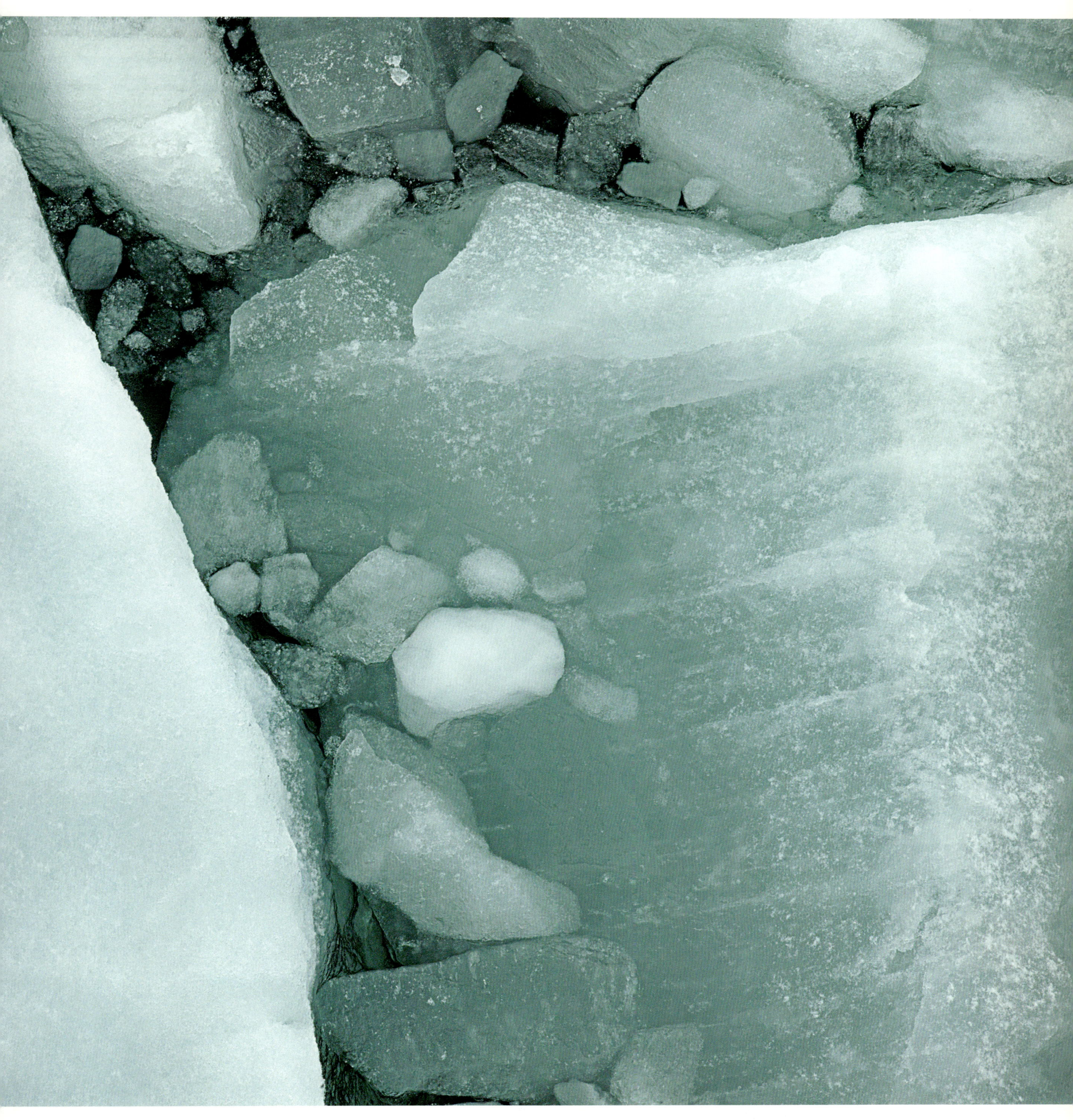

FRACTURES, NORTH POLE, 3:06 AM, 89 DEGREES N, -2 DEGREES C.
previous pages FIRE AND ICE, ARCTIC OCEAN, 5:12 PM, 88 DEGREES N.
following pages THEMES AND VARIATIONS, ARCTIC OCEAN, 84 DEGREES N, -2 DEGREES C.

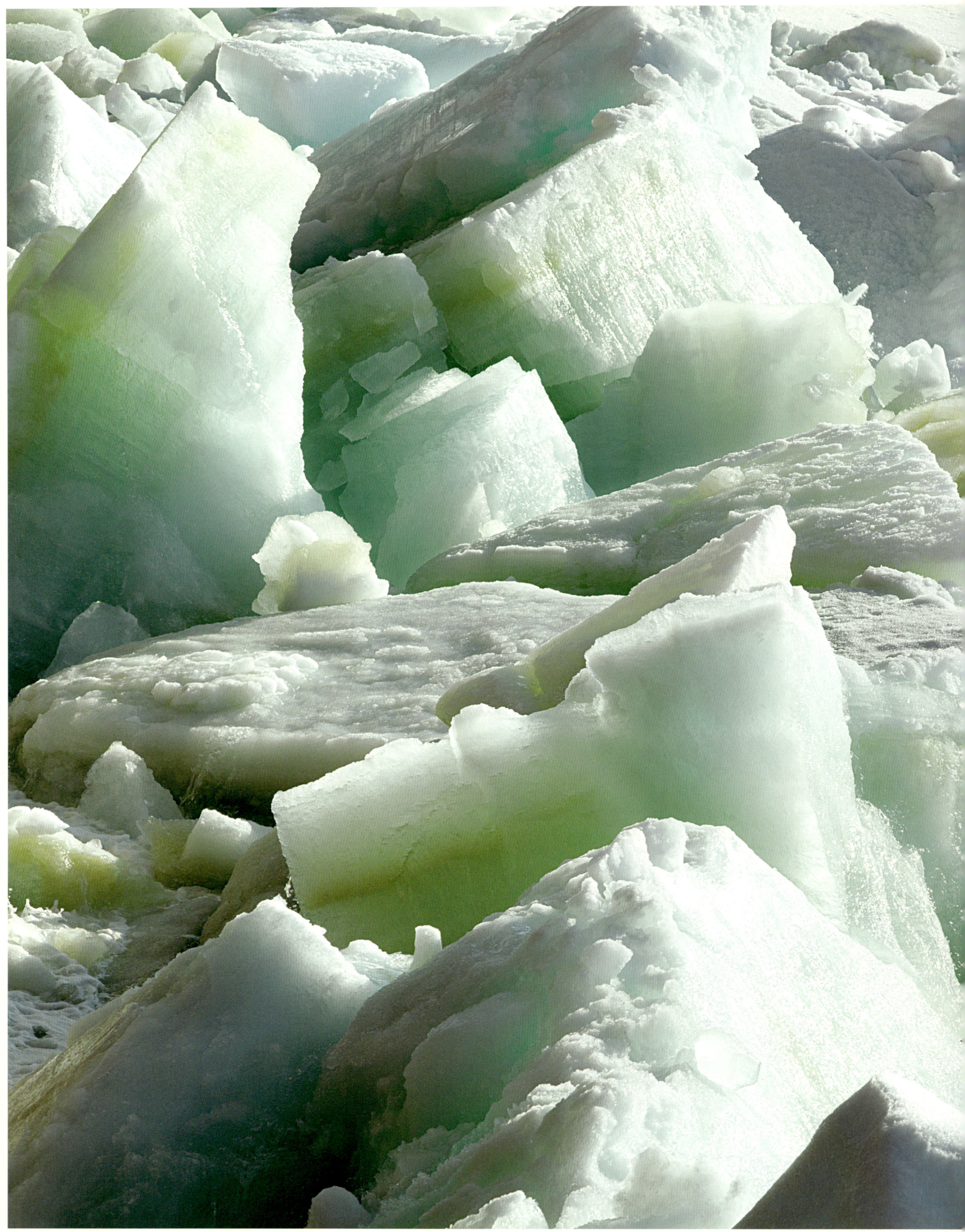

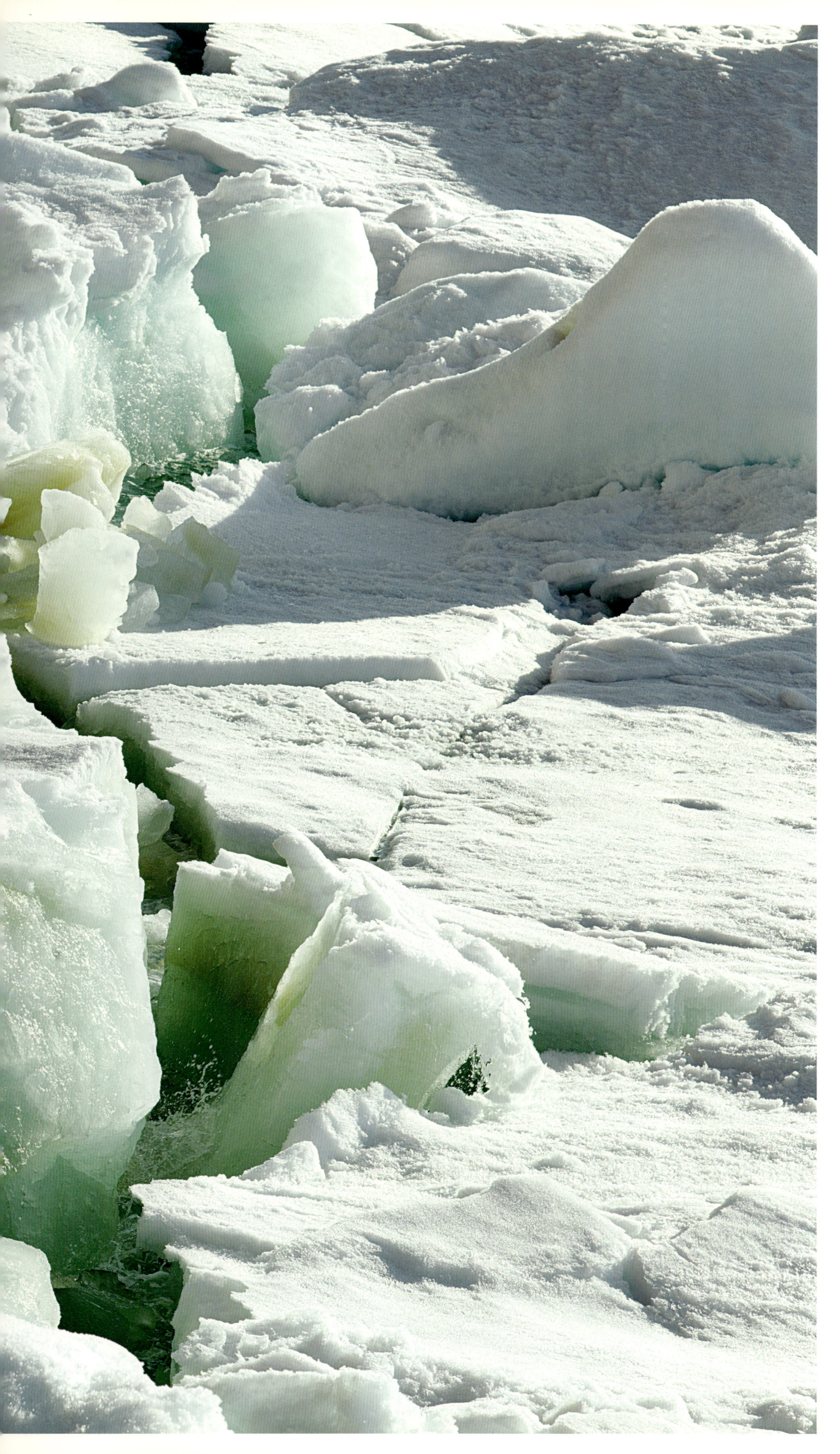

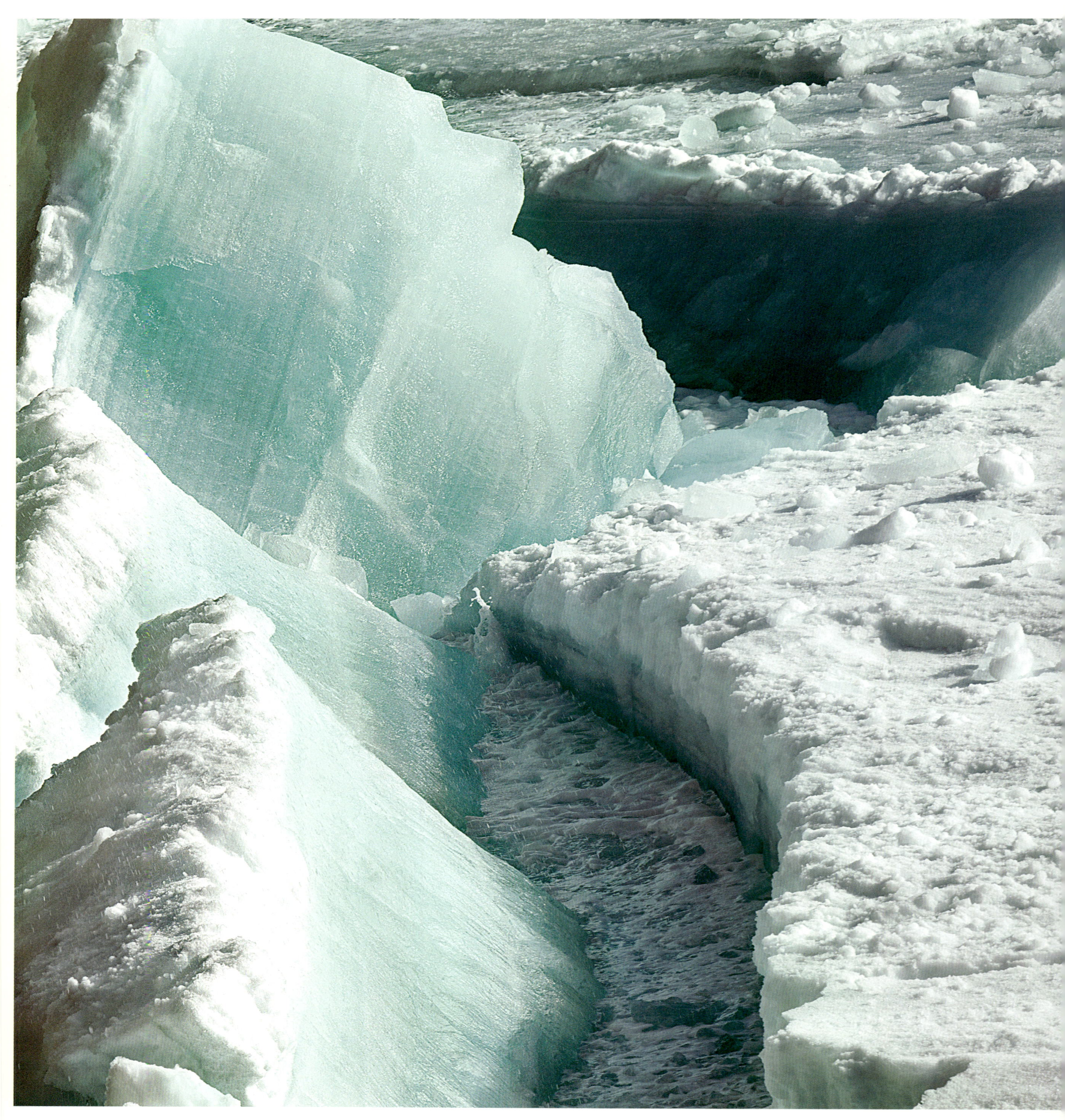

CADENCE, ARCTIC OCEAN, 3:21 PM, 87 DEGREES N.

following pages PERMUTATIONS, ARCTIC OCEAN, 11:04 PM, 89 DEGREES N, ICE THICKNESS 1-2 METERS.

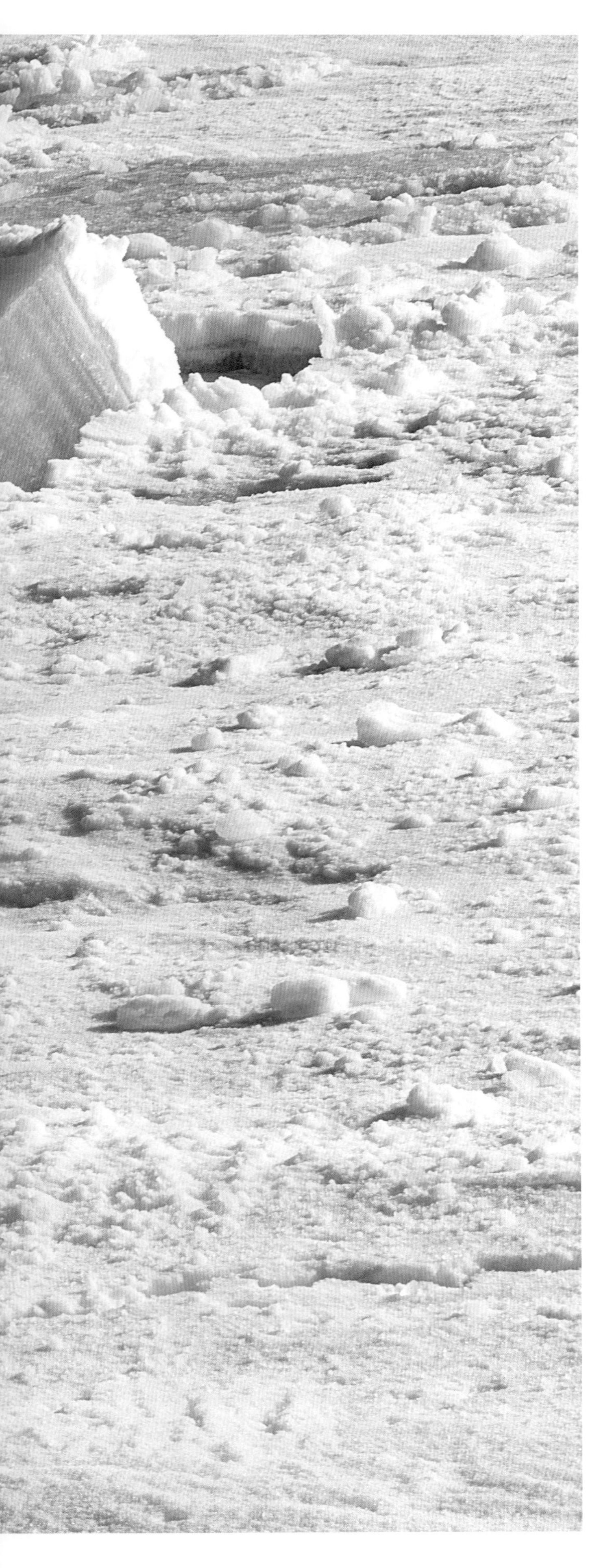

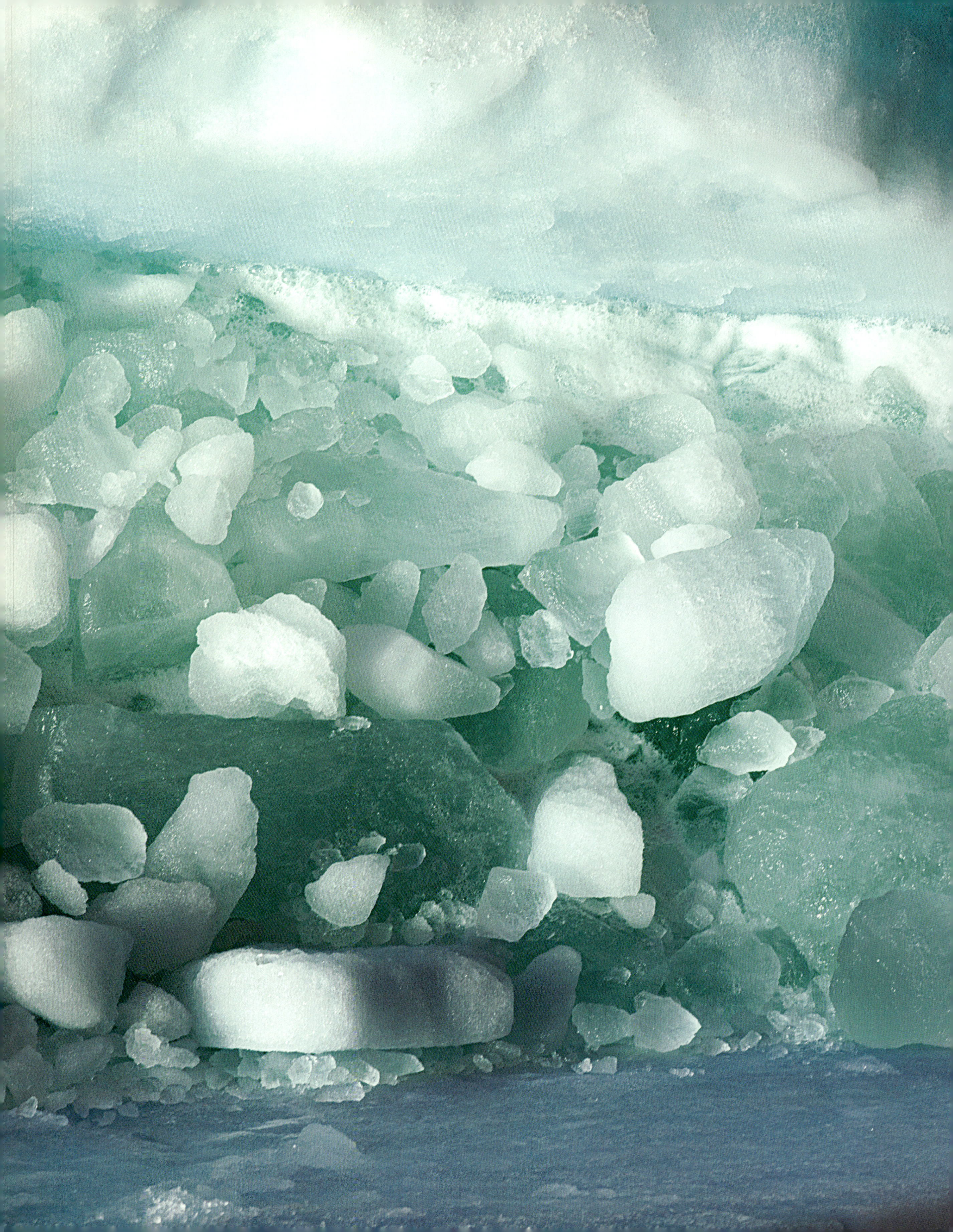

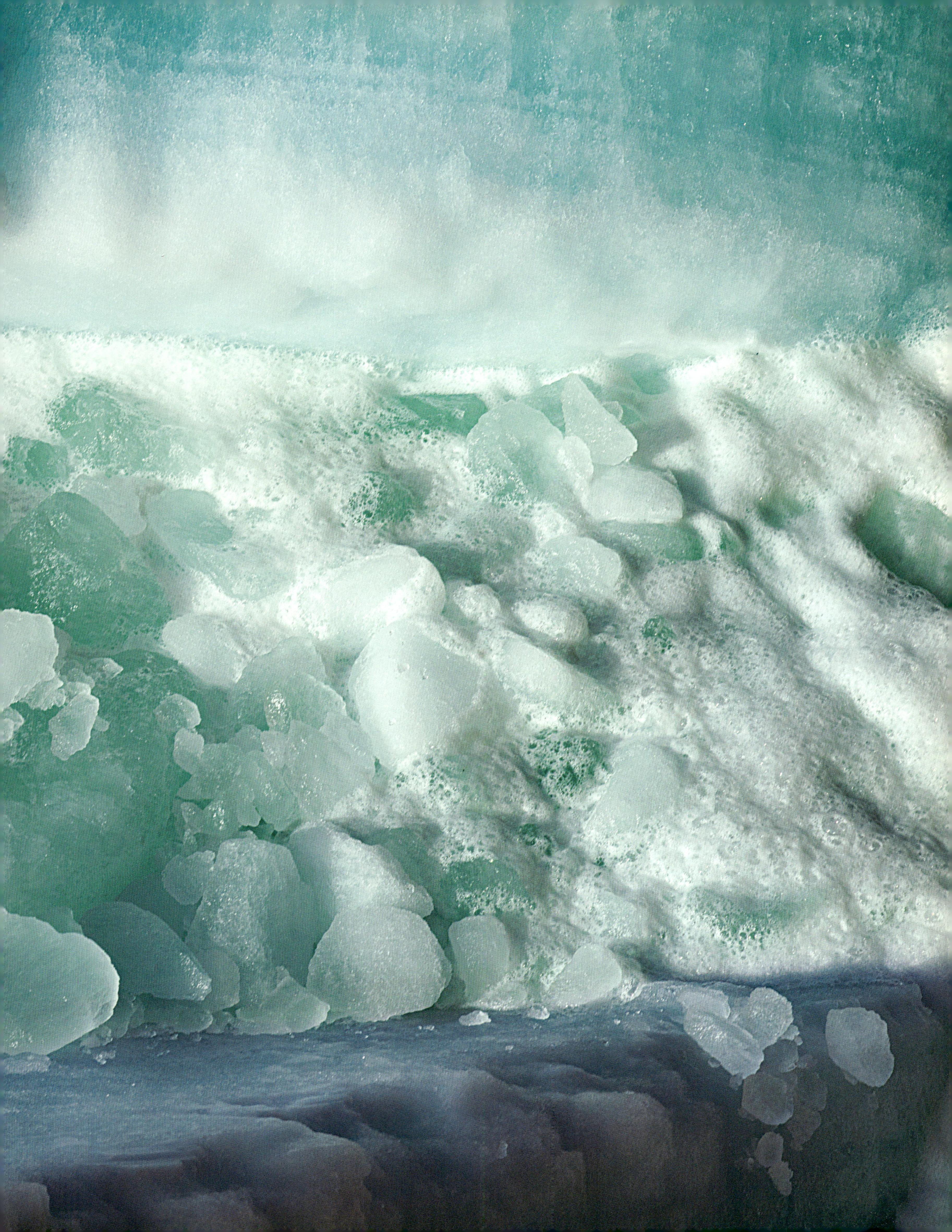

RETROGRADE, FRANZ JOSEPH LAND, AUSTRIAN CHANNEL, 11:37 PM, 81 DEGREES N, 0 DEGREES C.

following pages VIBRATIONS, ISFJORDEN, NORWAY.

pages 106-107 RELICS, ISFJORDEN, NORWAY.

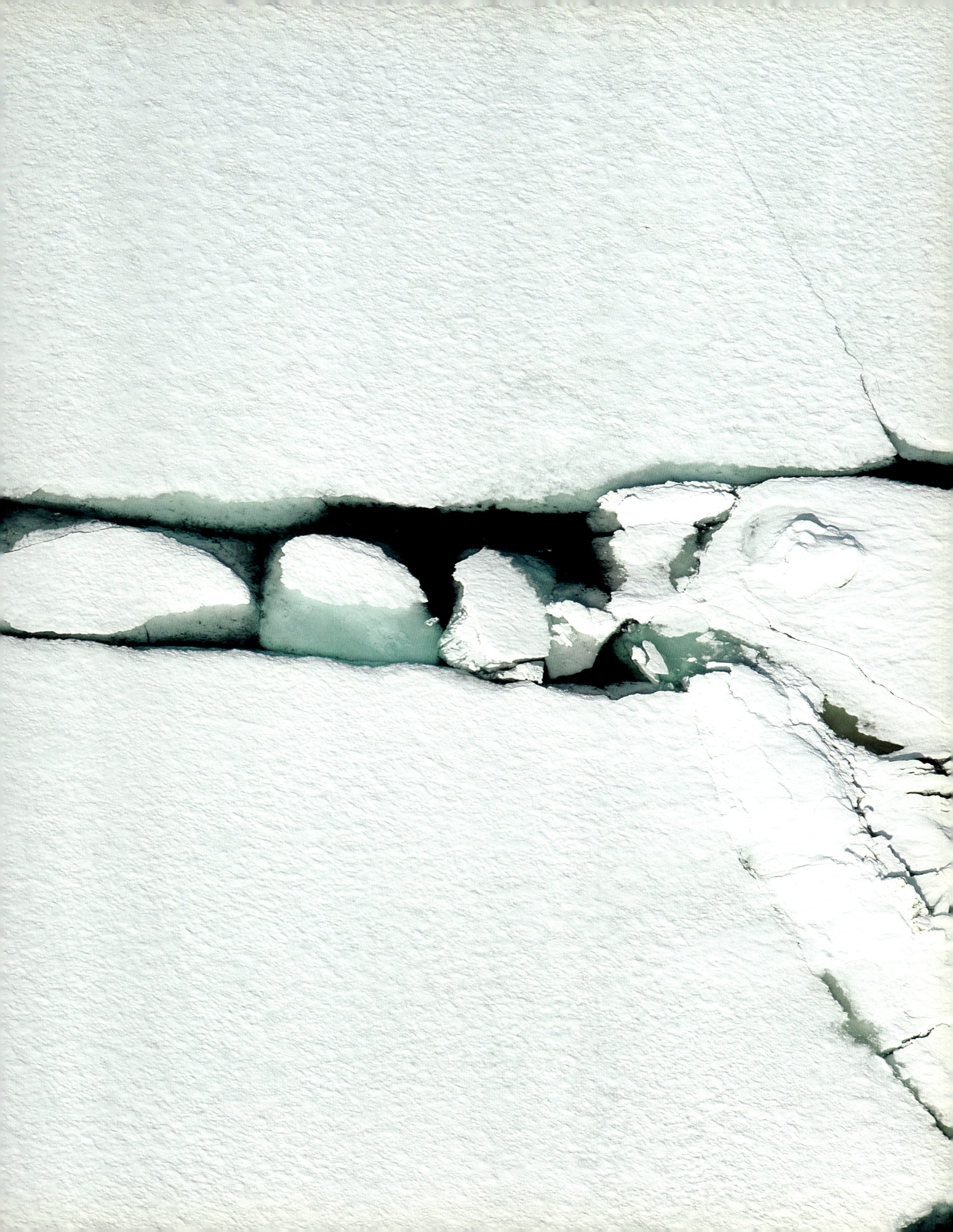

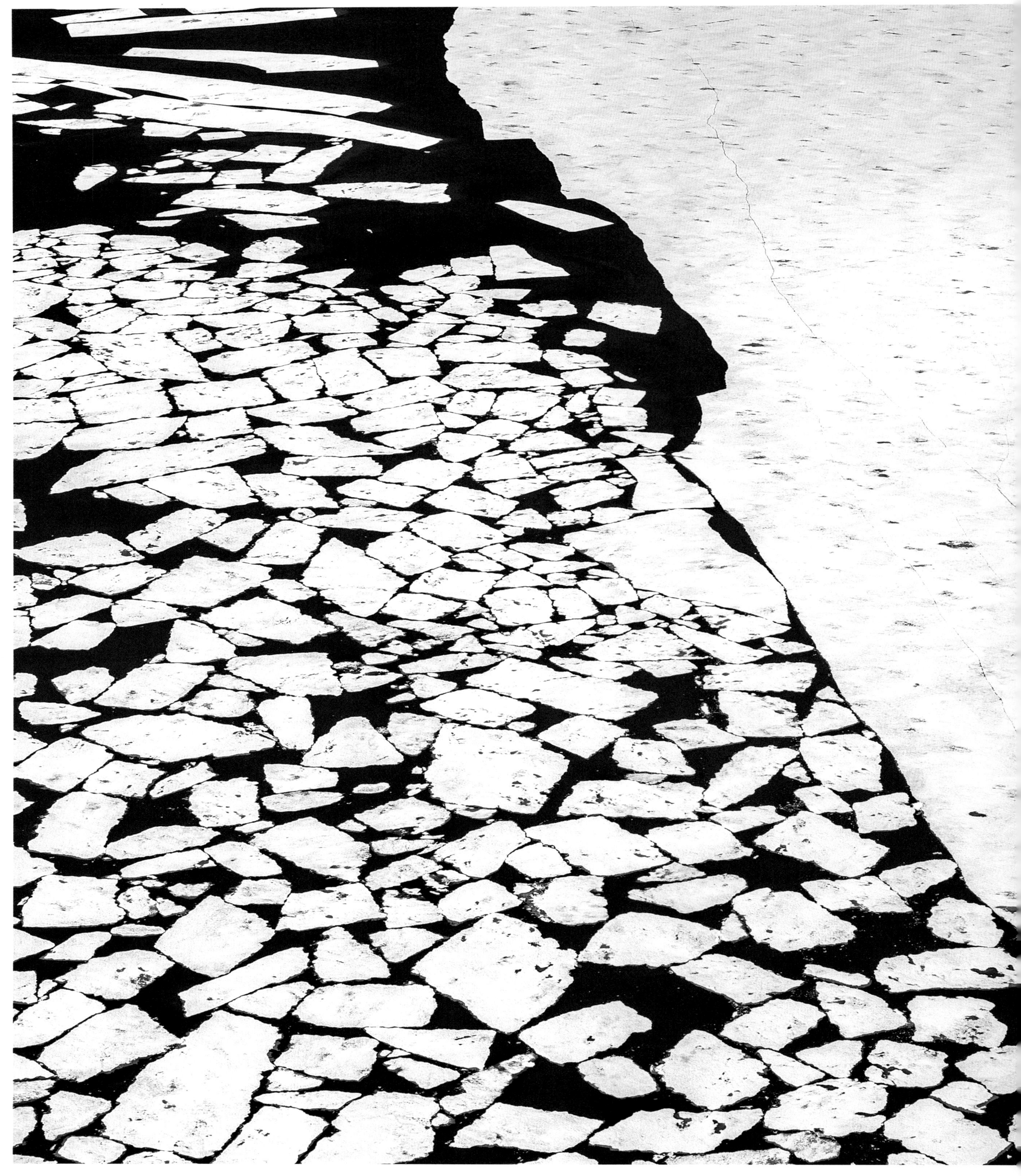

THE ARCTIC MELT, GREENLAND SEA, ARCTIC OCEAN, 4:48 PM, 79 DEGREES N.

previous pages ISFJORDEN, SVALBARD, NORWAY, 3:42 PM.

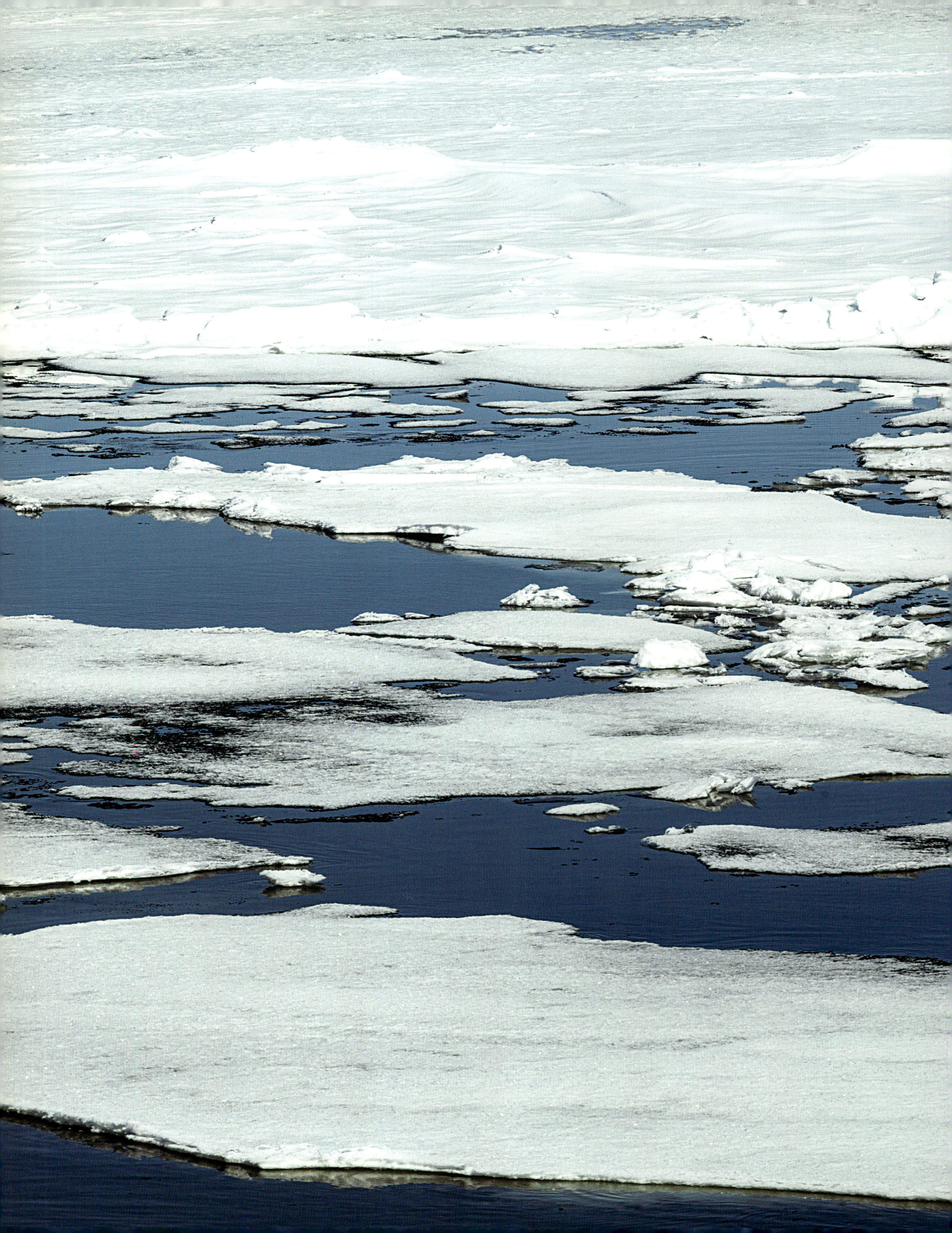

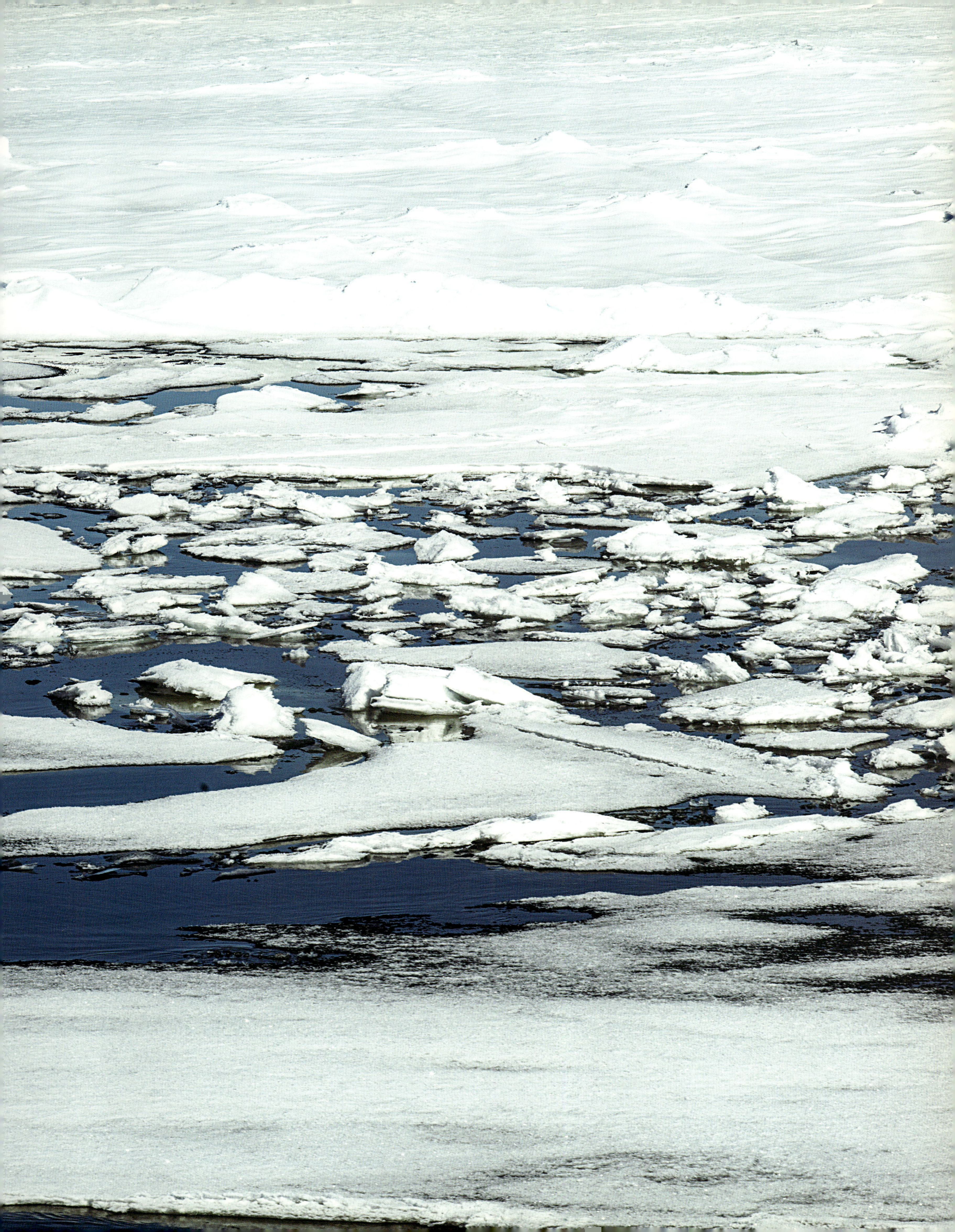

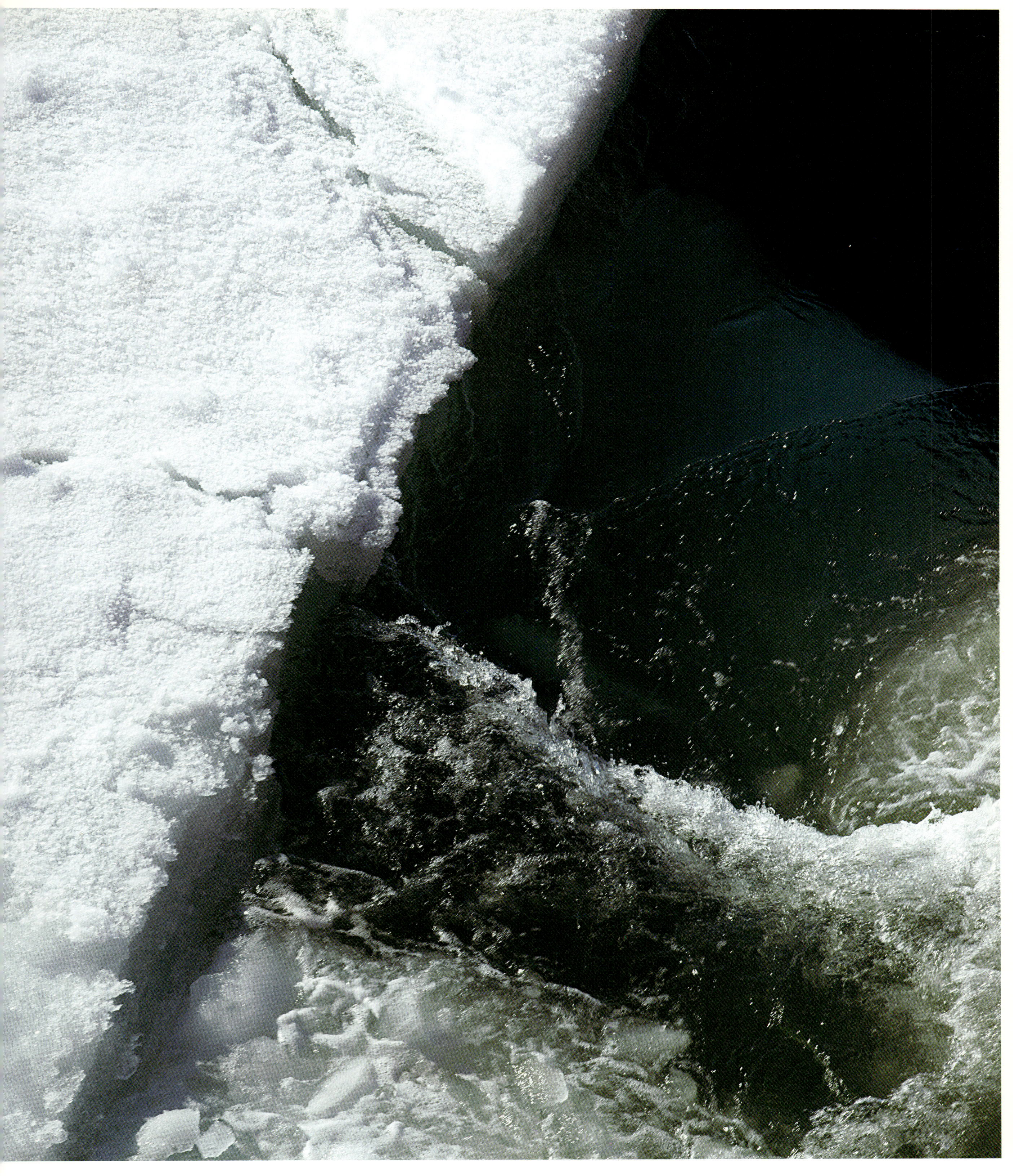

UNDER THE ICE, ARCTIC OCEAN, 12:00 PM, 85 DEGREES N.

previous pages OPEN WATERS, ARCTIC OCEAN, 1:22 PM, 83 DEGREES N, 0 DEGREES C.

> “The unity of Nature is an extremely artificial and fragile bridge, a garden net.”

T.E. HULME

TRANSITION, FRANZ JOSEPH LAND, NORTHERN BARENTS SEA, 79 DEGREES N, 0 DEGREES C.

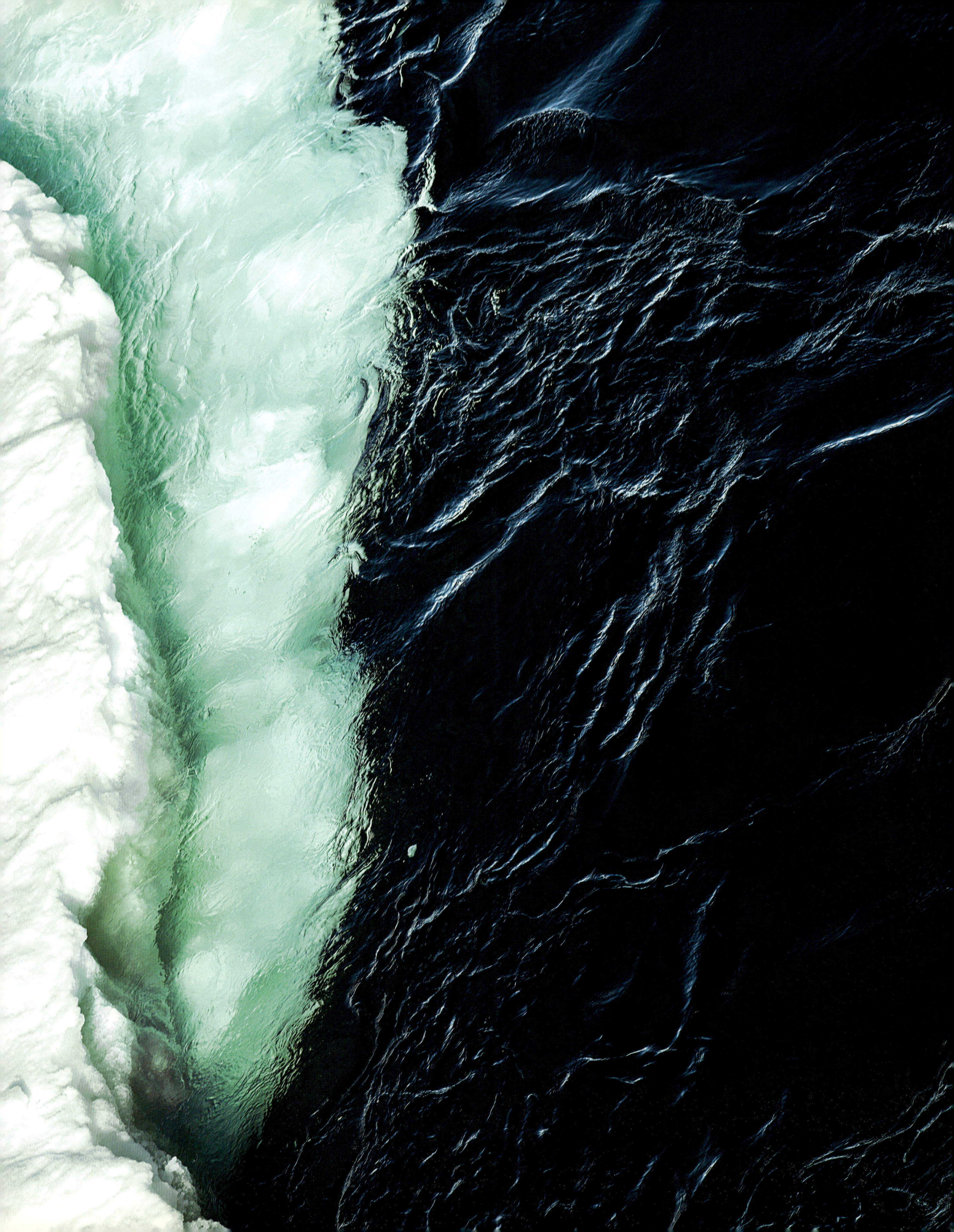

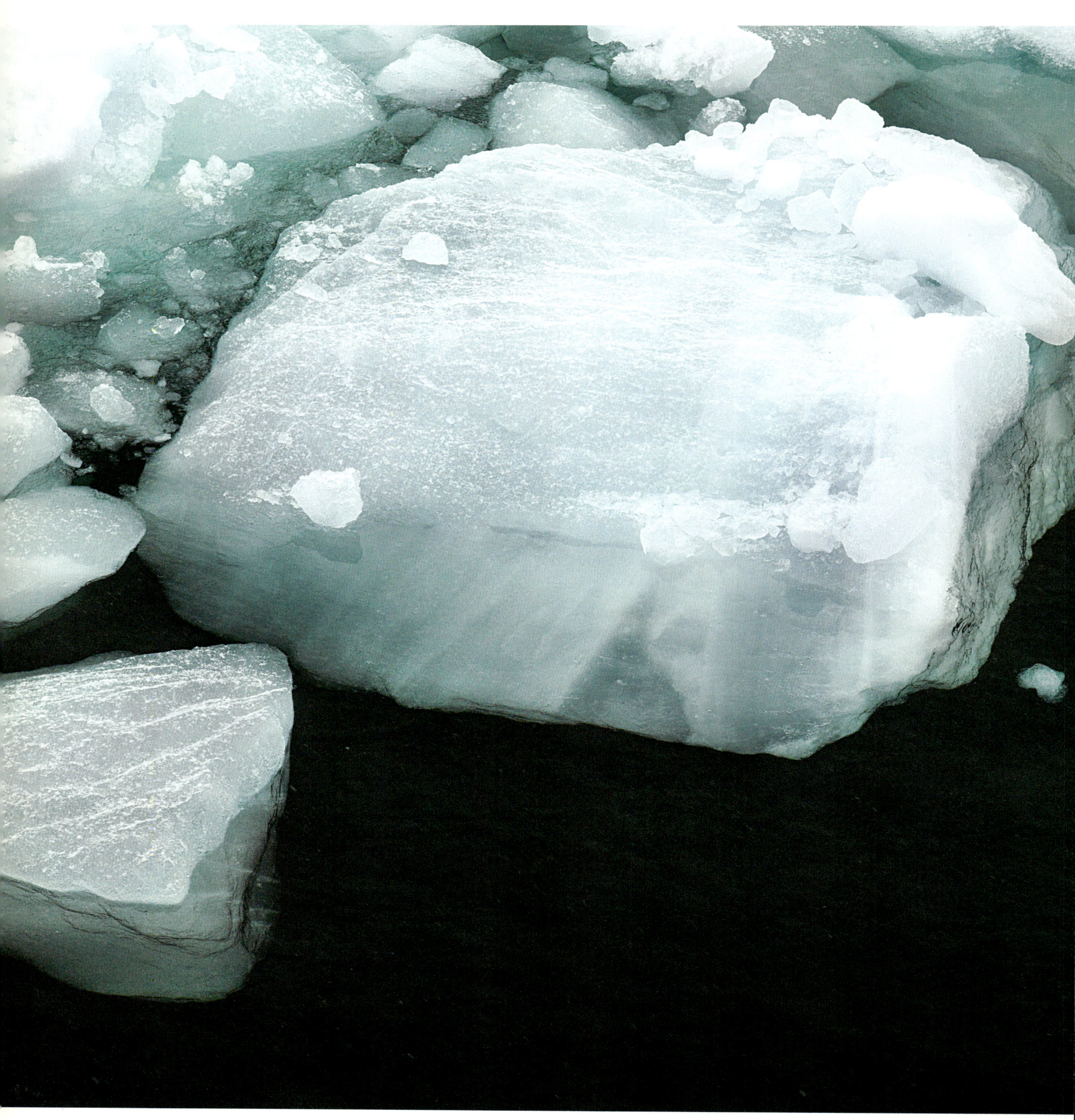

SEA ICE AT 89 DEGREES N, ARCTIC OCEAN, 3:01 AM, 0 DEGREES C.

following pages SUMMER SOLSTICE AT 90 DEGREES N, JUNE 21, 2015, 5:38 PM.

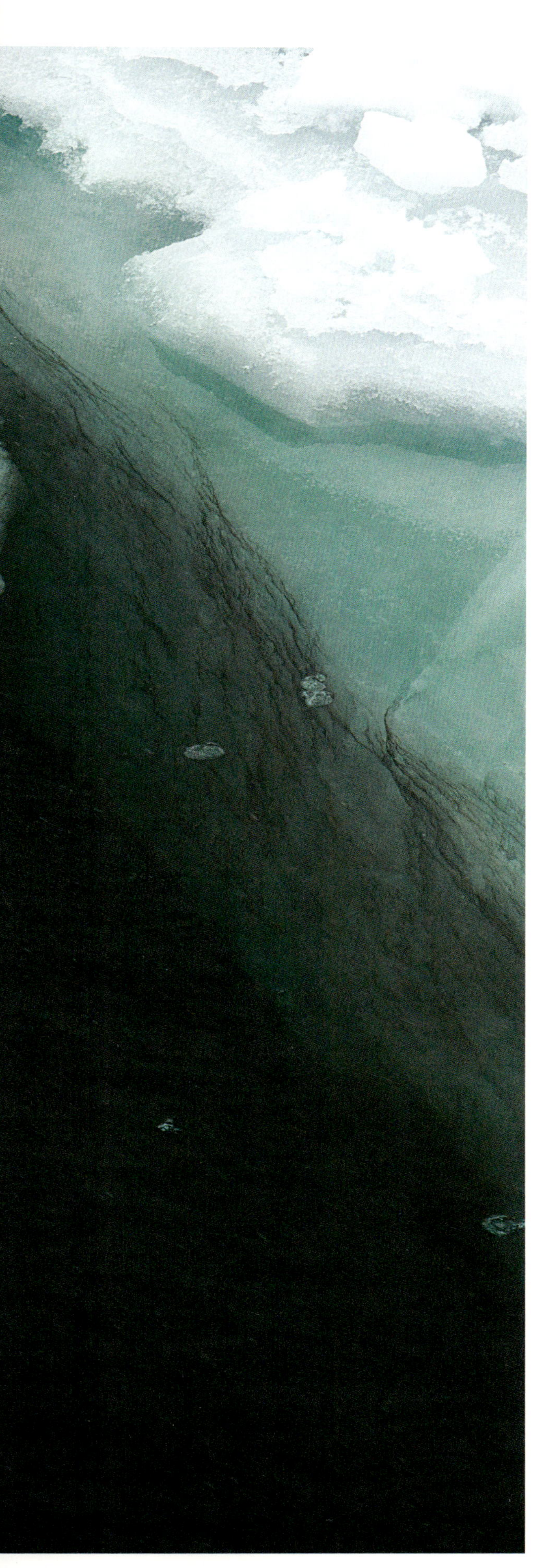

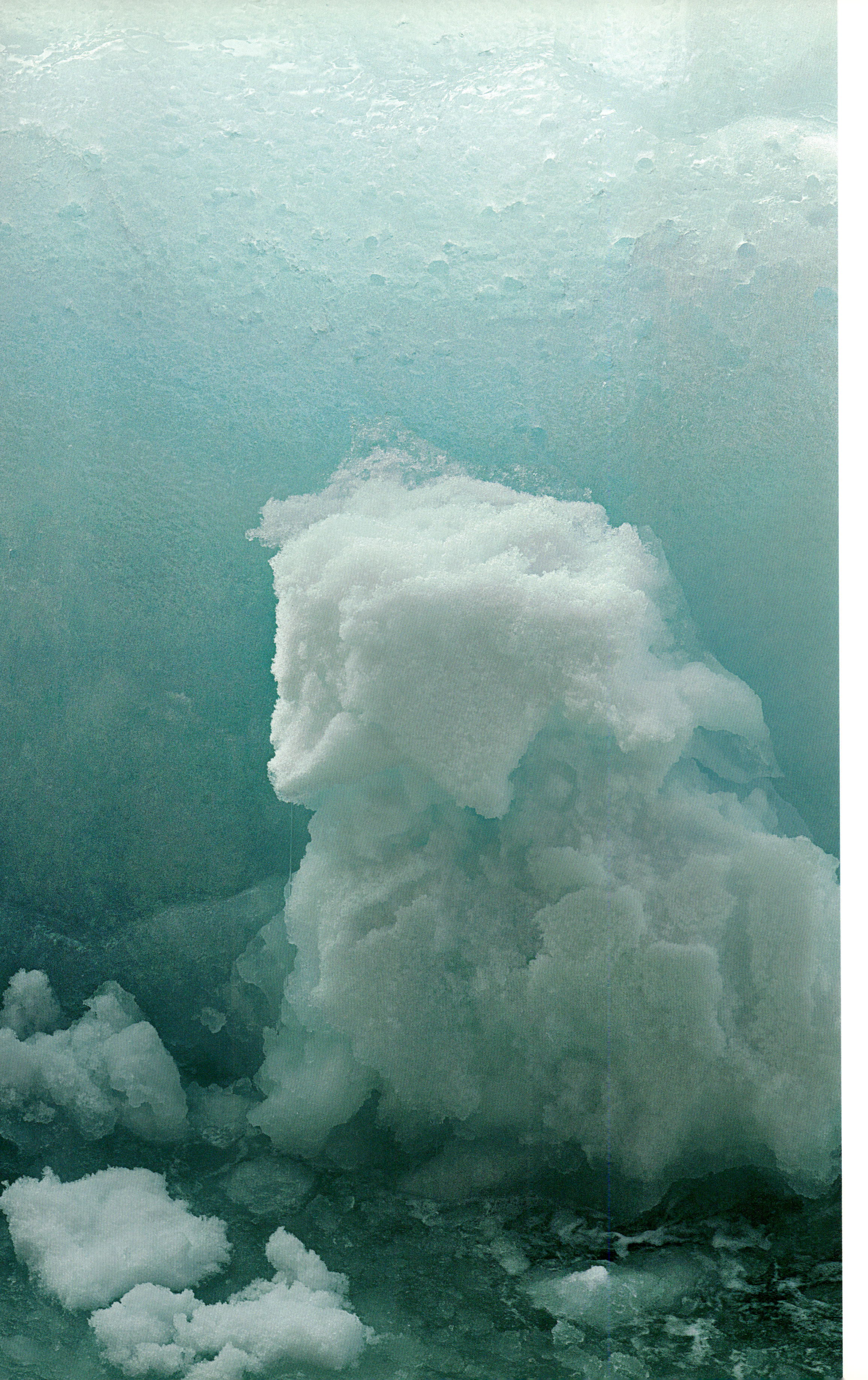

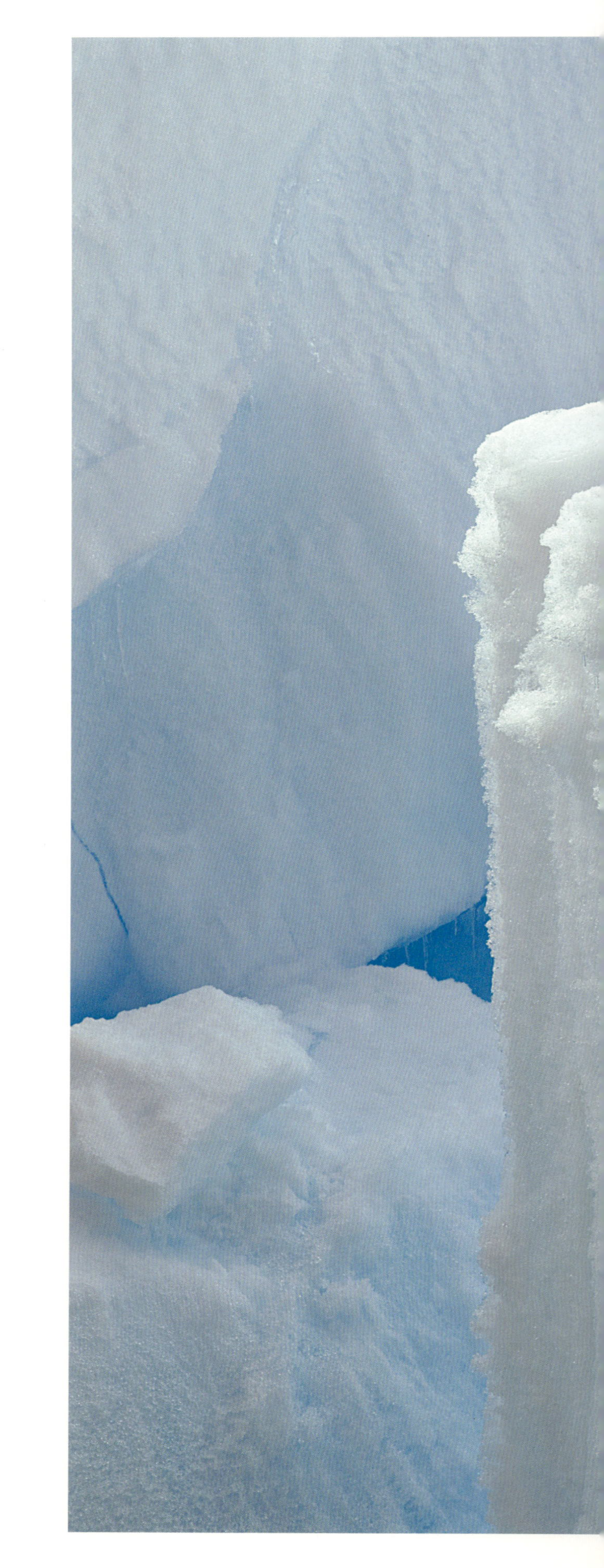

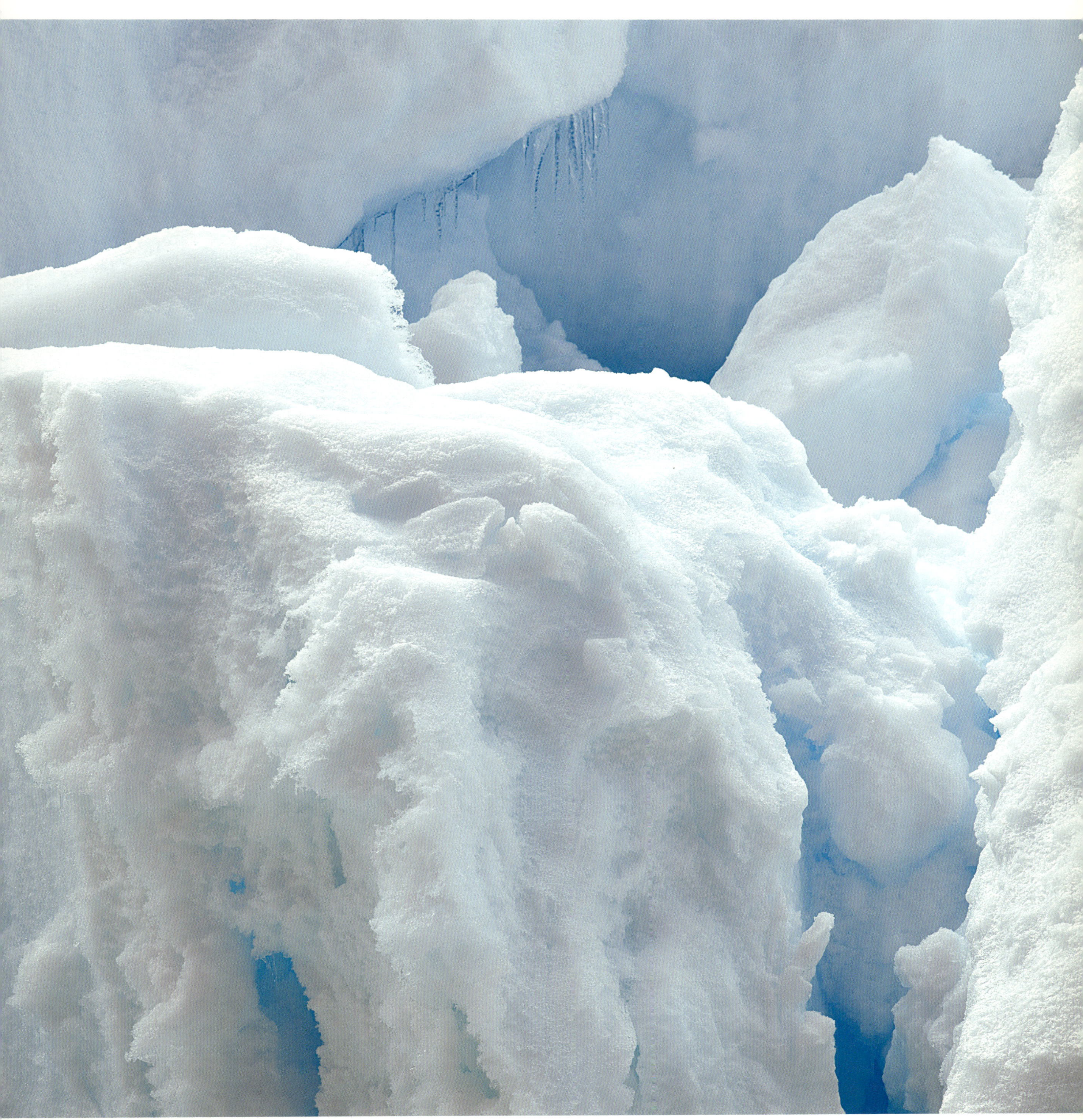

DRIFT AT THE NORTH POLE, 12:03 AM, 0 DEGREES C.

previous pages INSIDE THE MELT, ISFJORDEN, NORWAY, 4:54 PM, 79 DEGREES N.

“We won’t have a society if we destroy the environment.”

MARGARET MEAD

WITHIN THE PACK ICE, ARCTIC OCEAN, 88 DEGREES N, -1 DEGREES C, 12:05 AM.

previous pages SONATA ON THE ICE, 86 DEGREES N, -2 DEGREES C.

following pages SHORELINE, CAPE NORWAY, FRANZ JOSEPH LAND, 81 DEGREES N, 1 DEGREE C.

pages 132-133 BROKEN MELODY, ICE PACK, ARCTIC OCEAN, 84 DEGREES N, -2 DEGREES C.

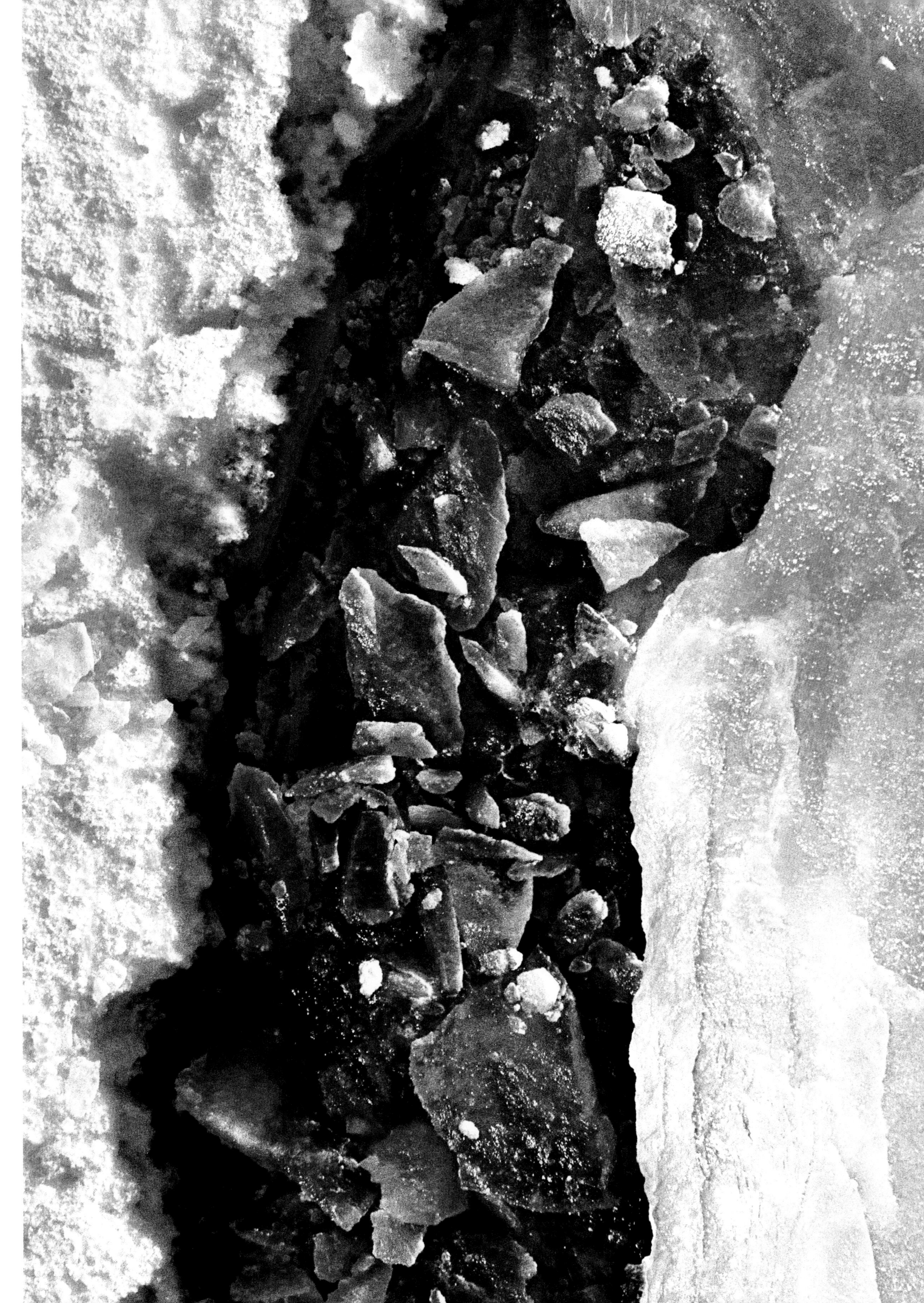

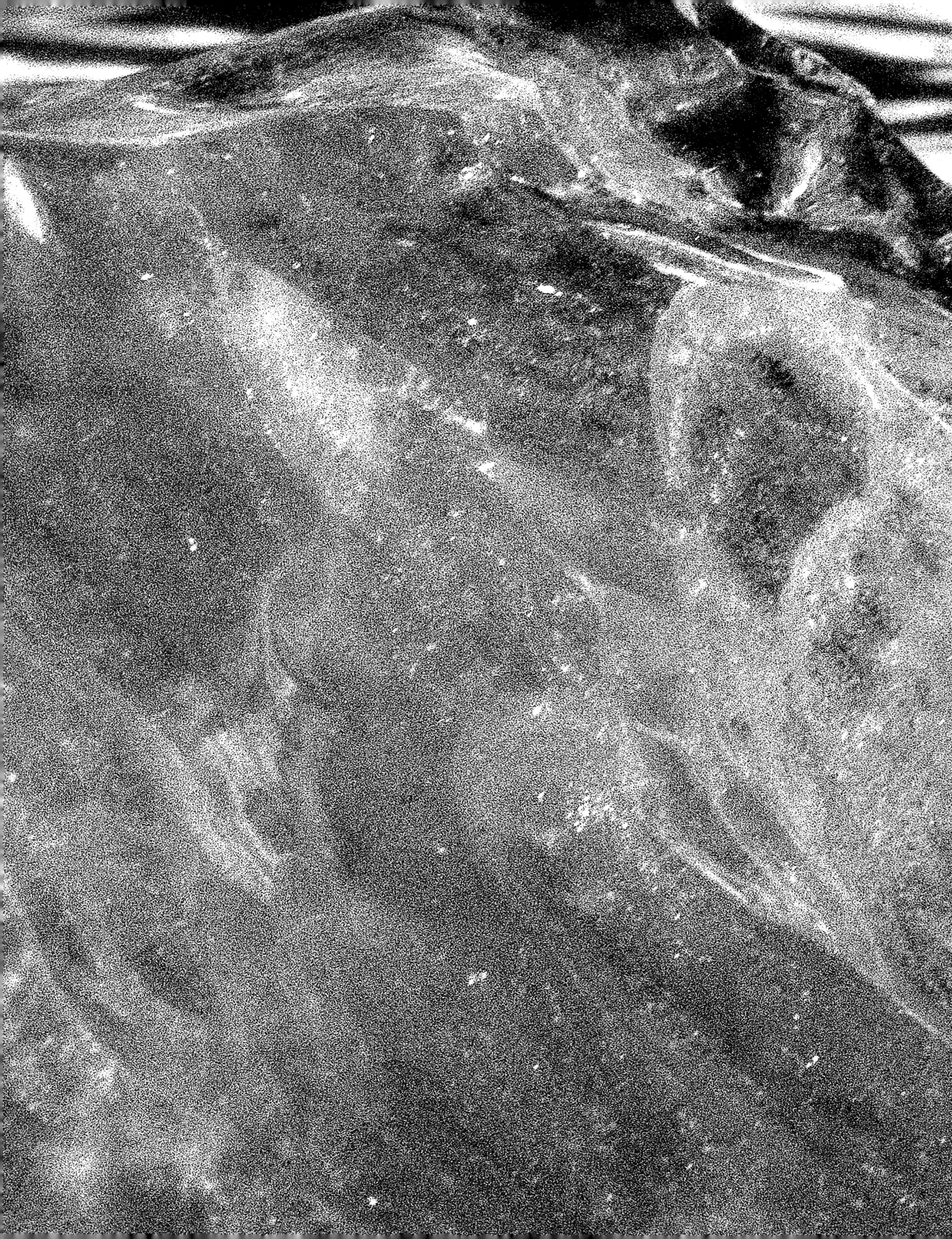

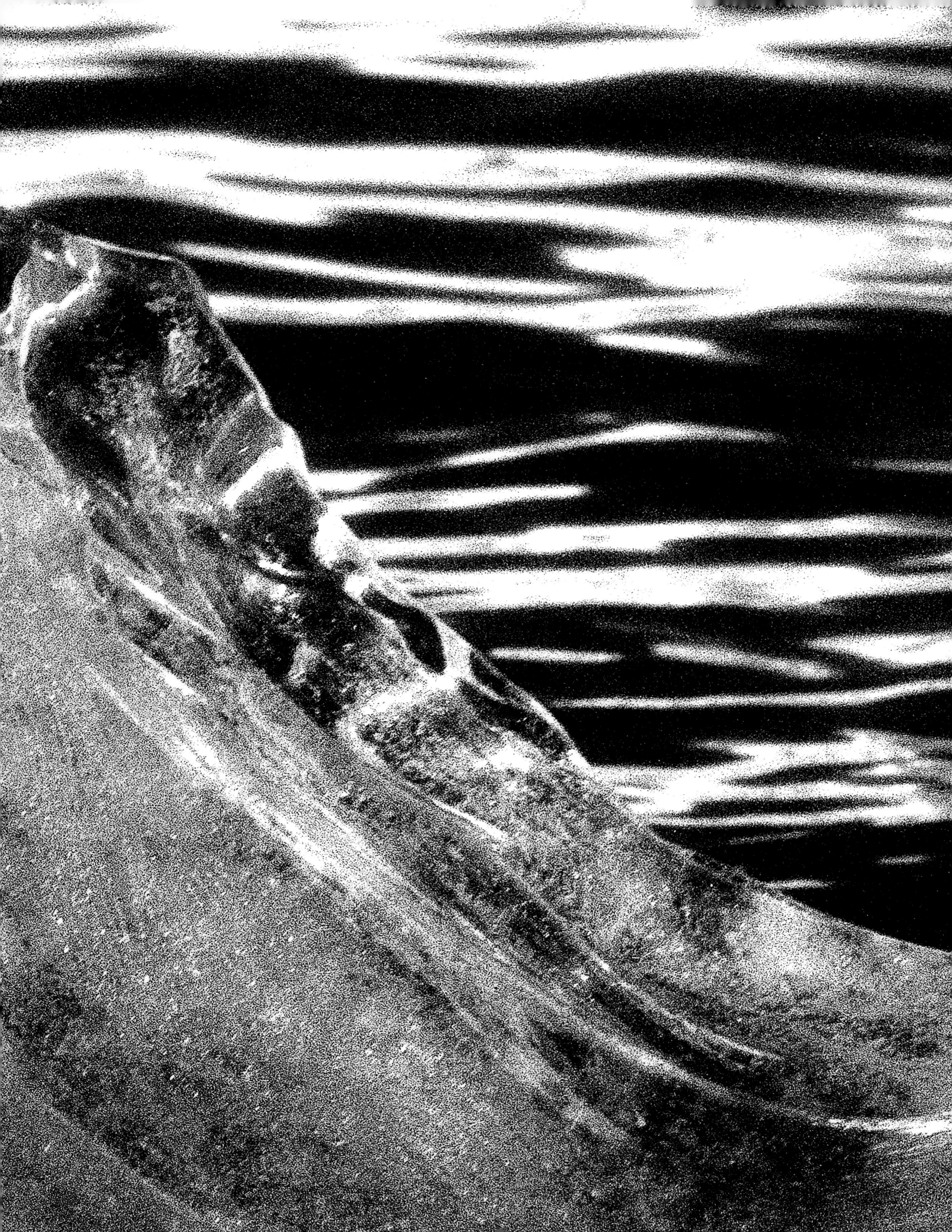

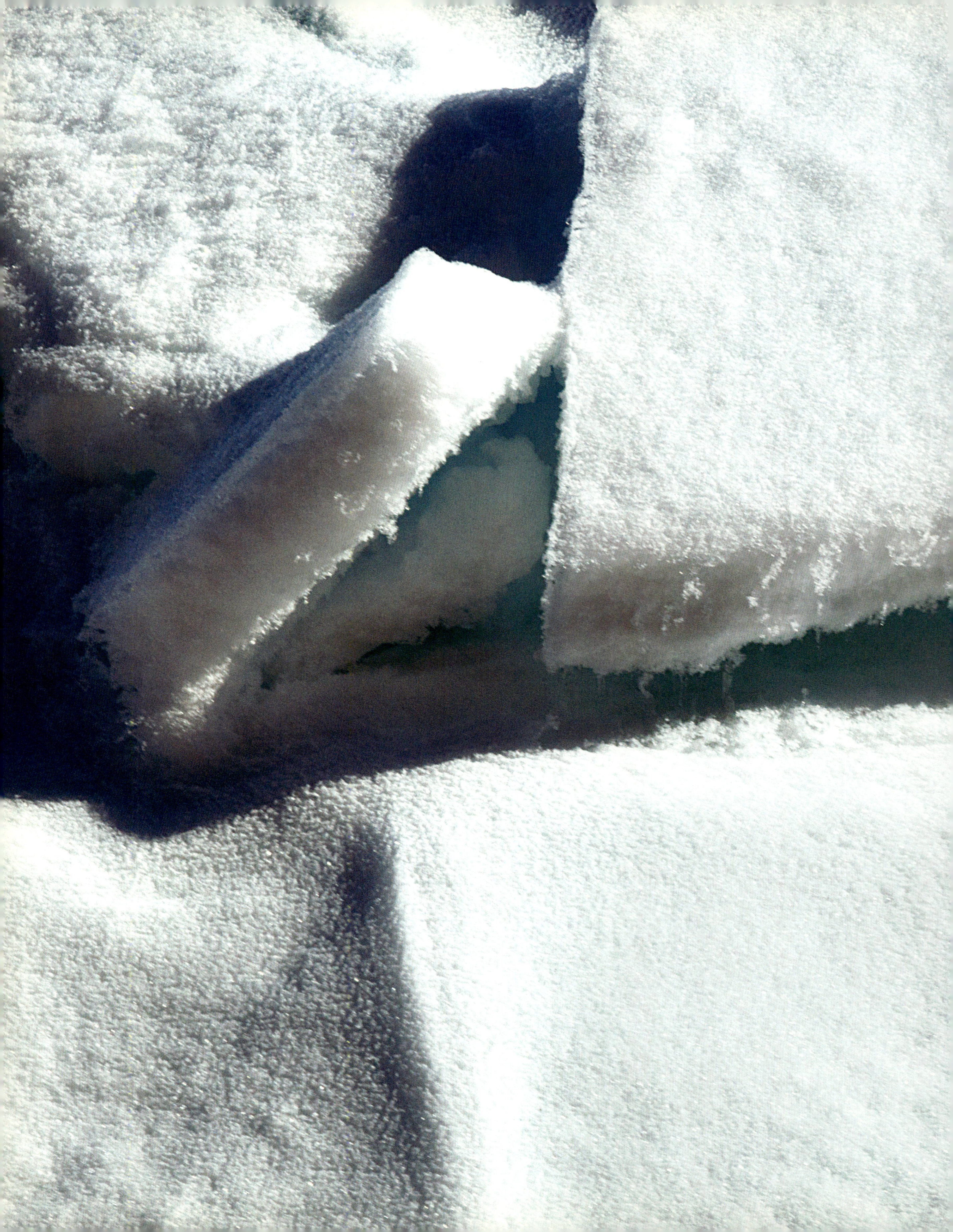

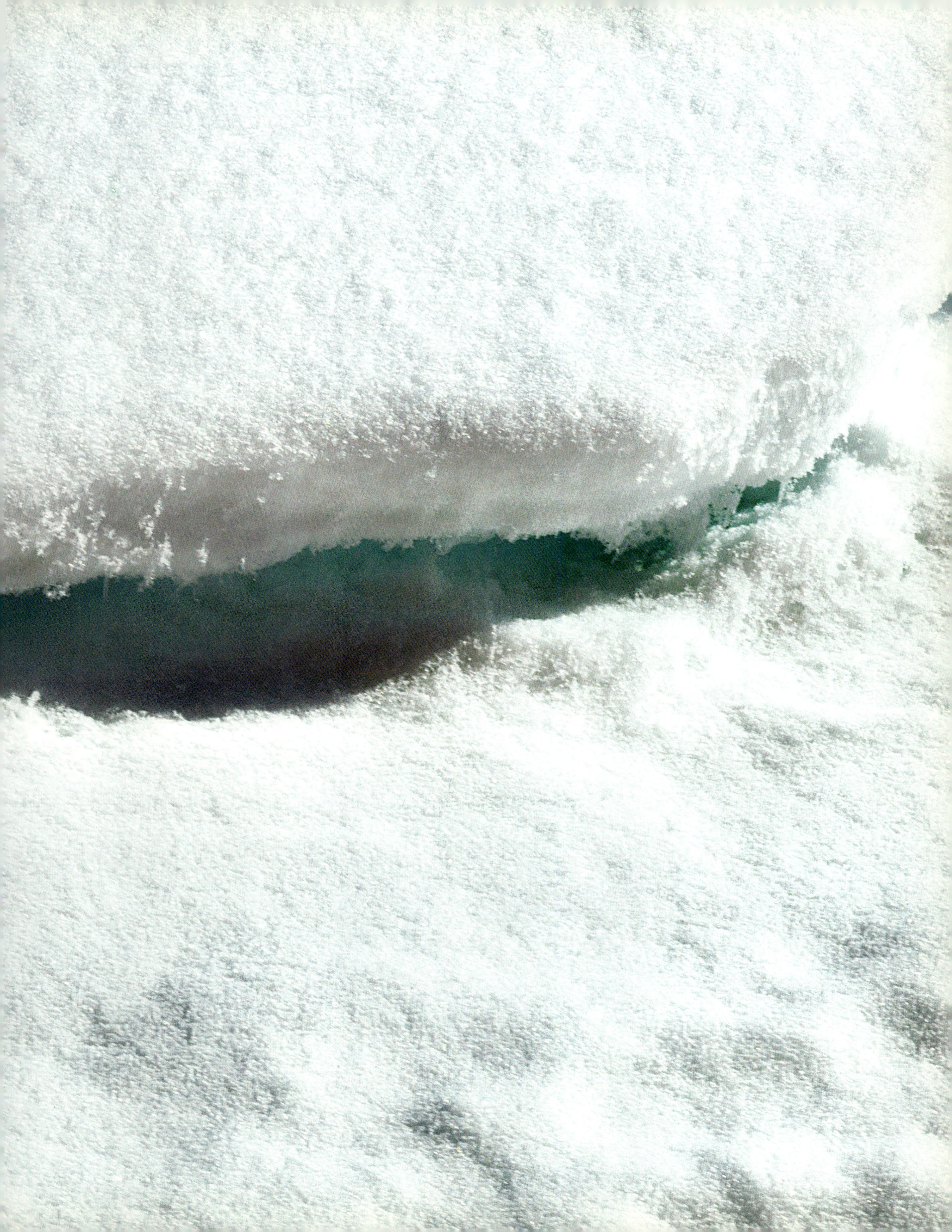

ICEBERG

the iceberg's saga
escaping from glacial strife
countless sculptures move

broken landscapes spill
disparate shapes intertwine
rising from the sea

incandescent rays
vibrate within slits of blue
enclosing sun's breath

waterfalls descend
light sculpting imagined forms
inhabiting dreams

concave to convex
ripples undulate, folds crease
envelop color

blue transforms to pink
secret melodies wander
ice puddles in melt

shattered reflections
float on the waters of time
shimmer and sparkle

broken arches weep
icebergs soft soliloquy
fragile destiny

INTERNAL FLOW, DISKO BAY, GREENLAND.

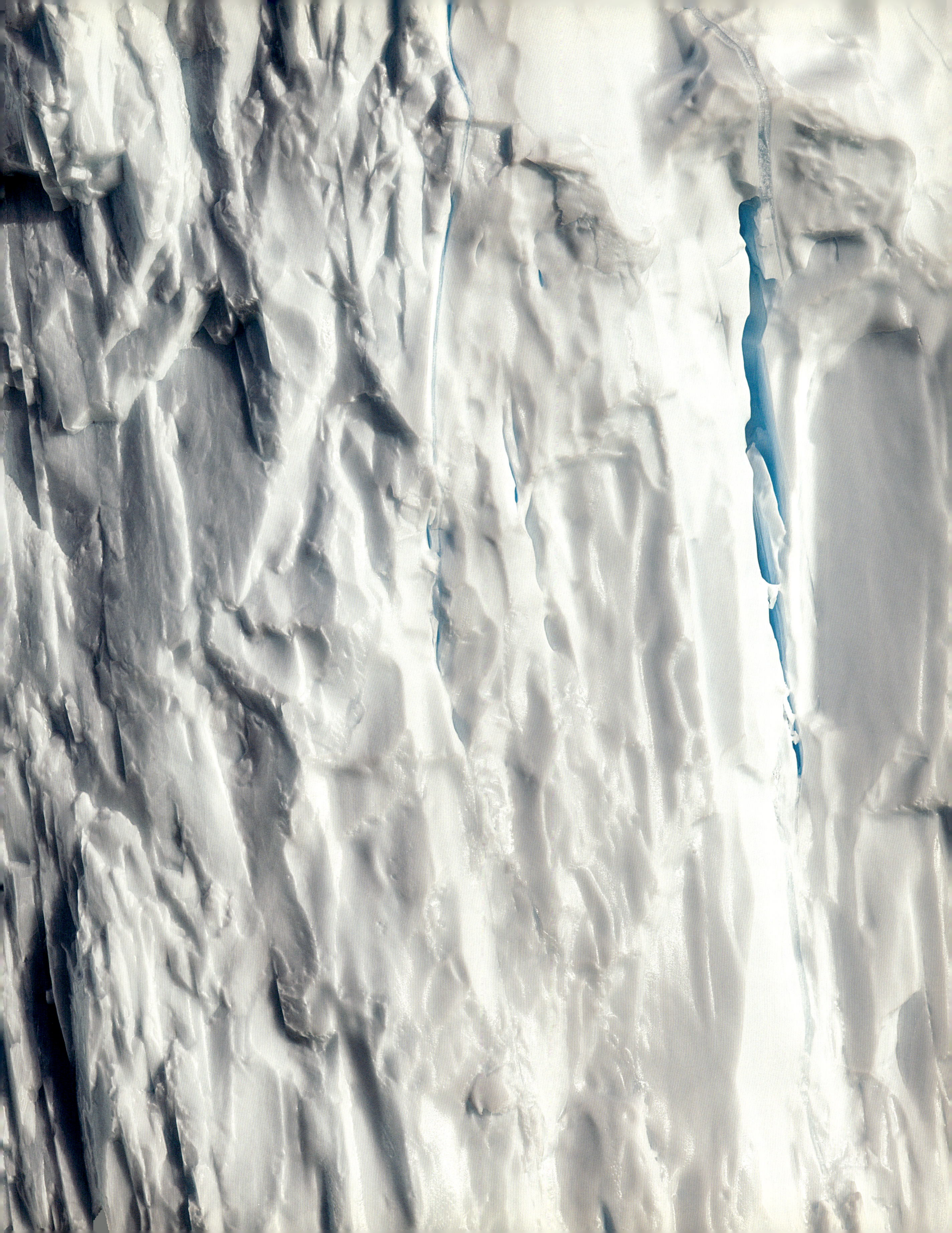

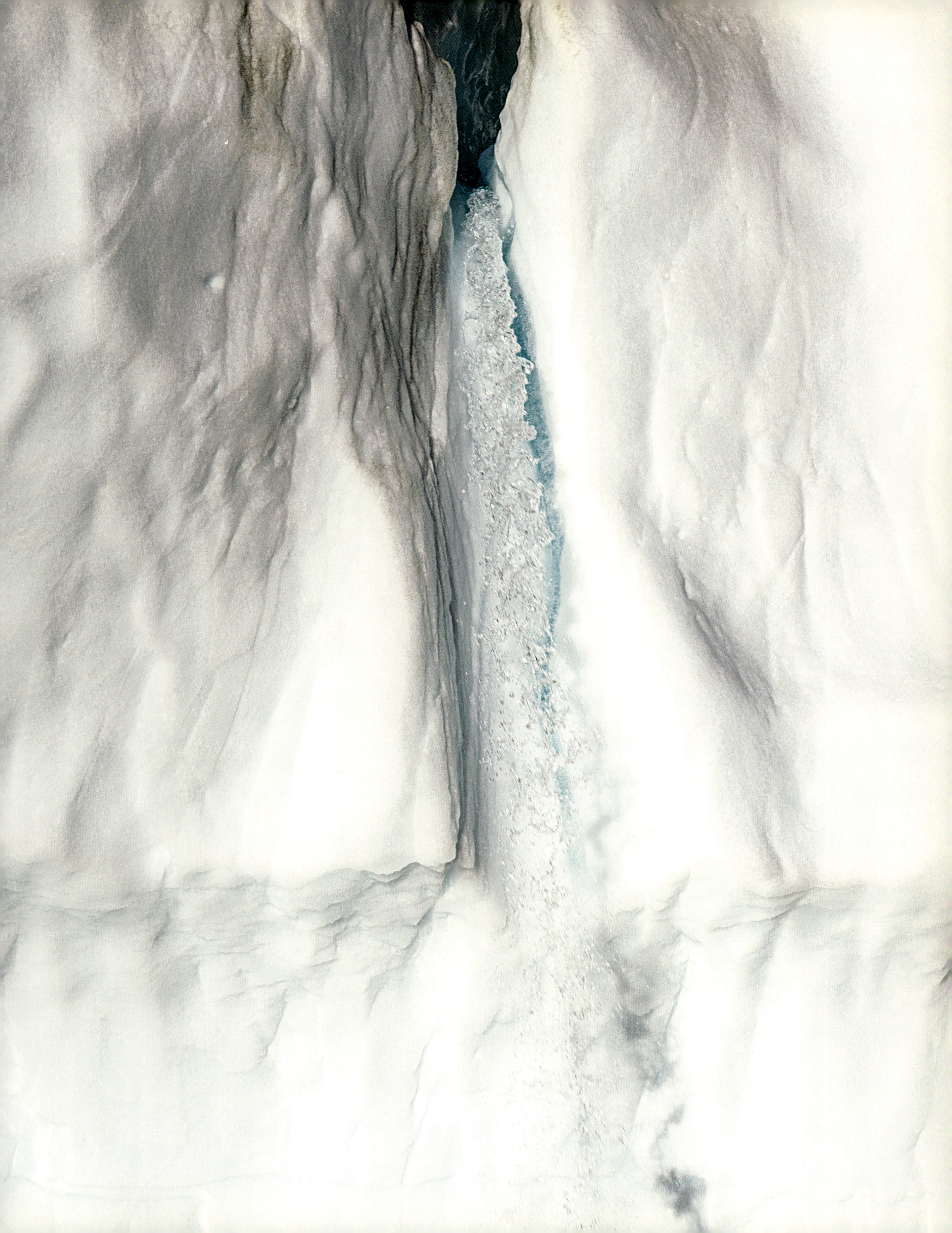

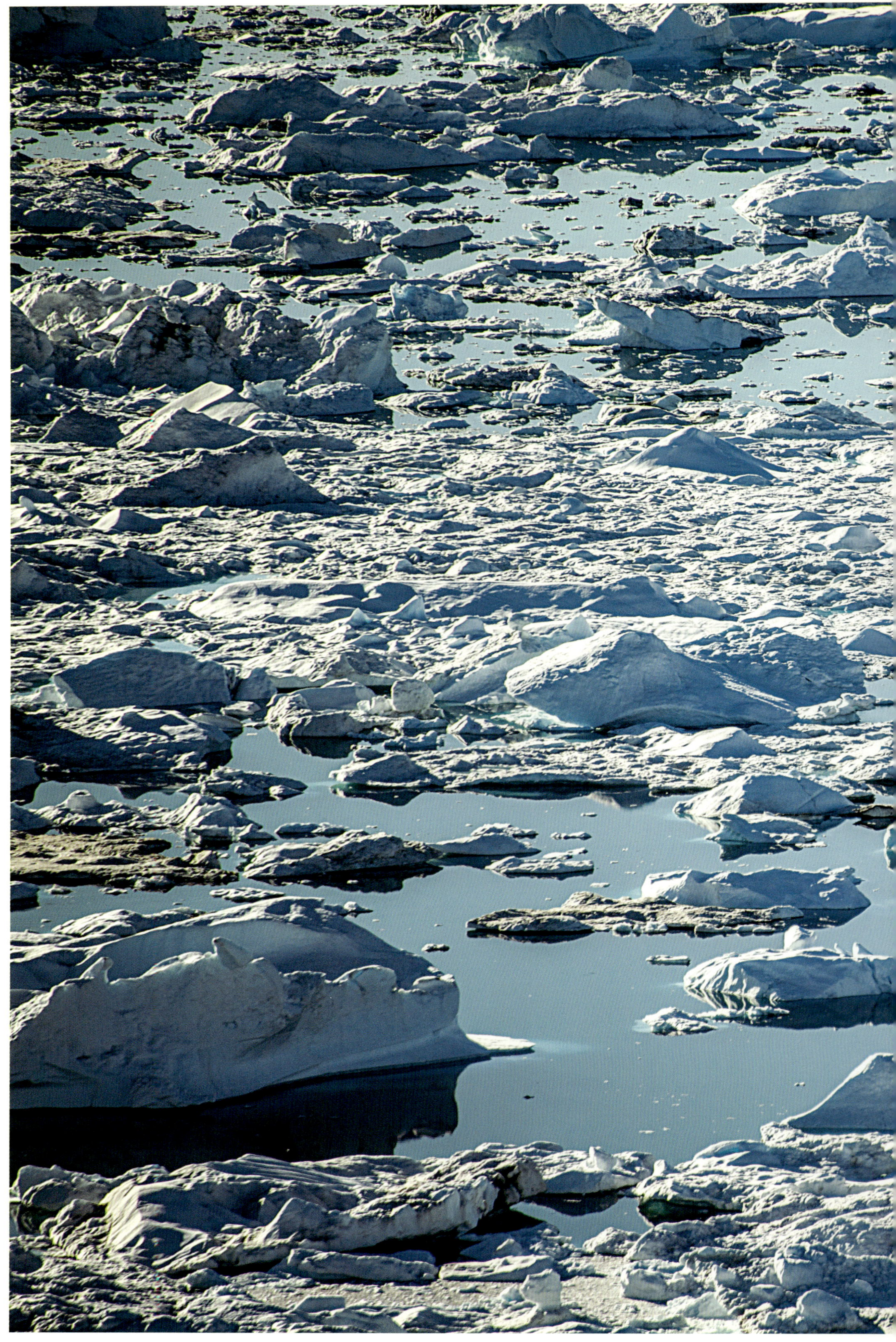

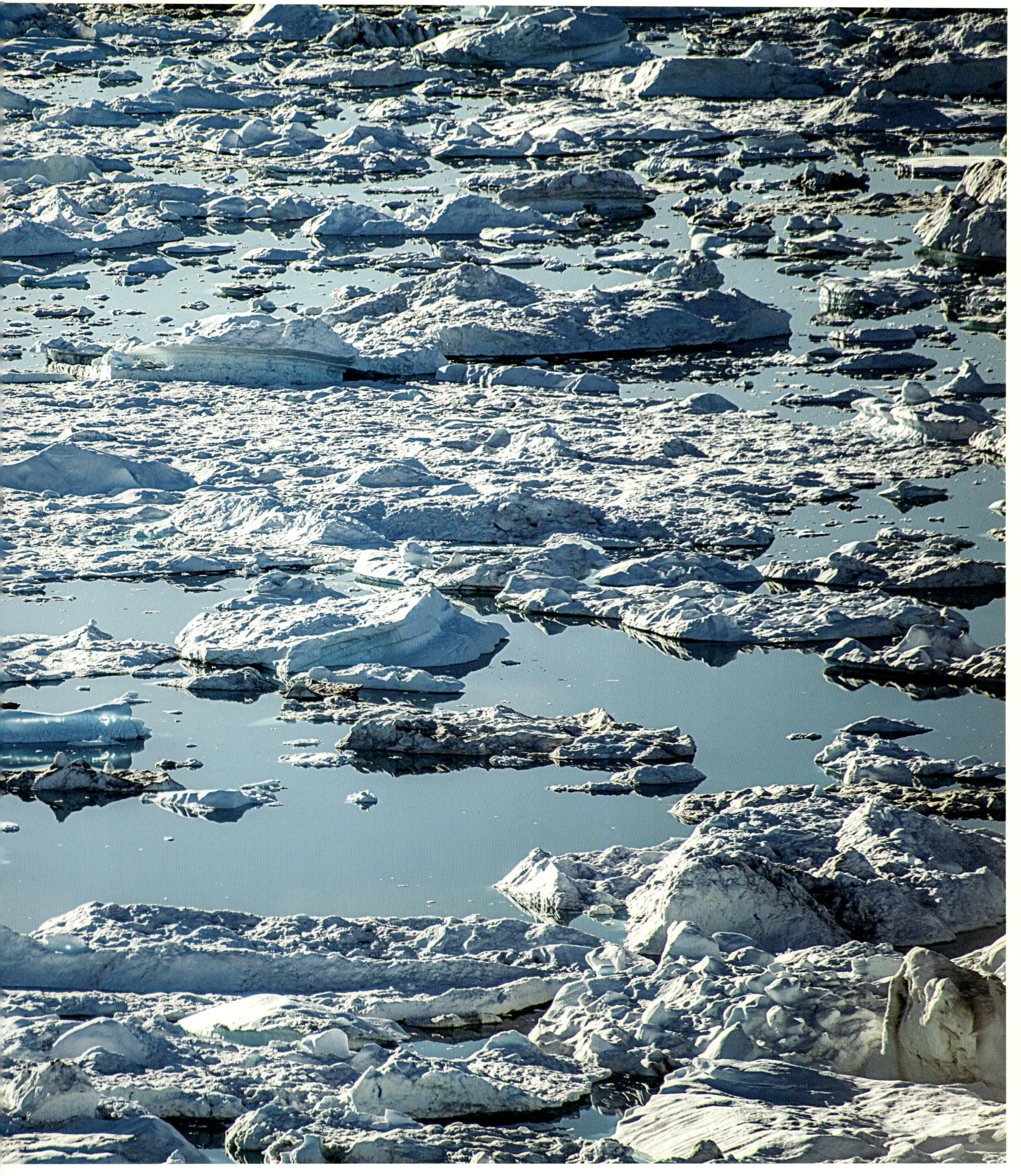

ILULISSAT ICEFJORD, GREENLAND.
previous pages BLUE SLIT, DISKO BAY, GREENLAND.
following pages BROKEN ARCHES, DISKO BAY, GREENLAND.

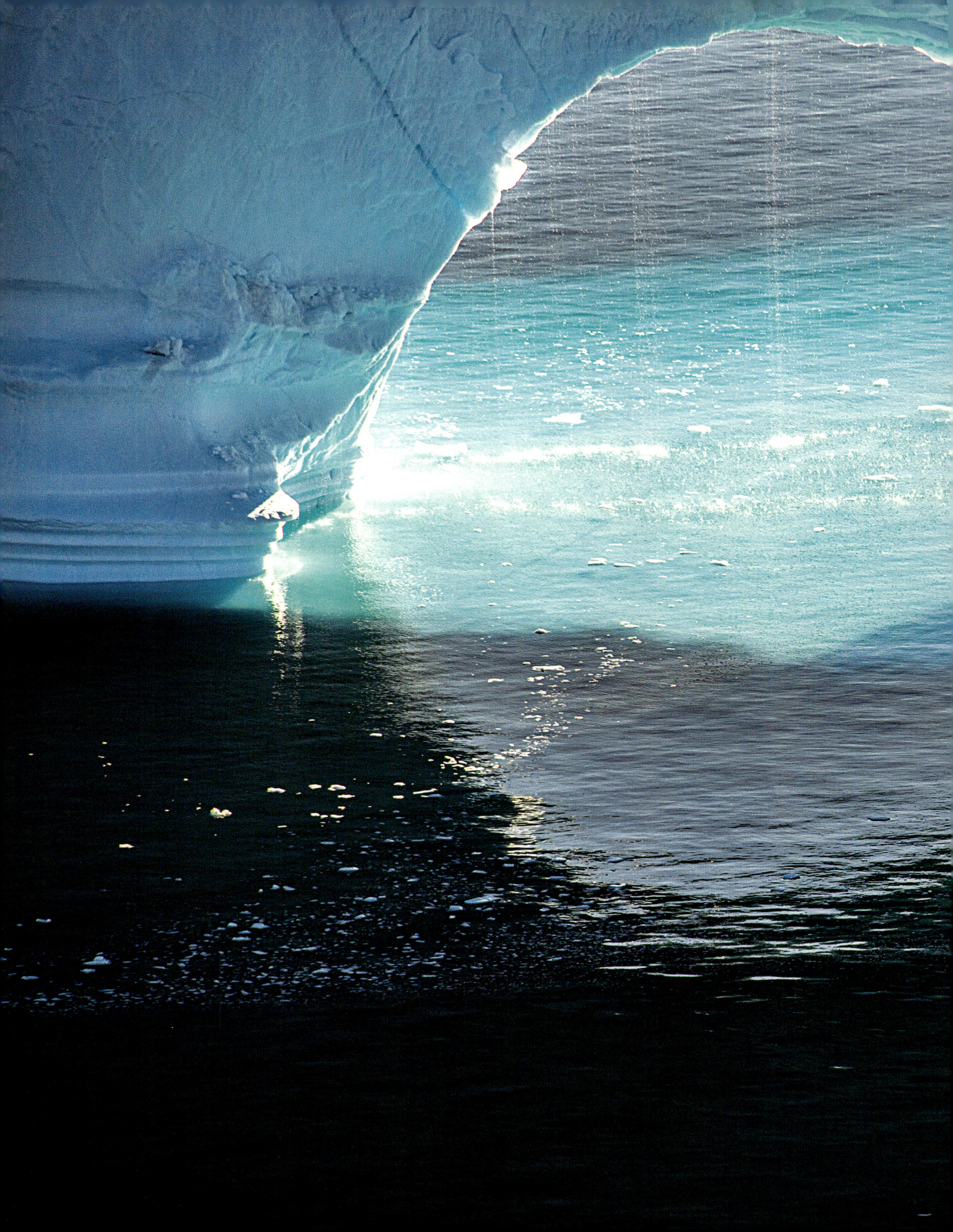

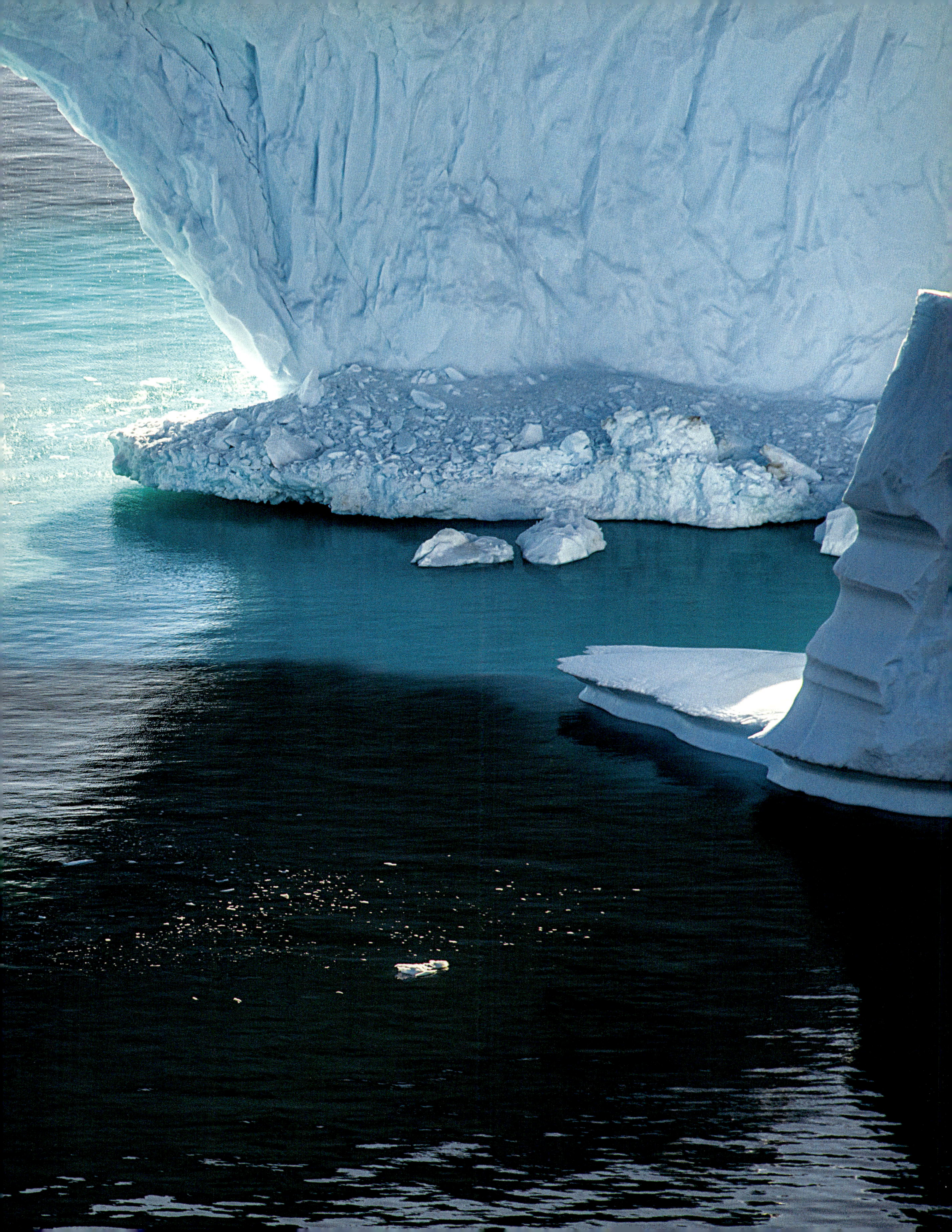

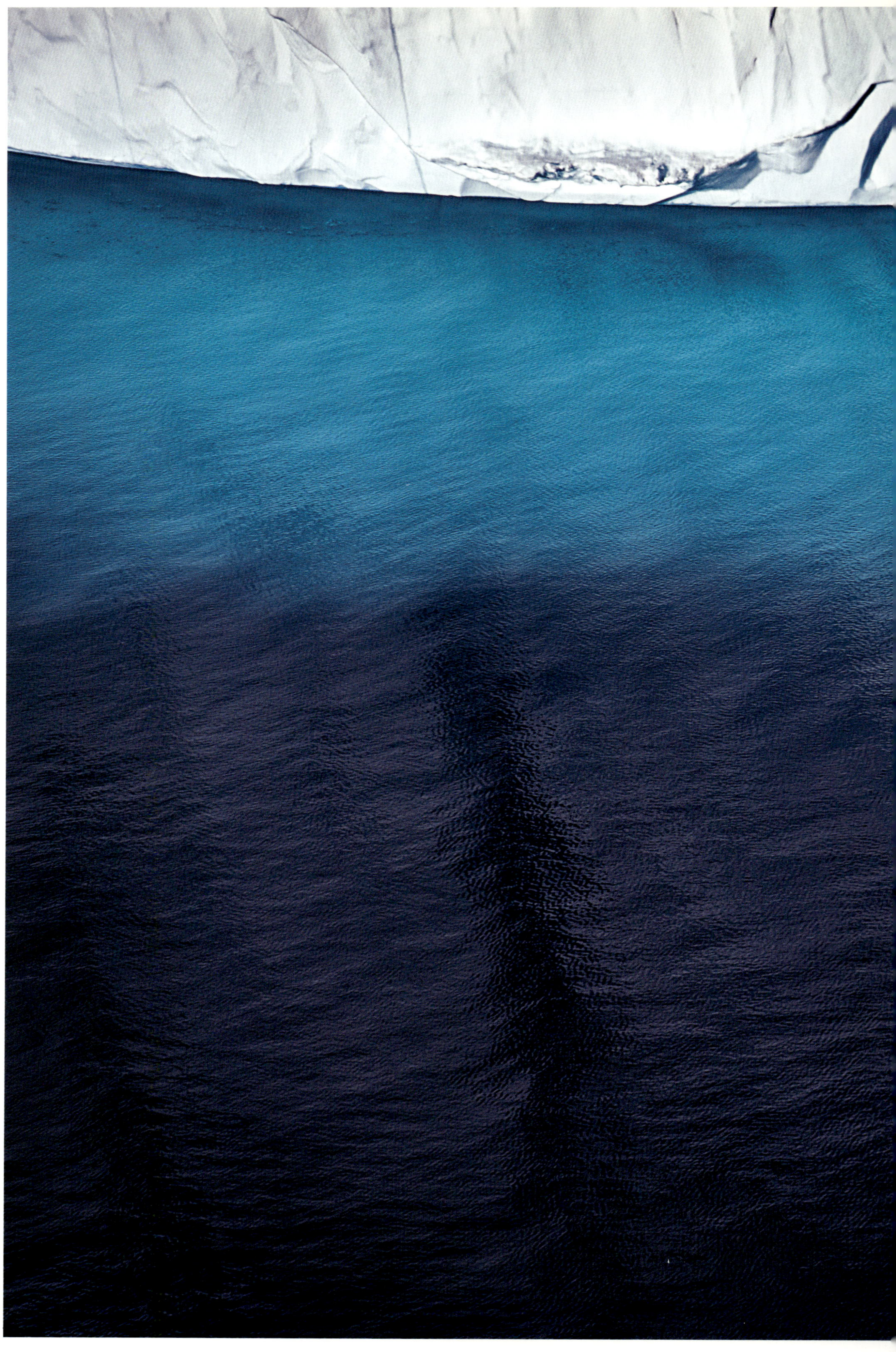

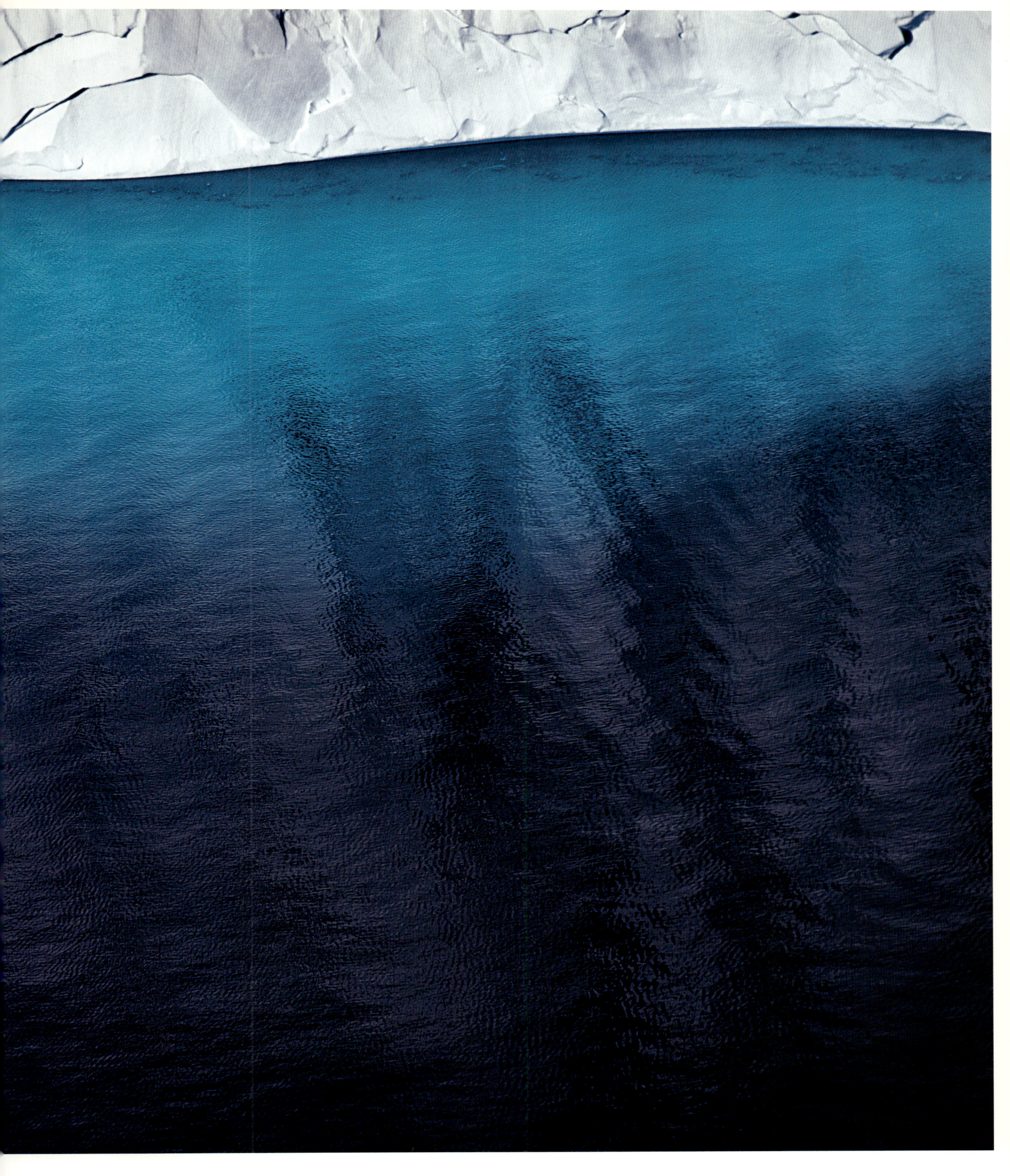

REFLECTIONS, SULLORSUAQ STRAIT, GREENLAND.

following pages AMIDST THE ICEBERGS, DISKO BAY, GREENLAND, 9:20 PM.

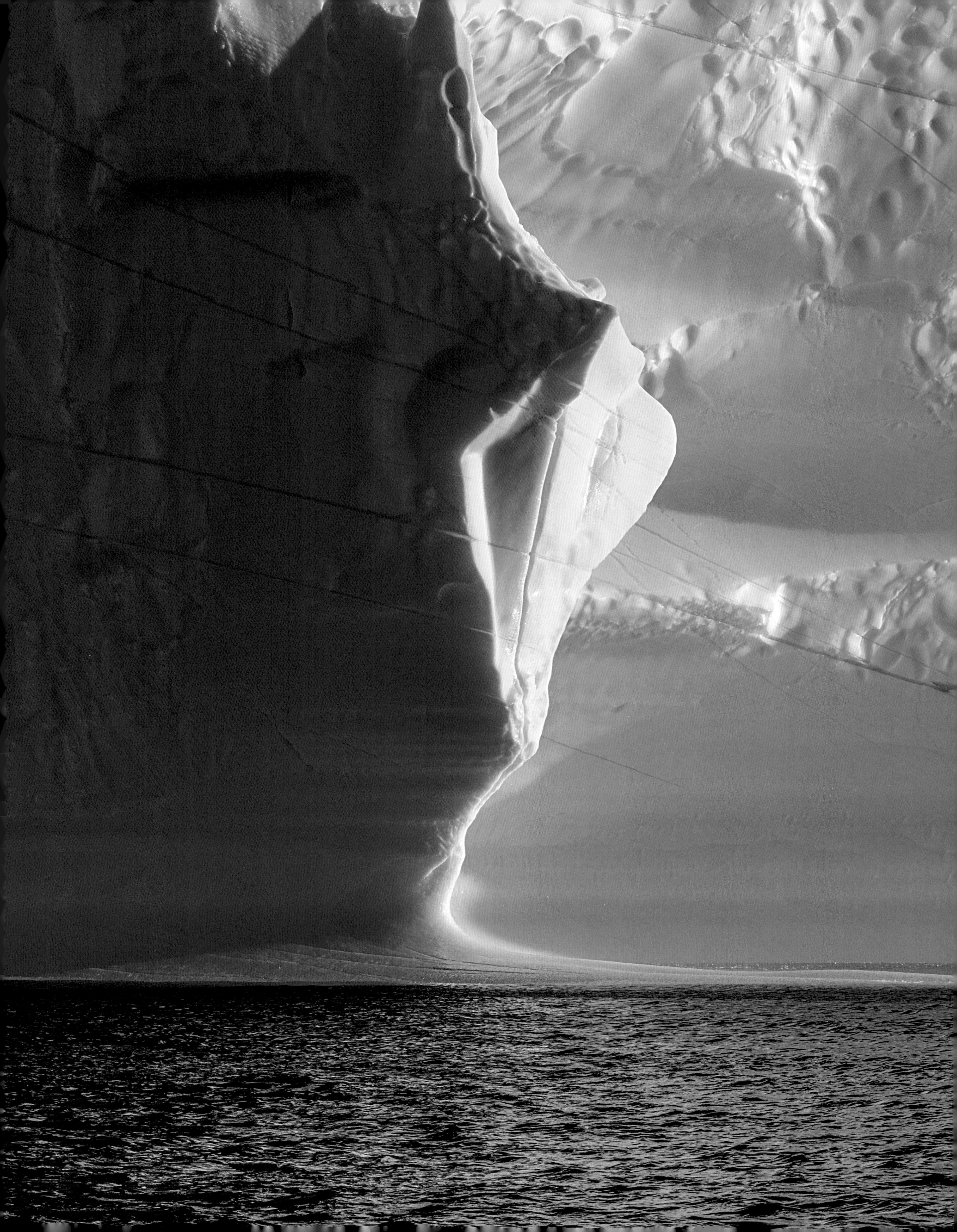

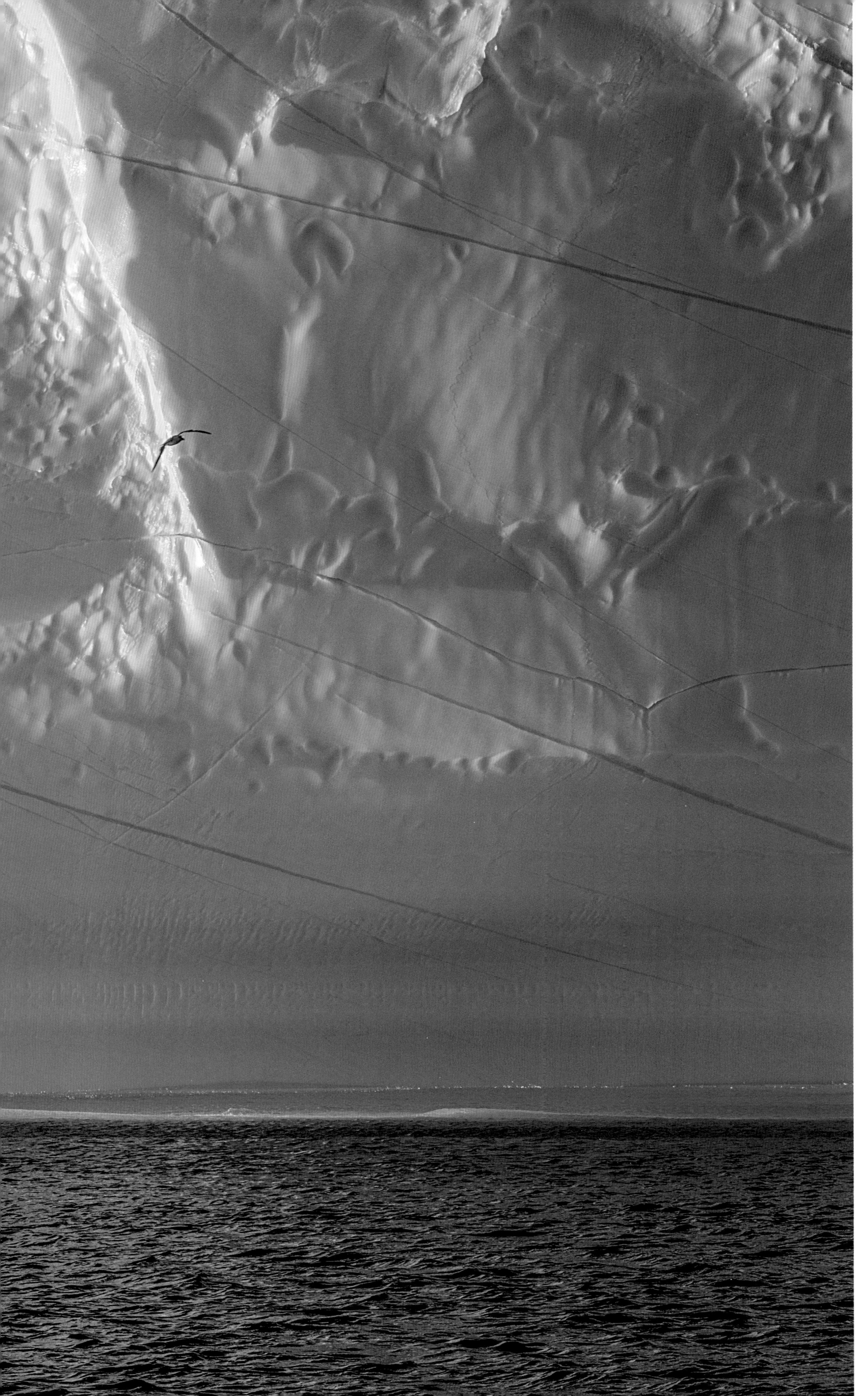

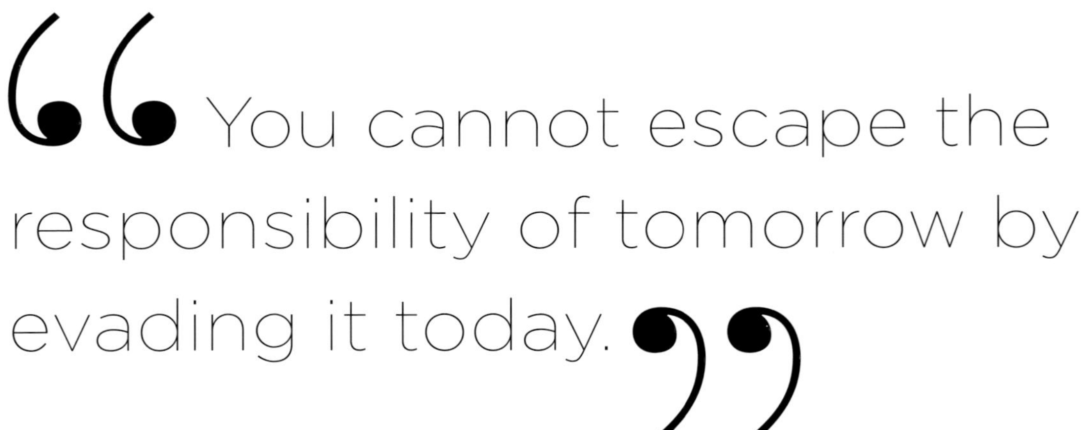

ABRAHAM LINCOLN

DISKO BAY, GREENLAND, 11:05 AM.

following pages CAPE NORWAY, FRANZ JOSEPH LAND, 4:46 PM, 81 DEGREES N, 1 DEGREE C.

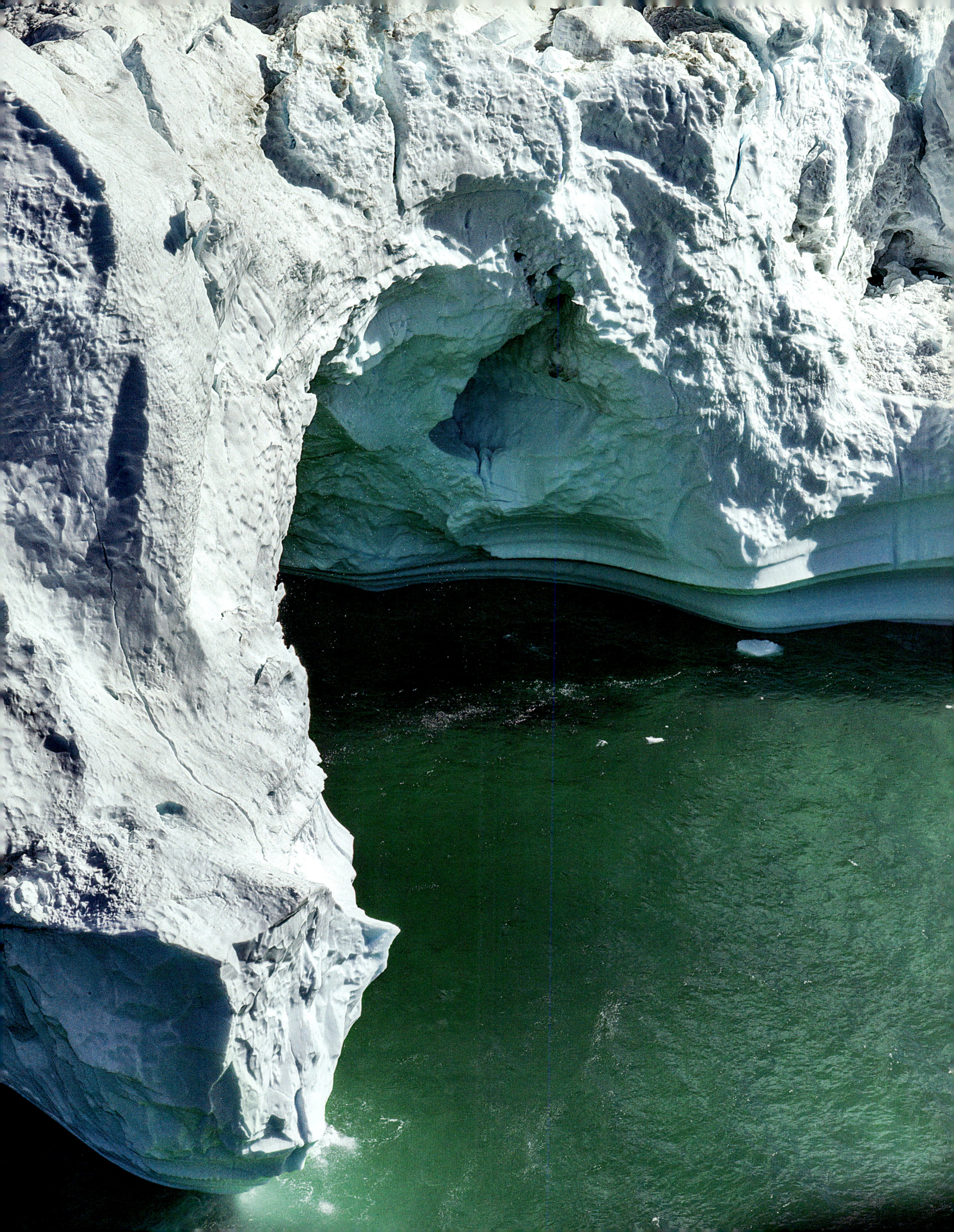

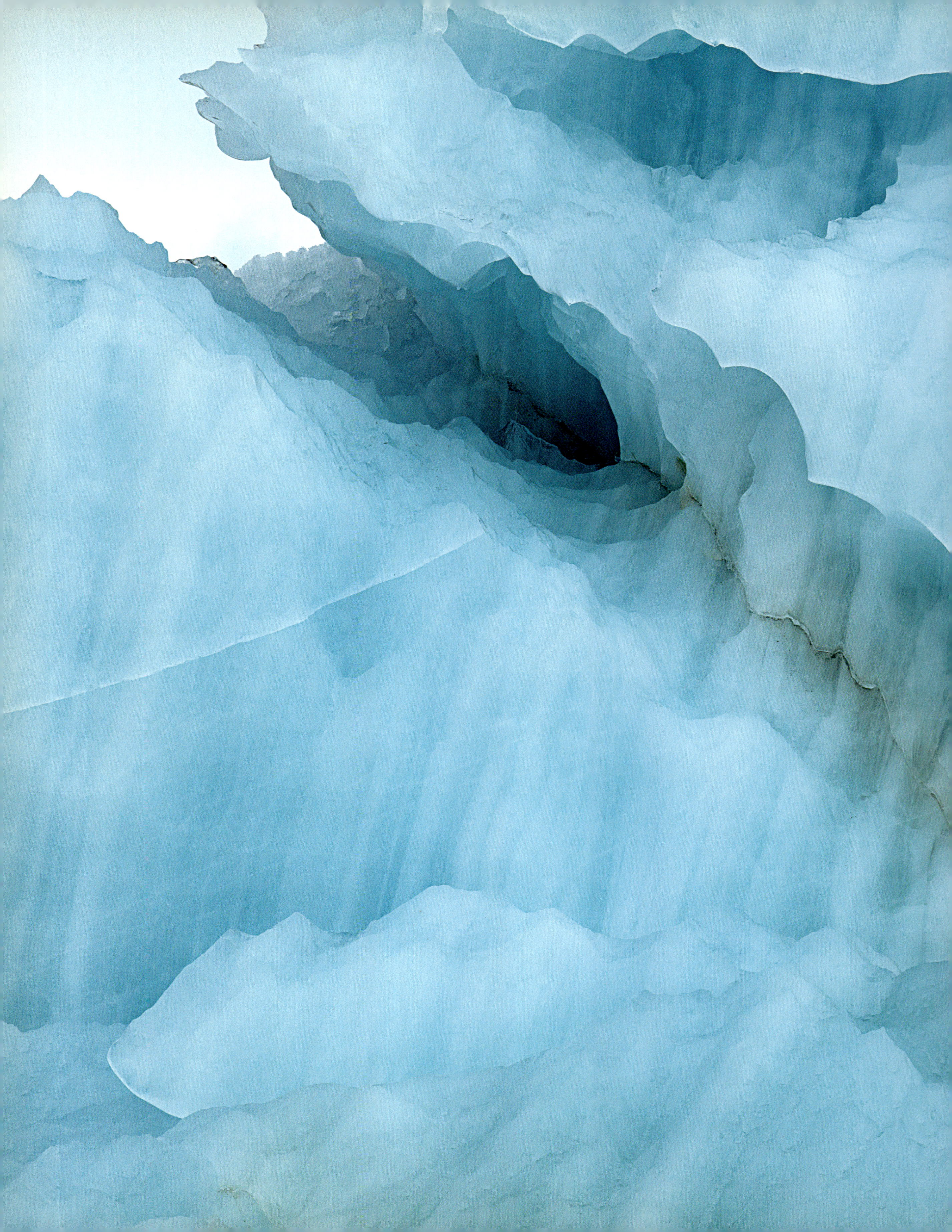

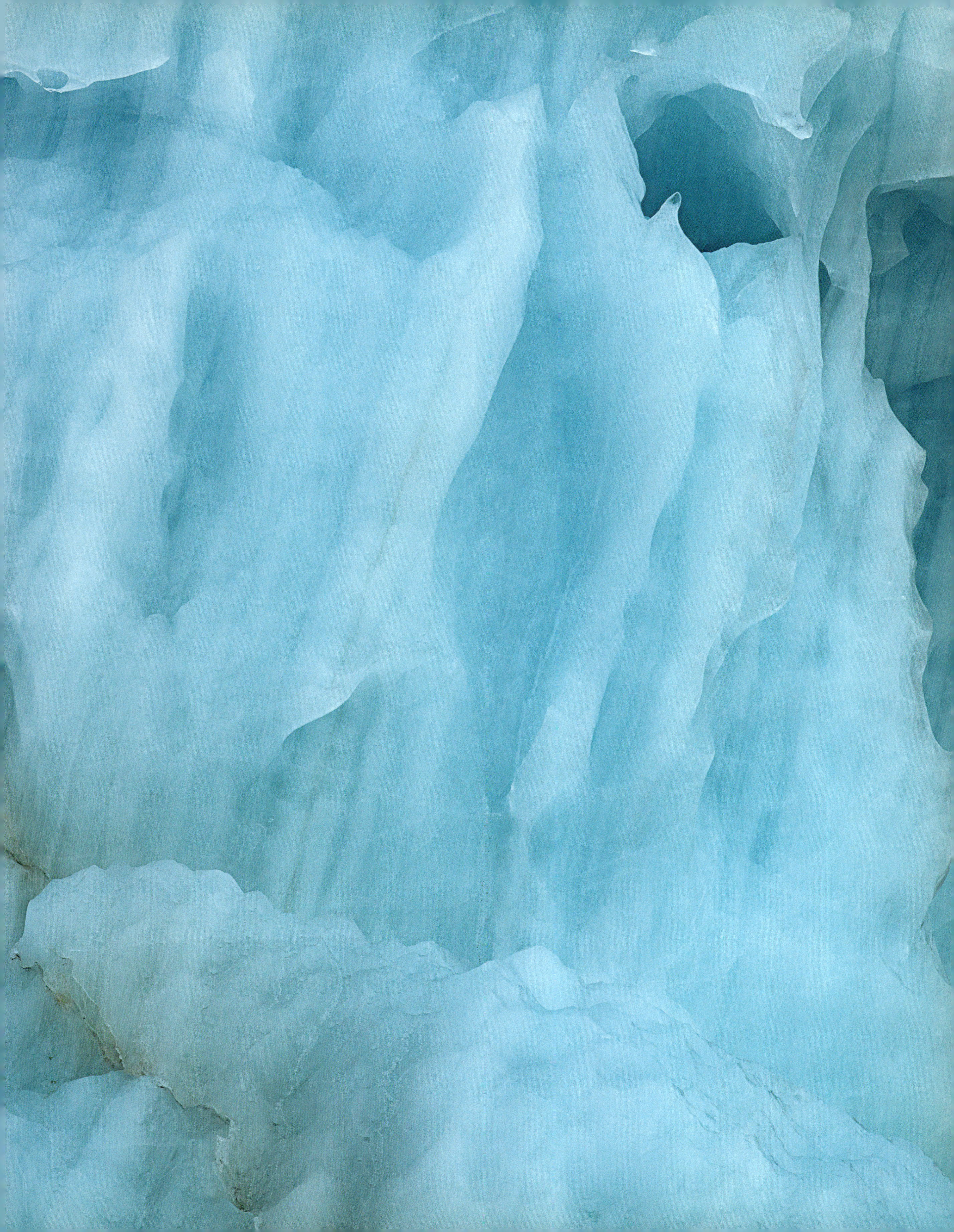

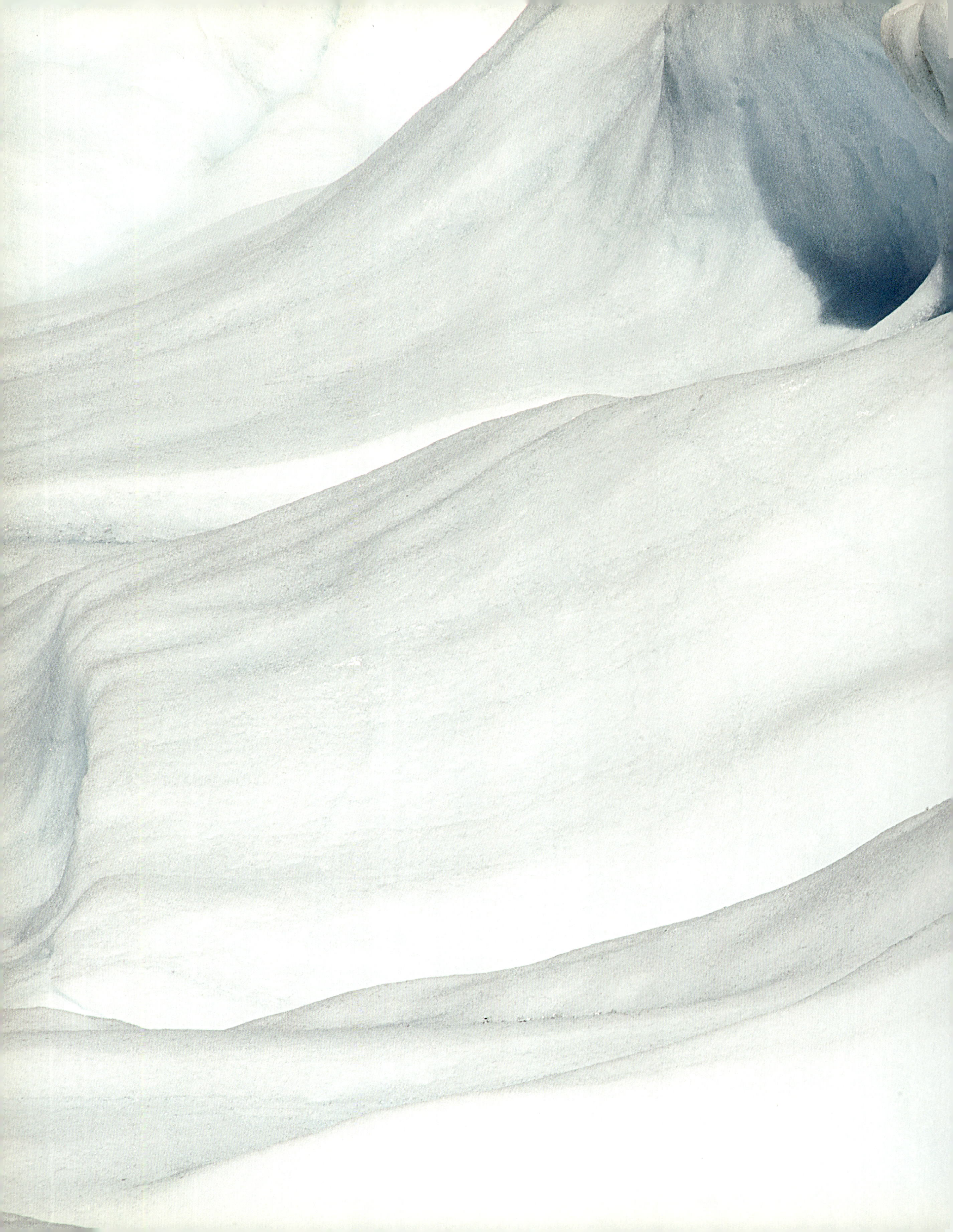

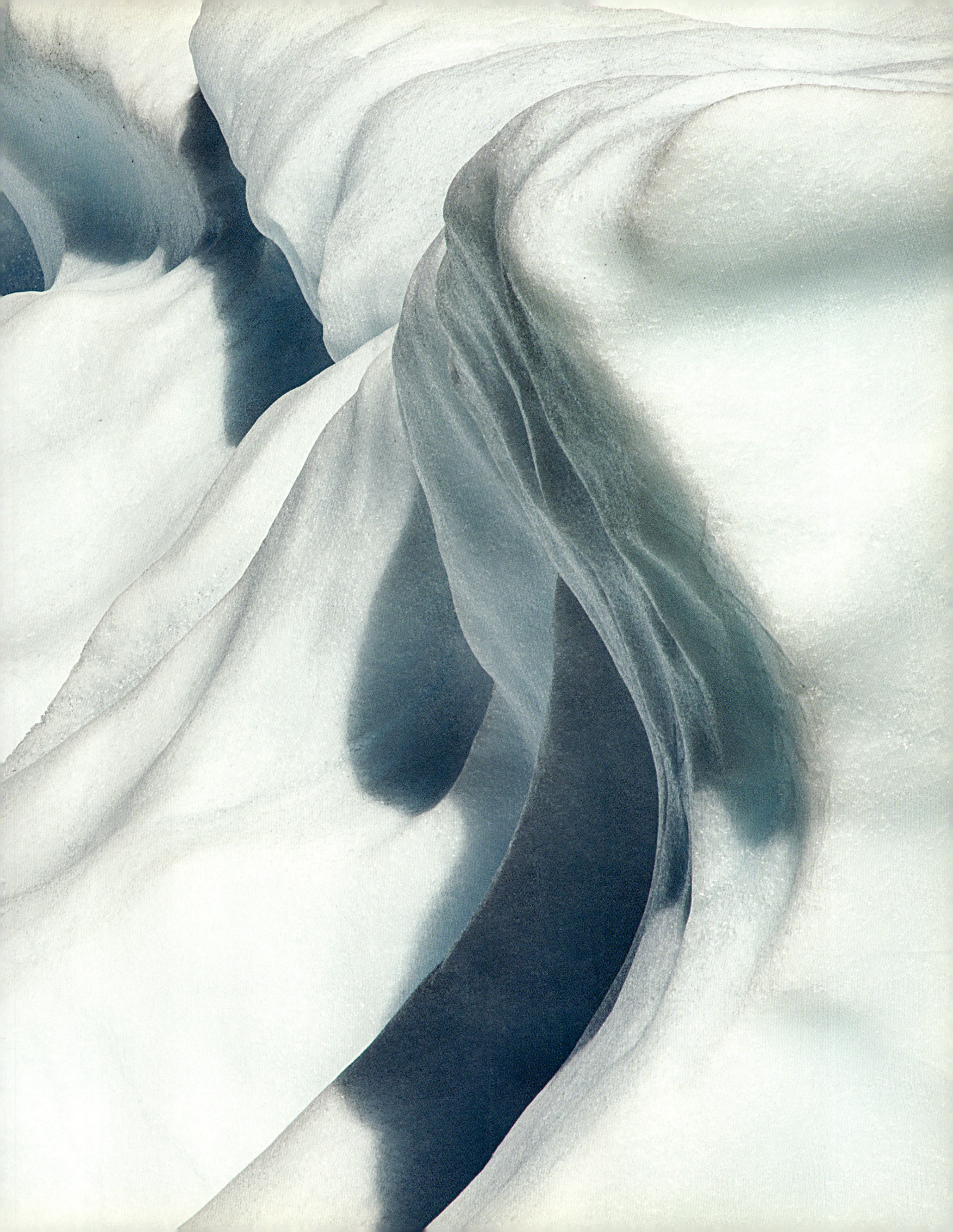

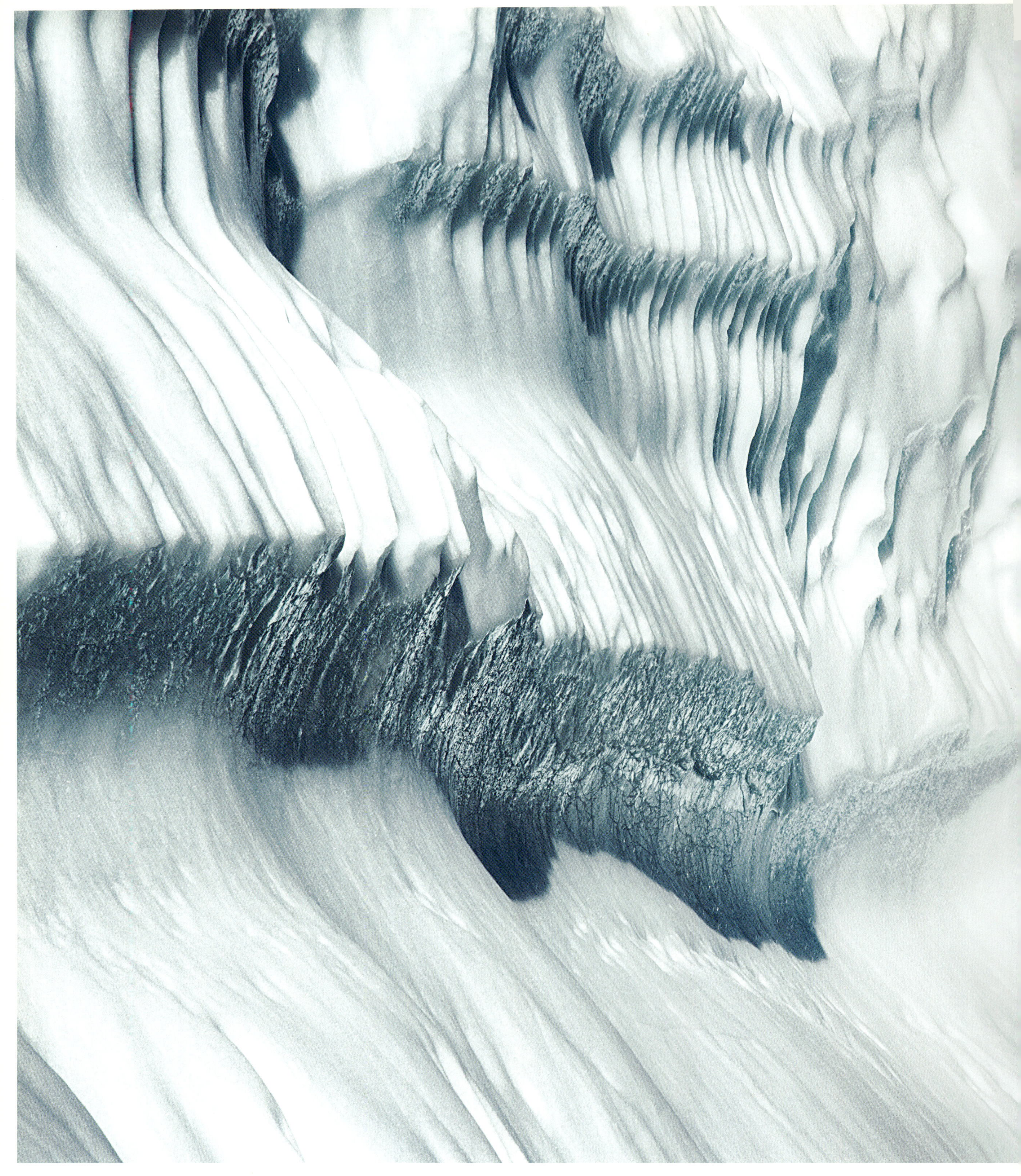

REACHING OUT, DE QUERVAIN HAVN, GREENLAND.
previous pages UNDULATION, DE QUERVAIN HAVN, GREENLAND.

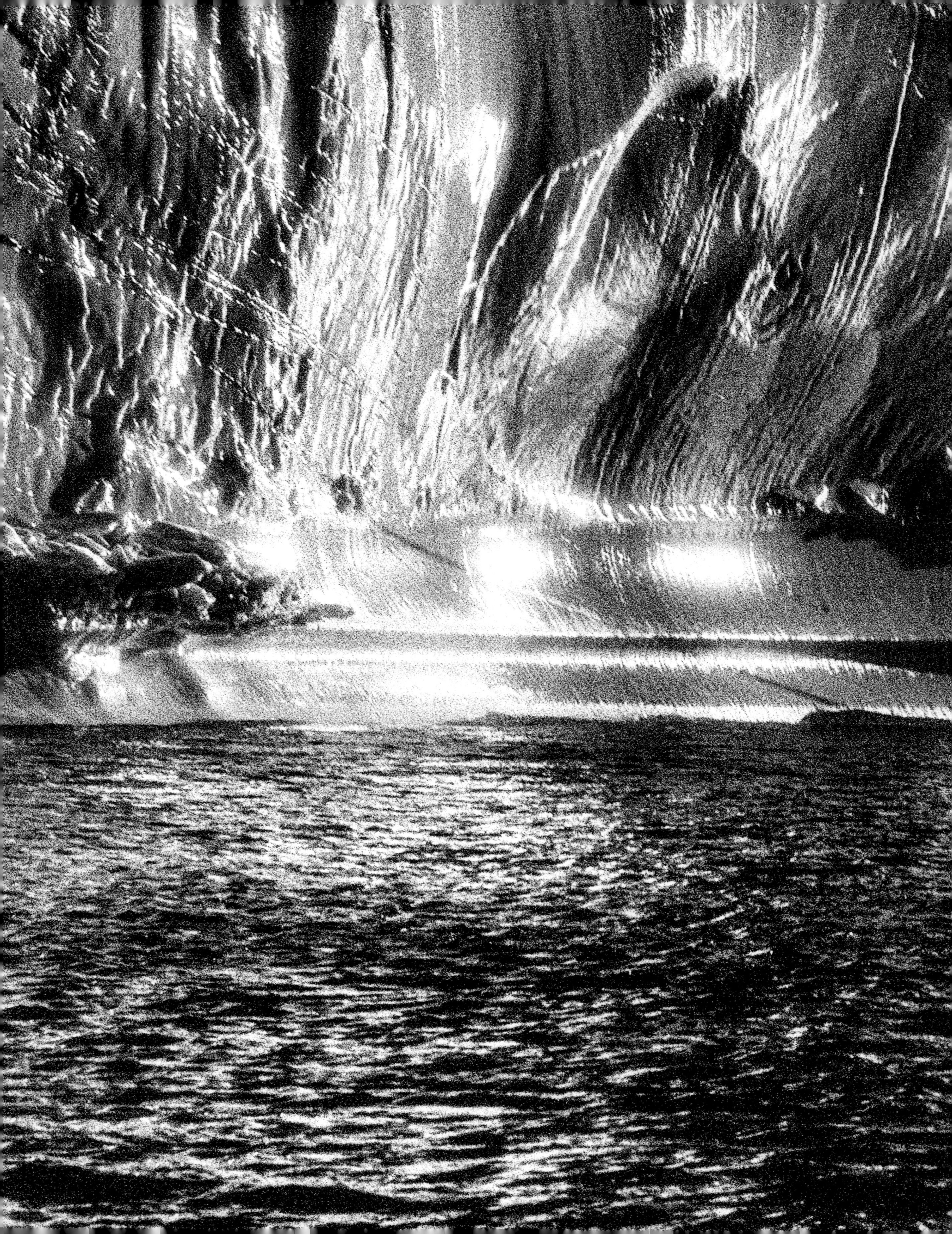

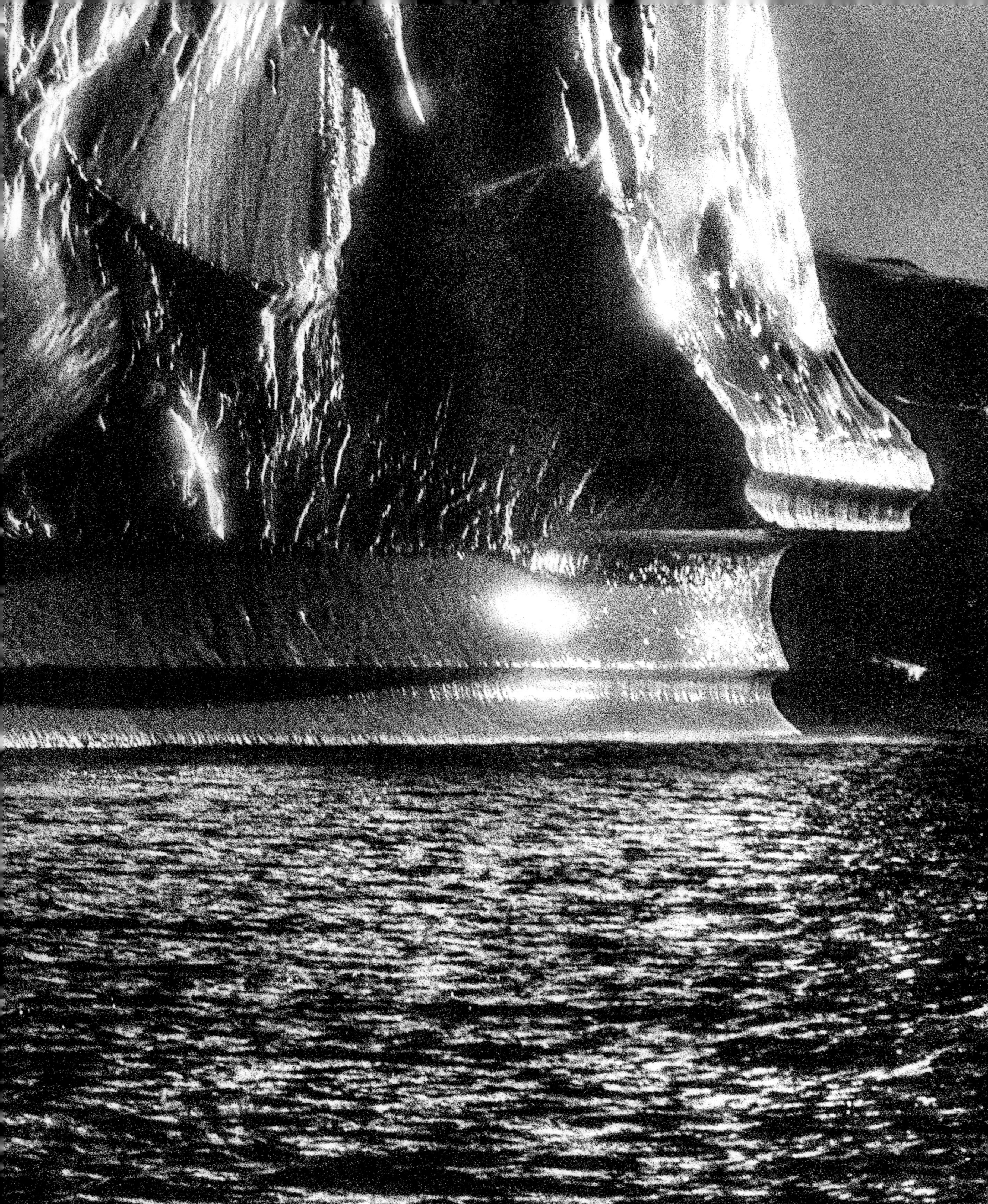

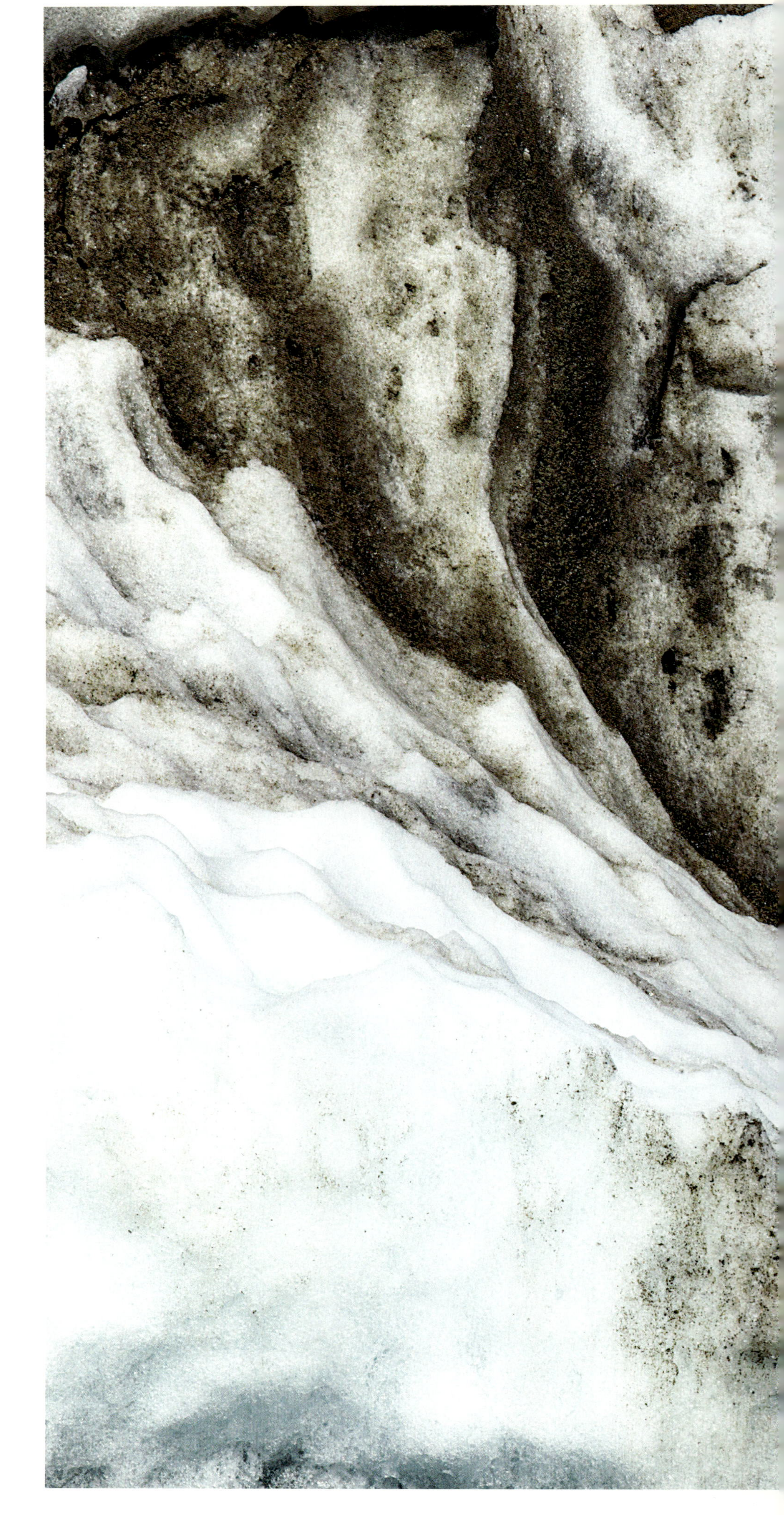

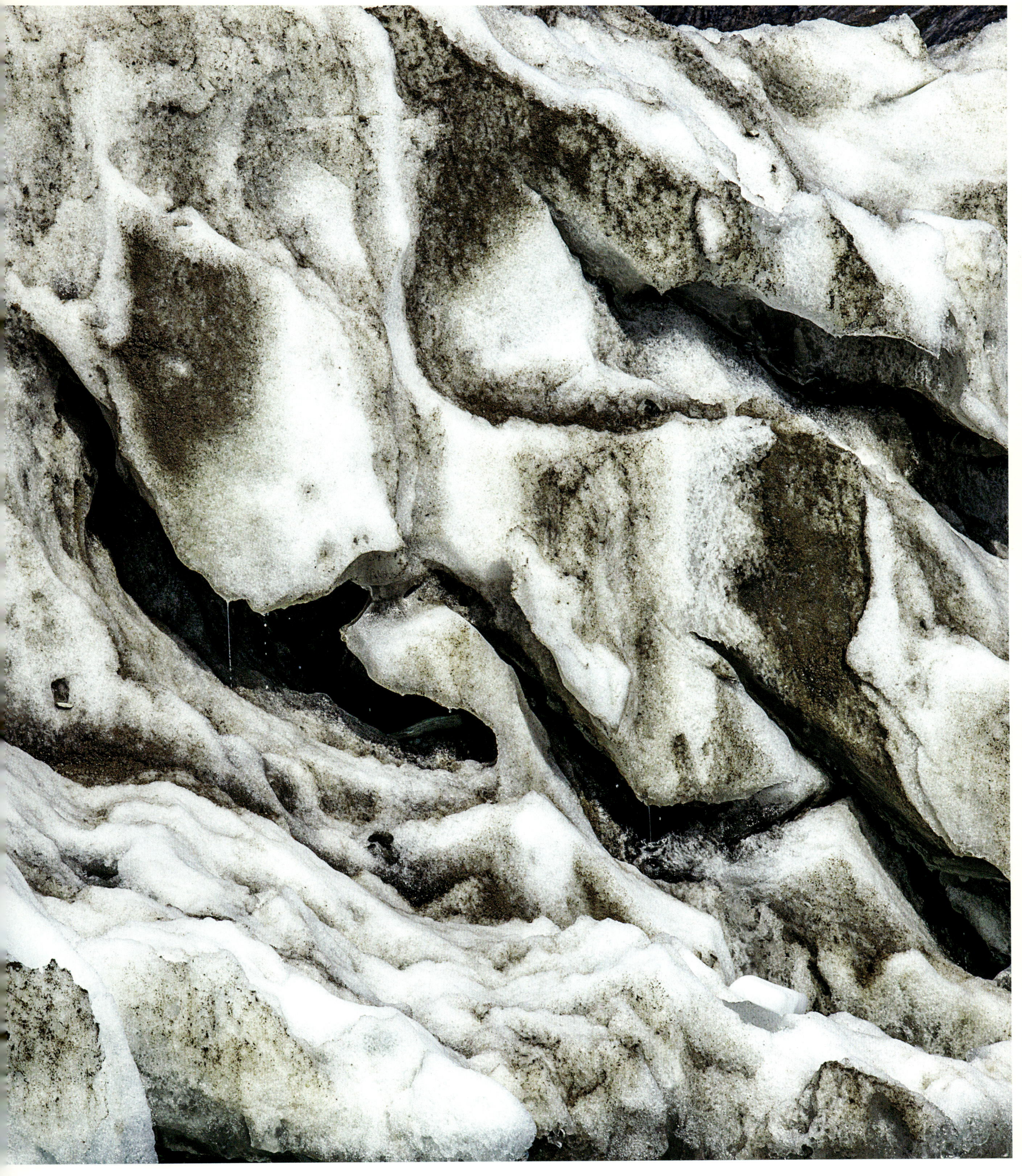

SILT AND ICE, DE QUERVAIN HAVN, GREENLAND.
previous pages ICEBERGS II, DISKO BAY, GREENLAND.

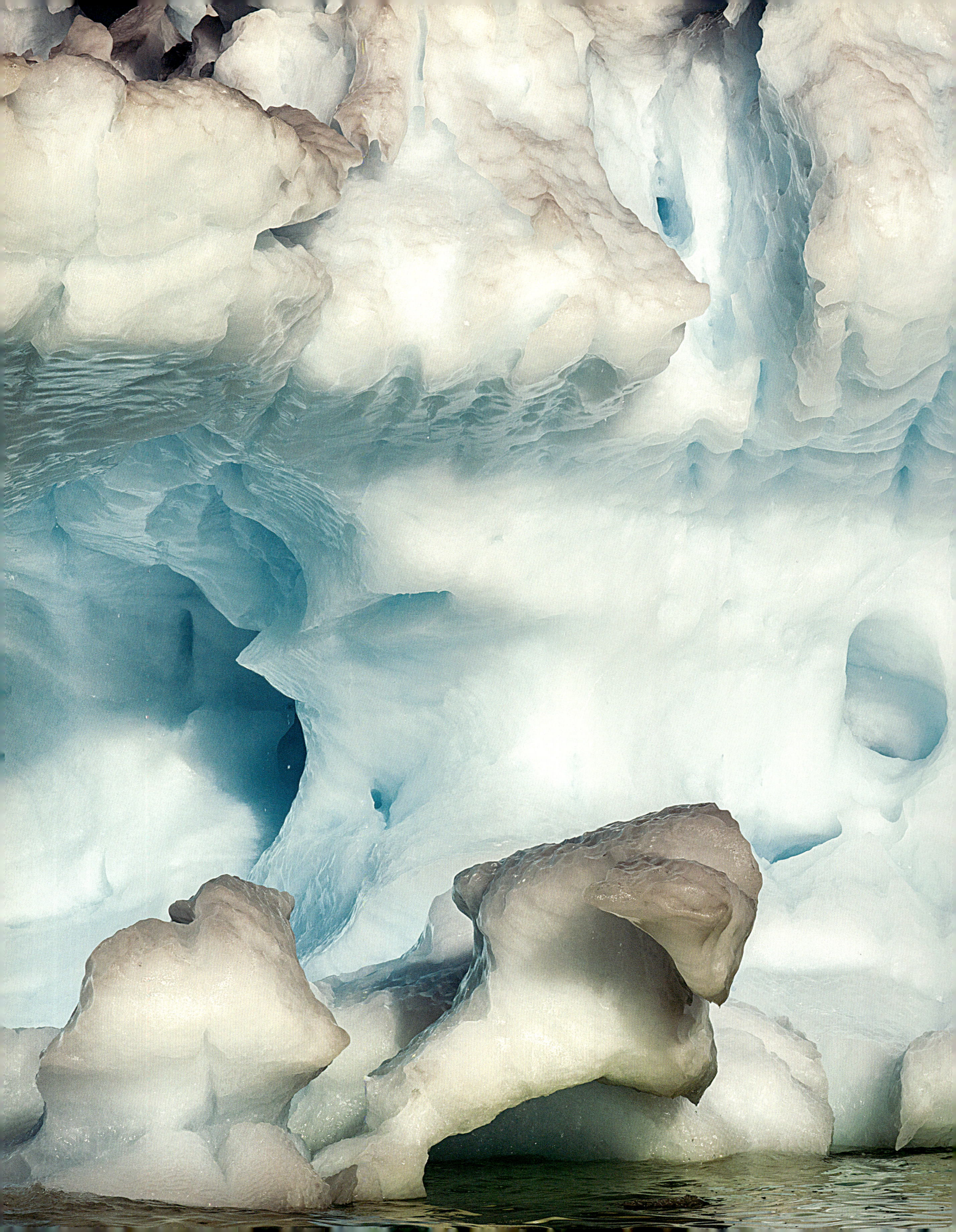

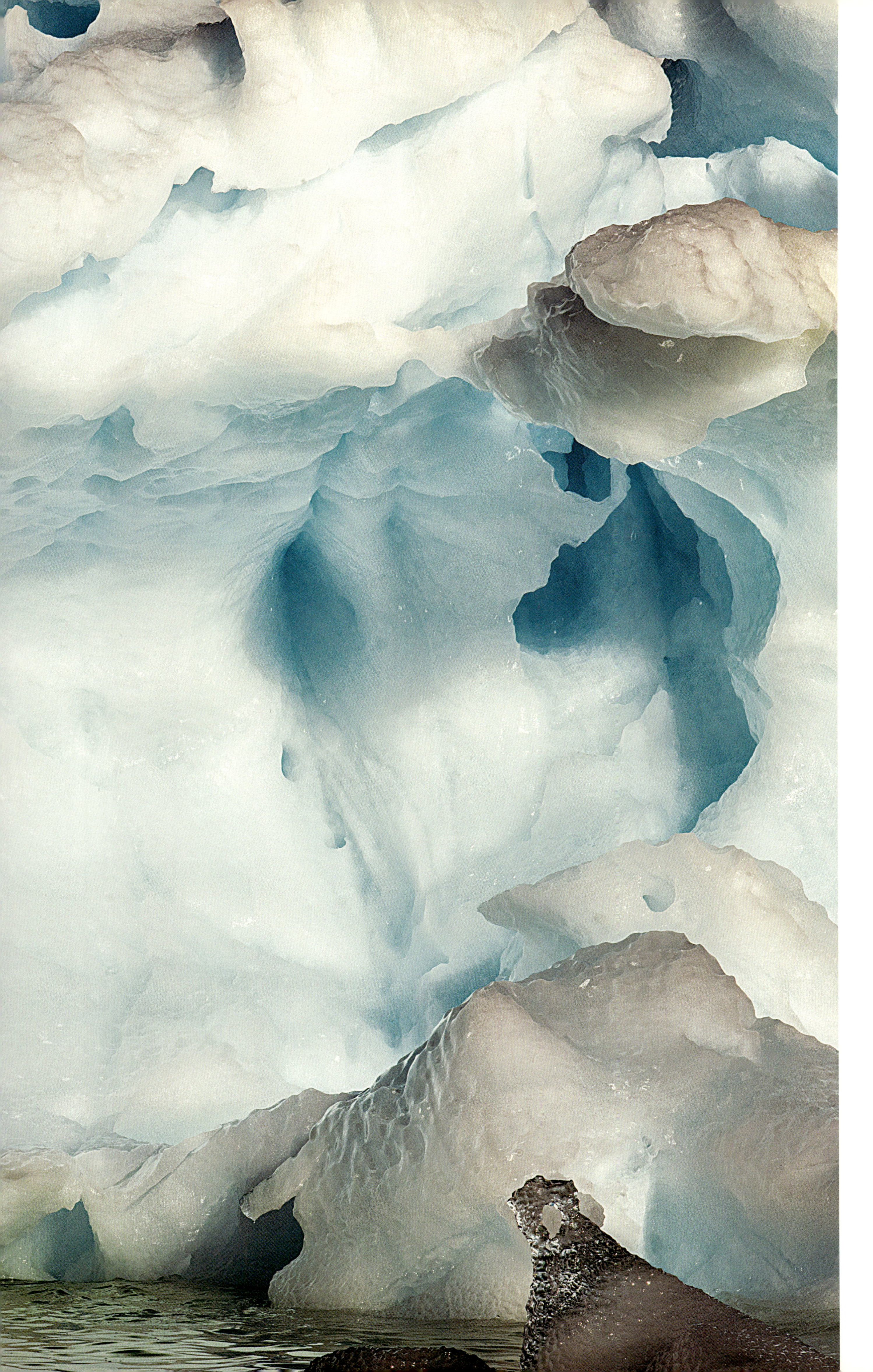

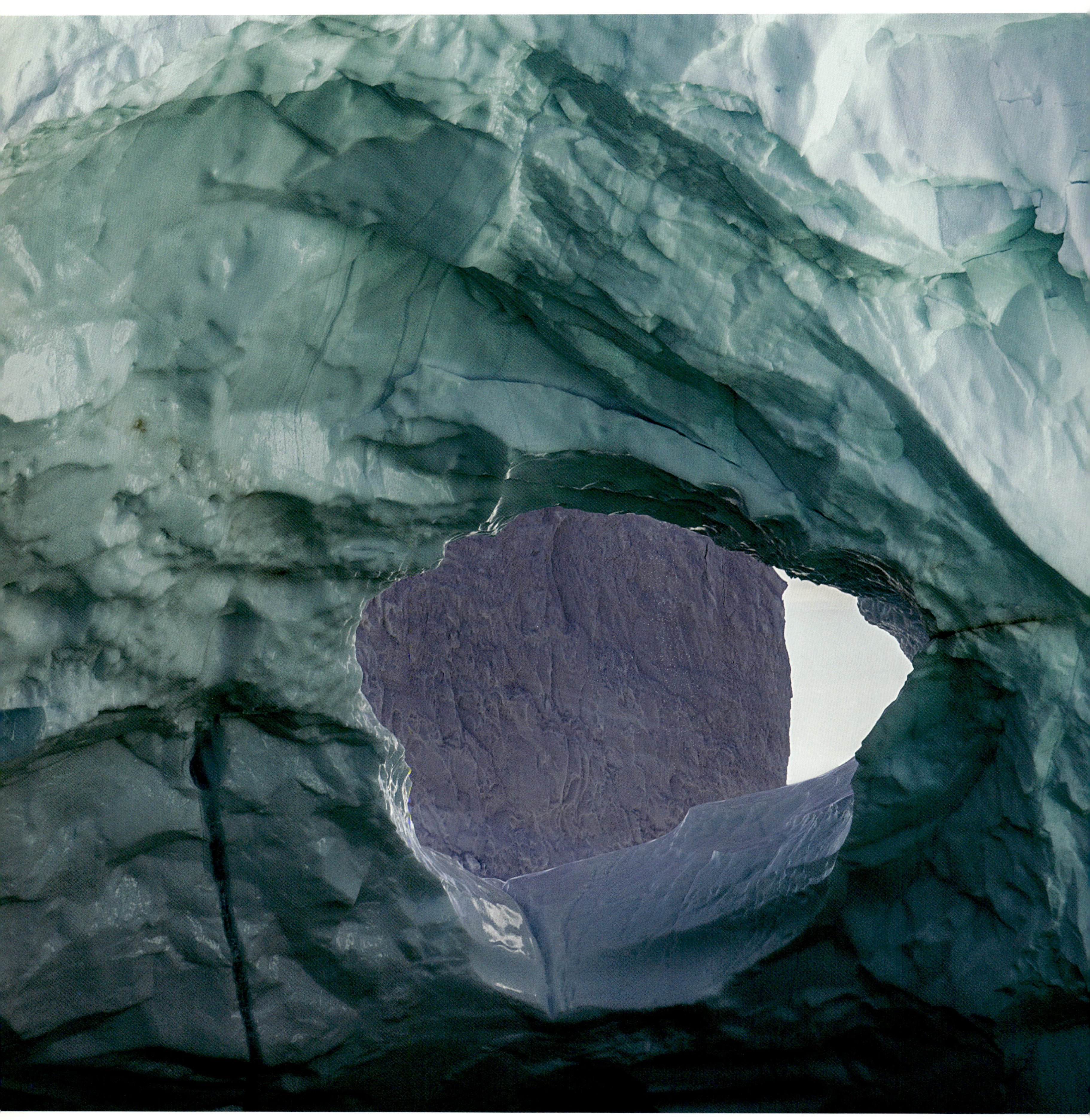

ULTRAVIOLET SHAPES, DISKO BAY, GREENLAND.

previous pages INSIDE THE ICE, SULLORSUAQ STRAIT, GREENLAND.

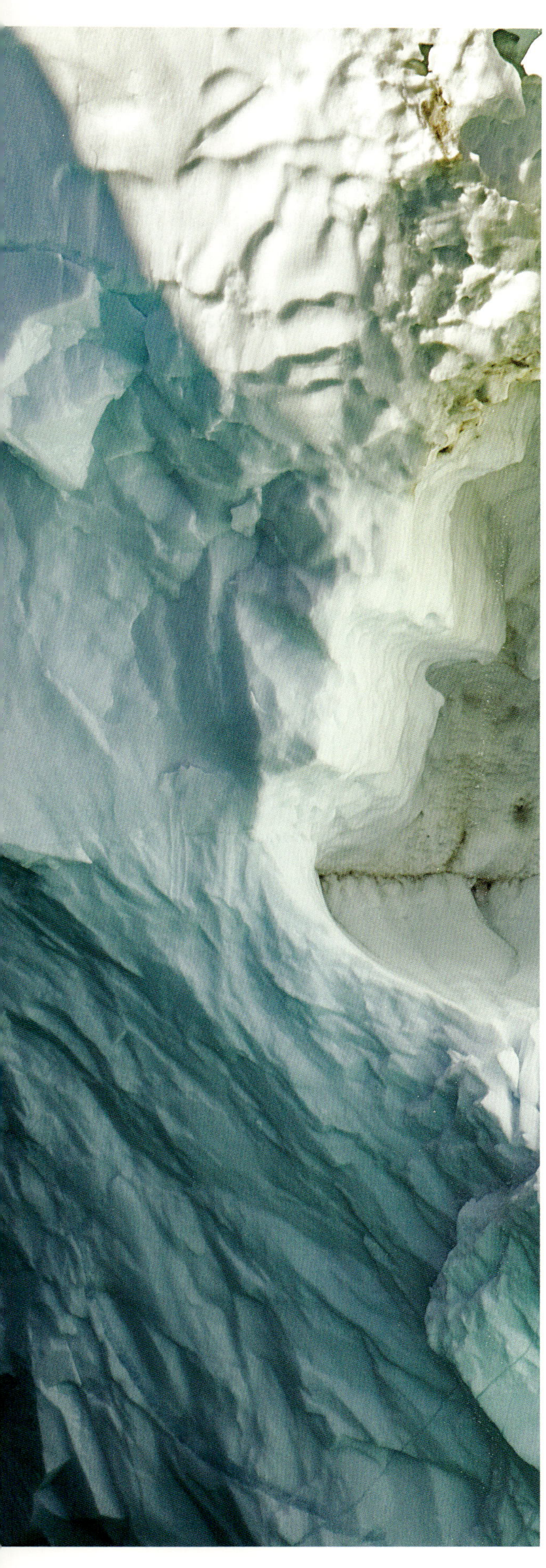

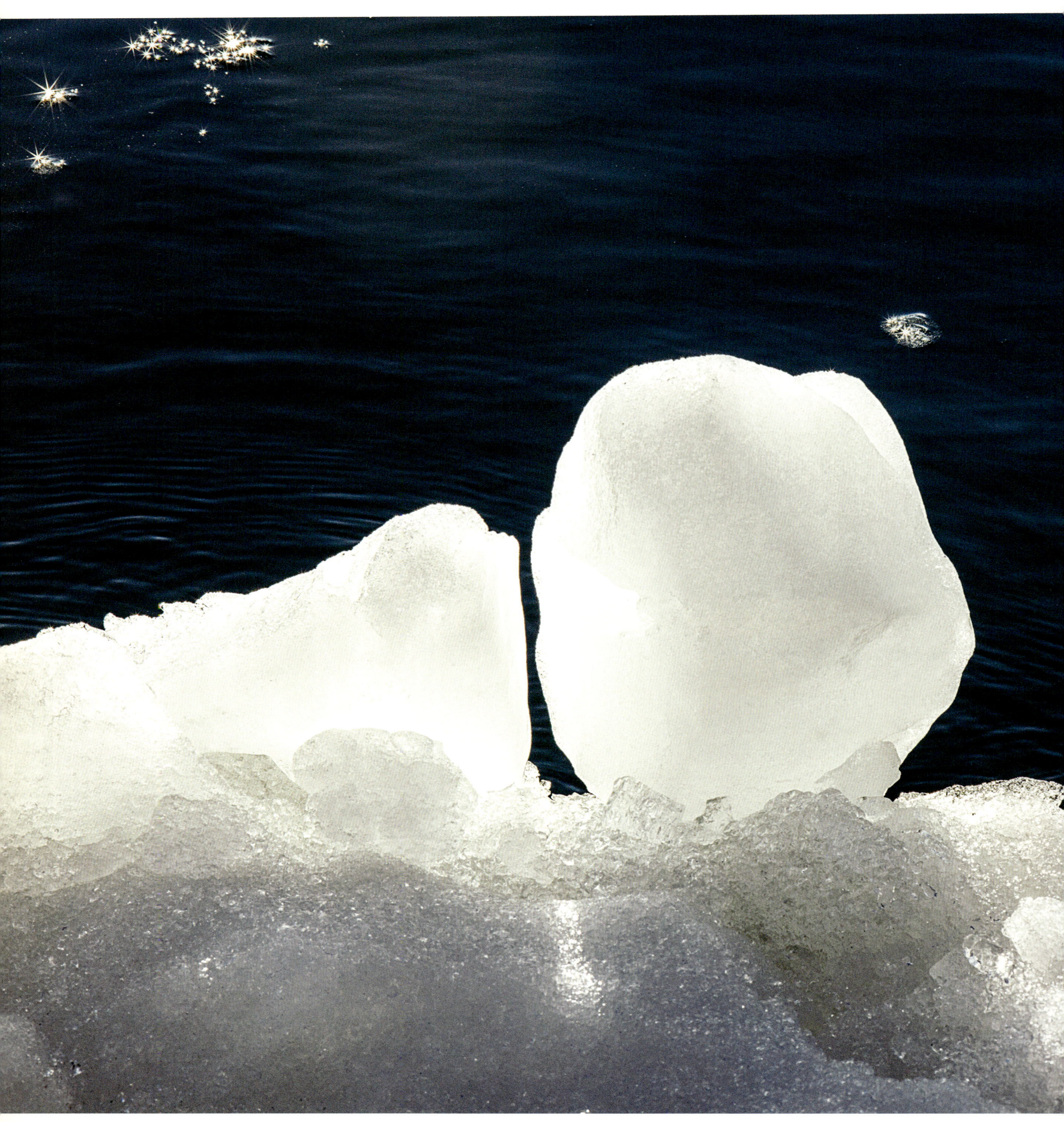

MEMORIES, DISKO BAY, GREENLAND.

following pages MORNING OVER DISKO BAY, GREENLAND.

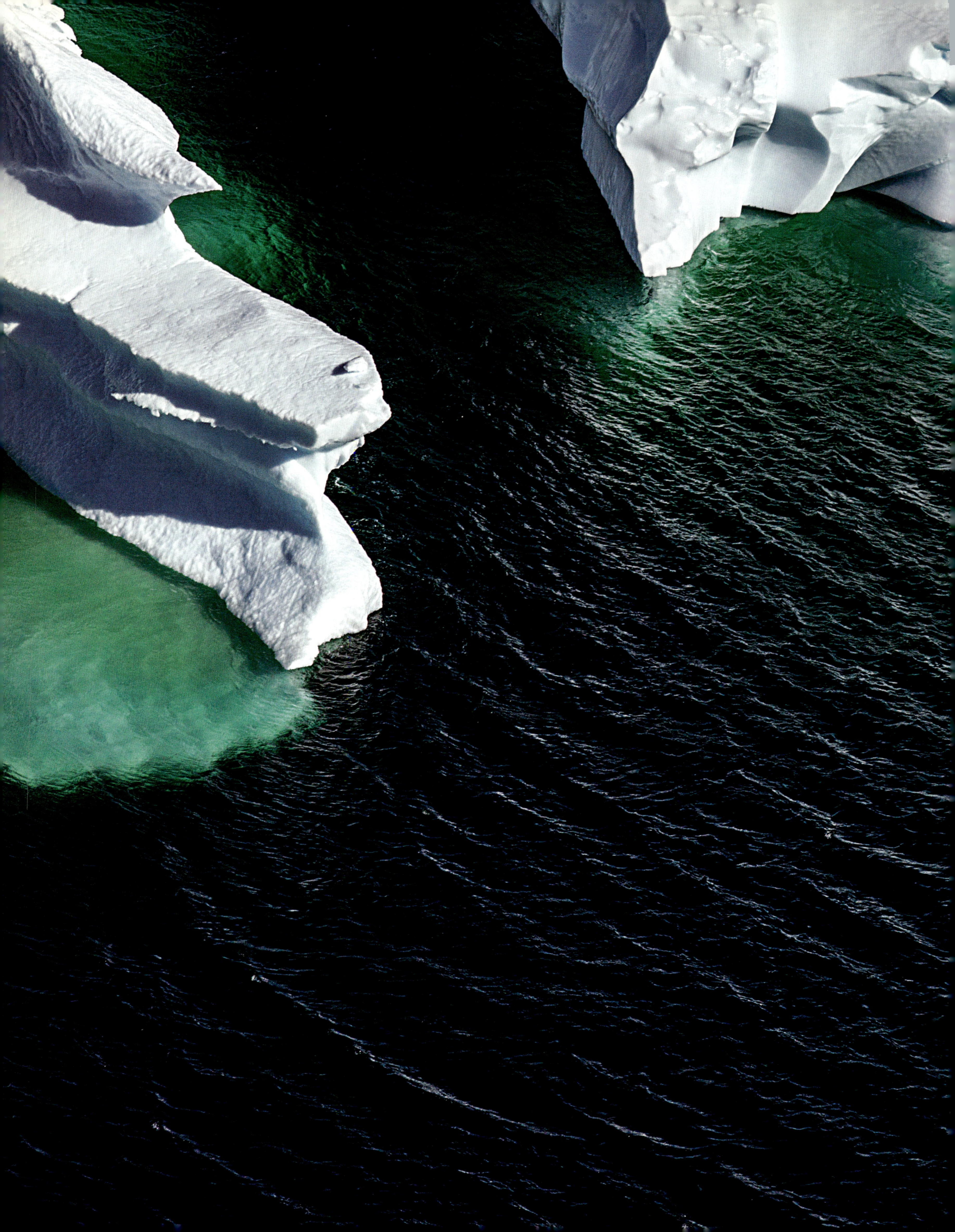

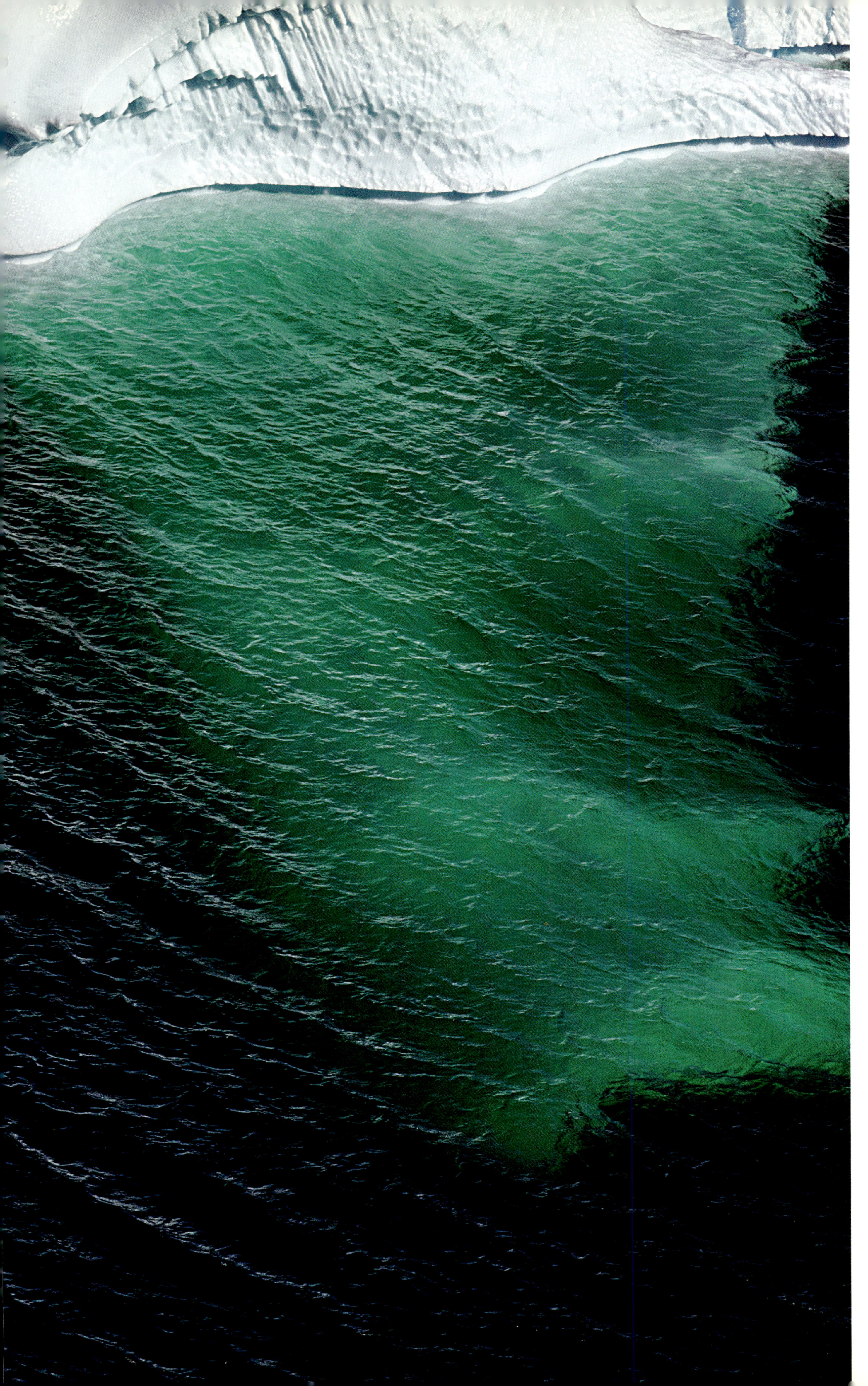

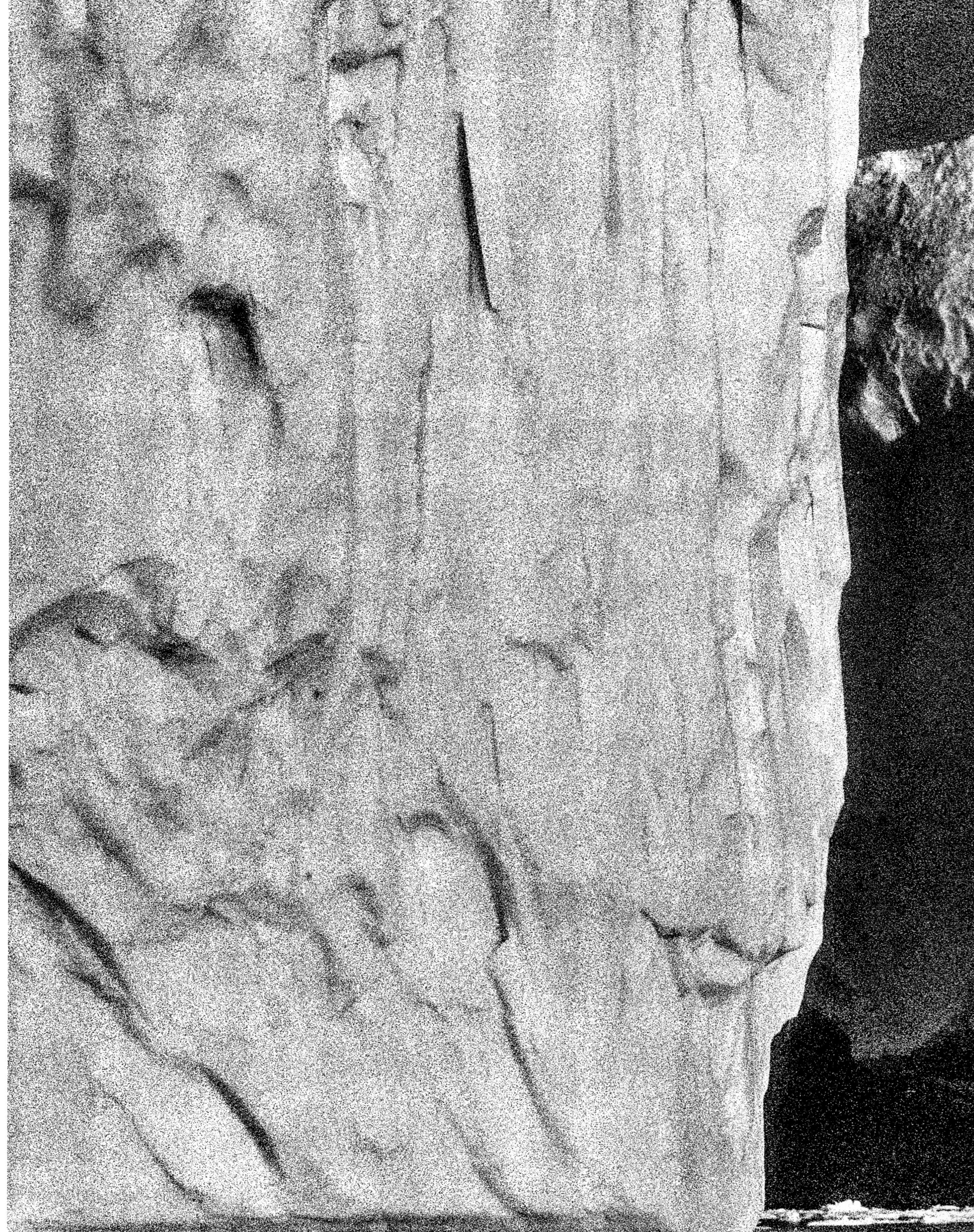

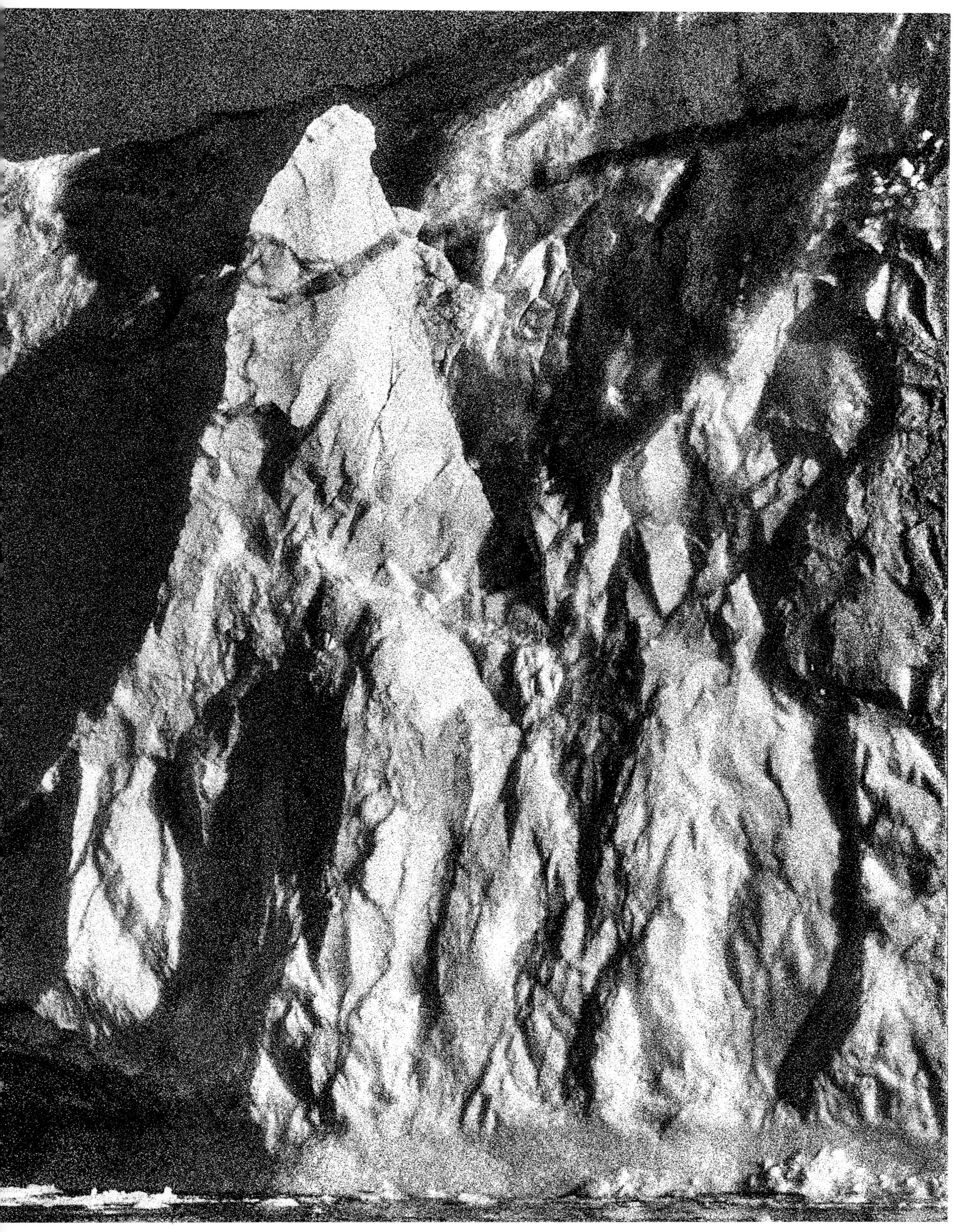

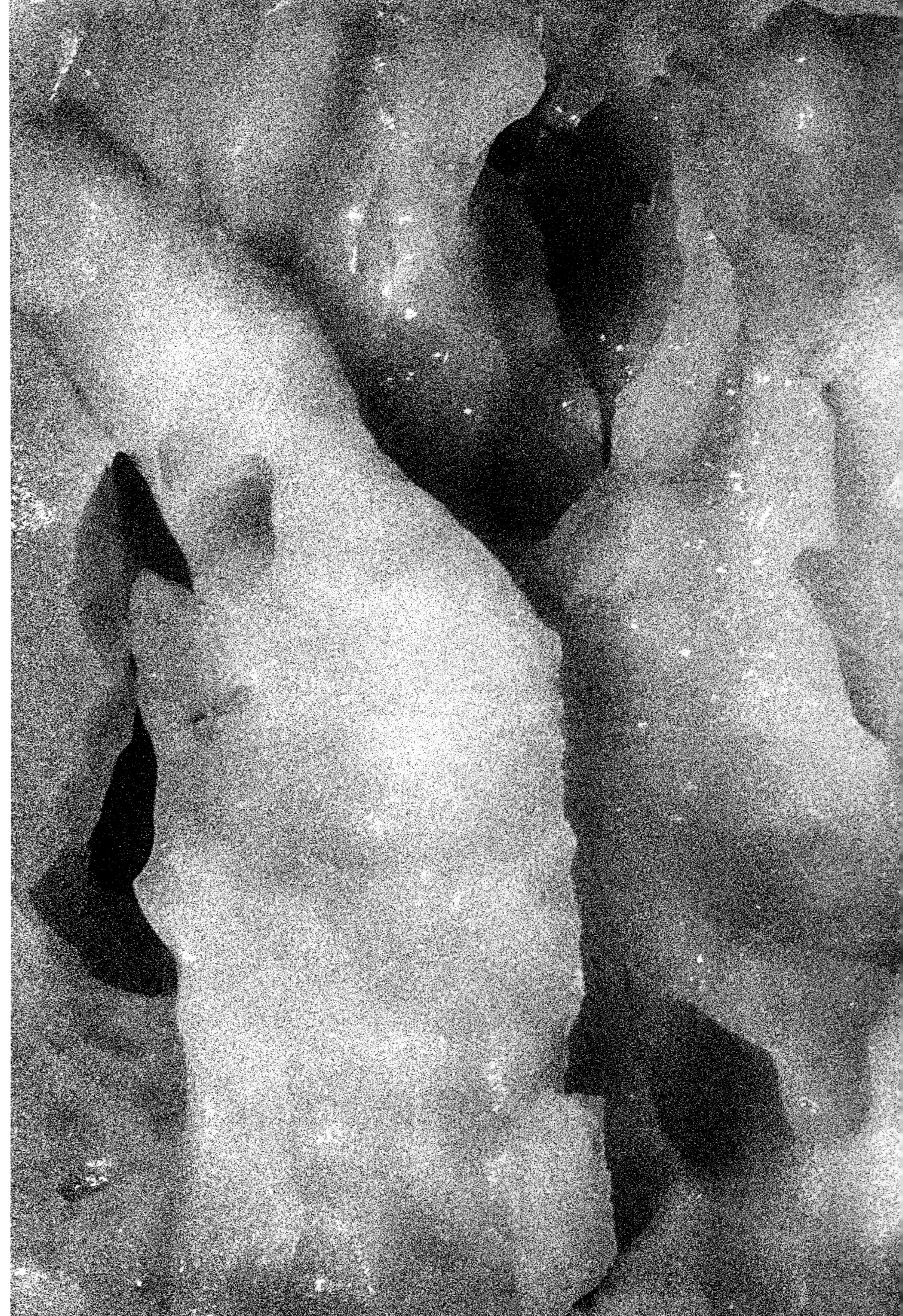

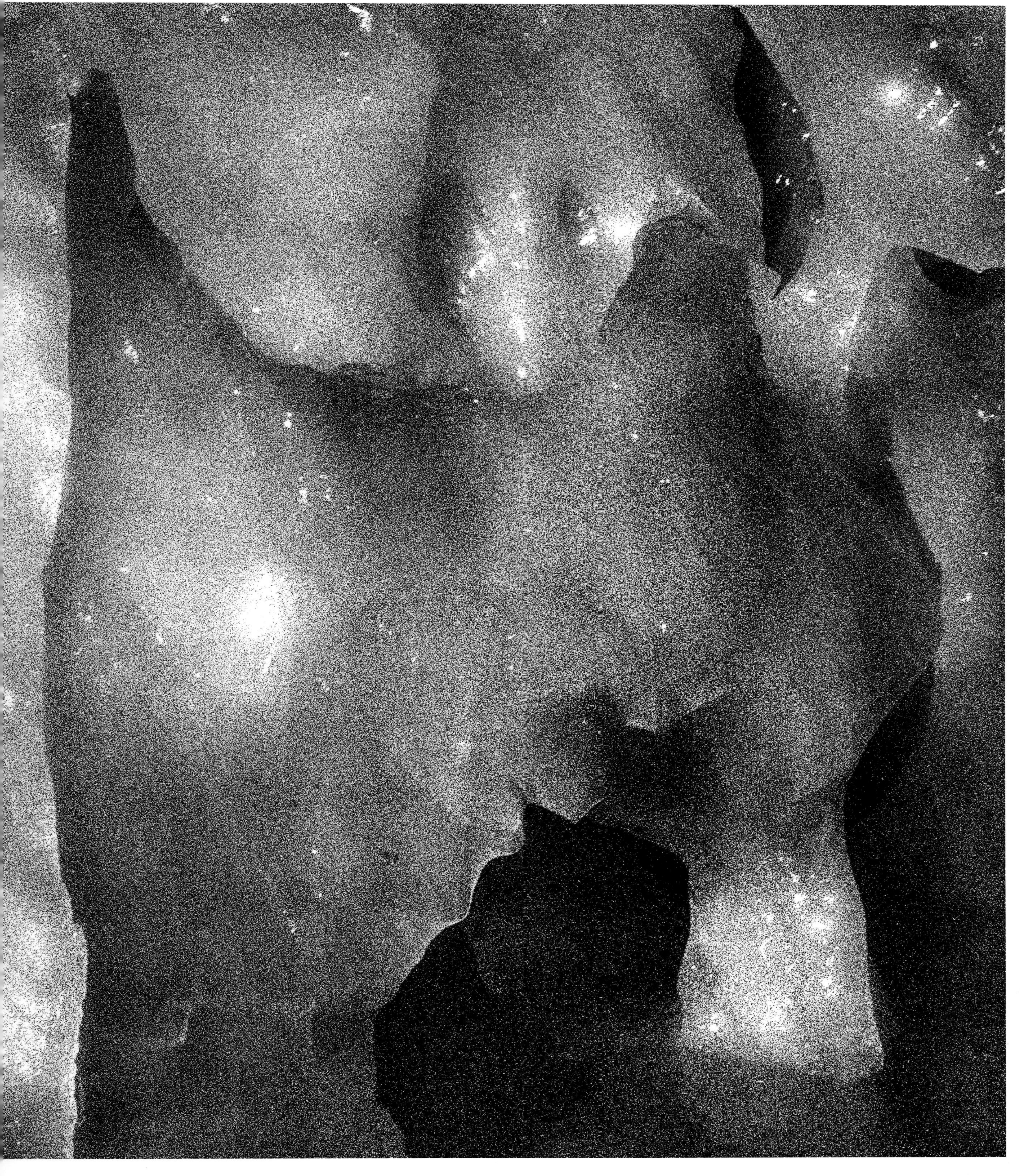

DISAPPEARANCE IN DISKO BAY, GREENLAND.

previous pages ICEBERGS I, DISKO BAY, GREENLAND.
following pages ARCTIC ICE, 86 DEGREES N, -2 DEGREES C.

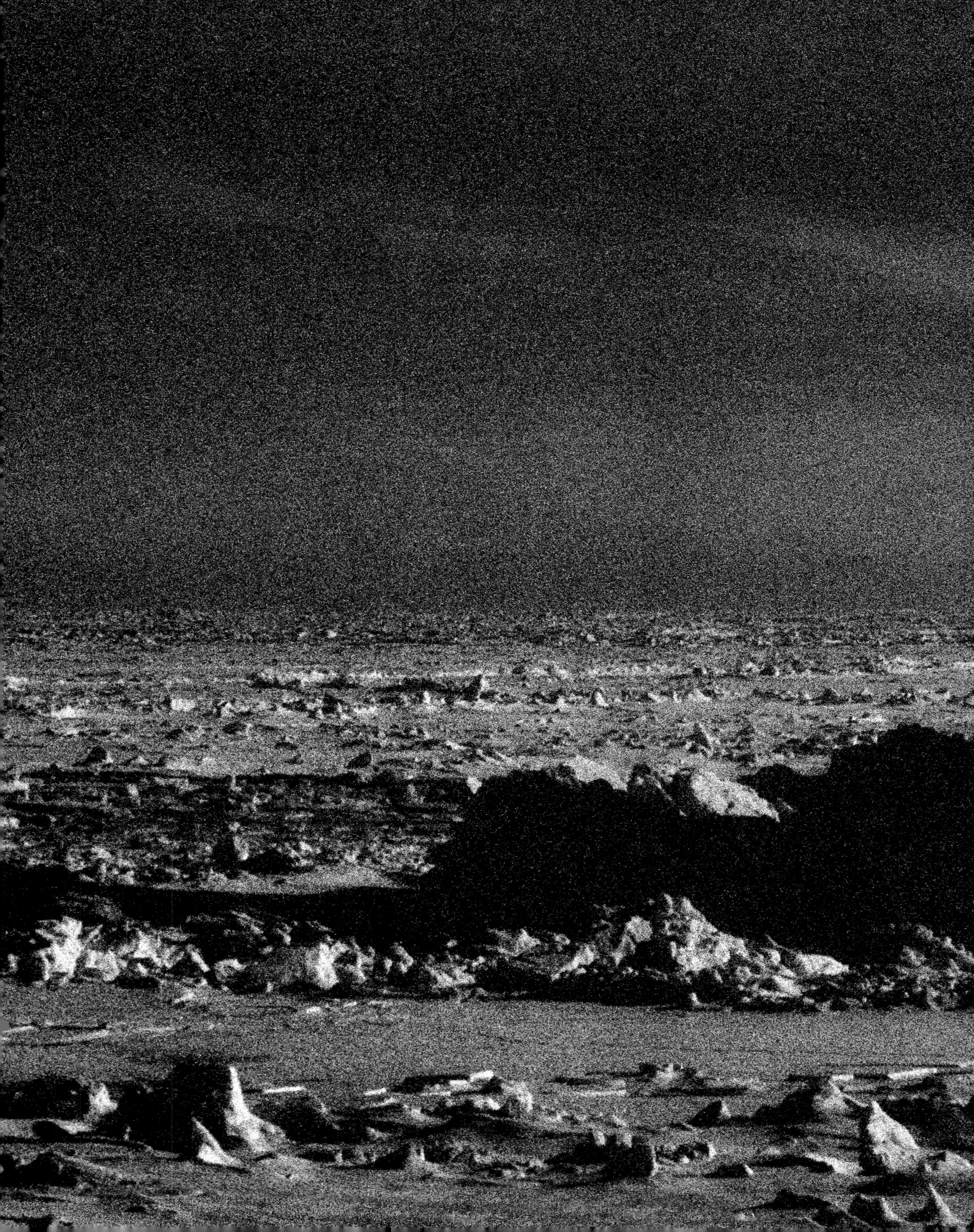

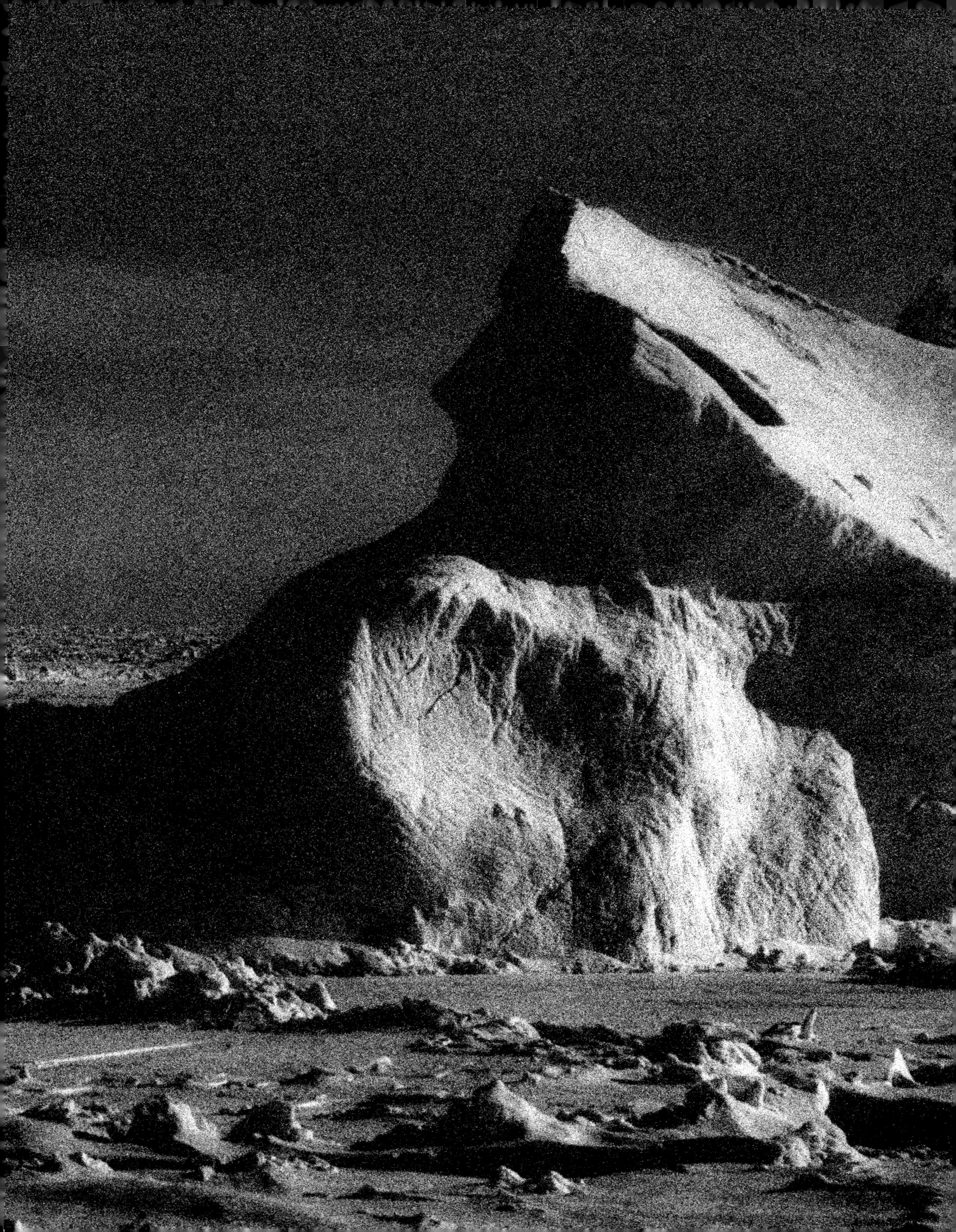

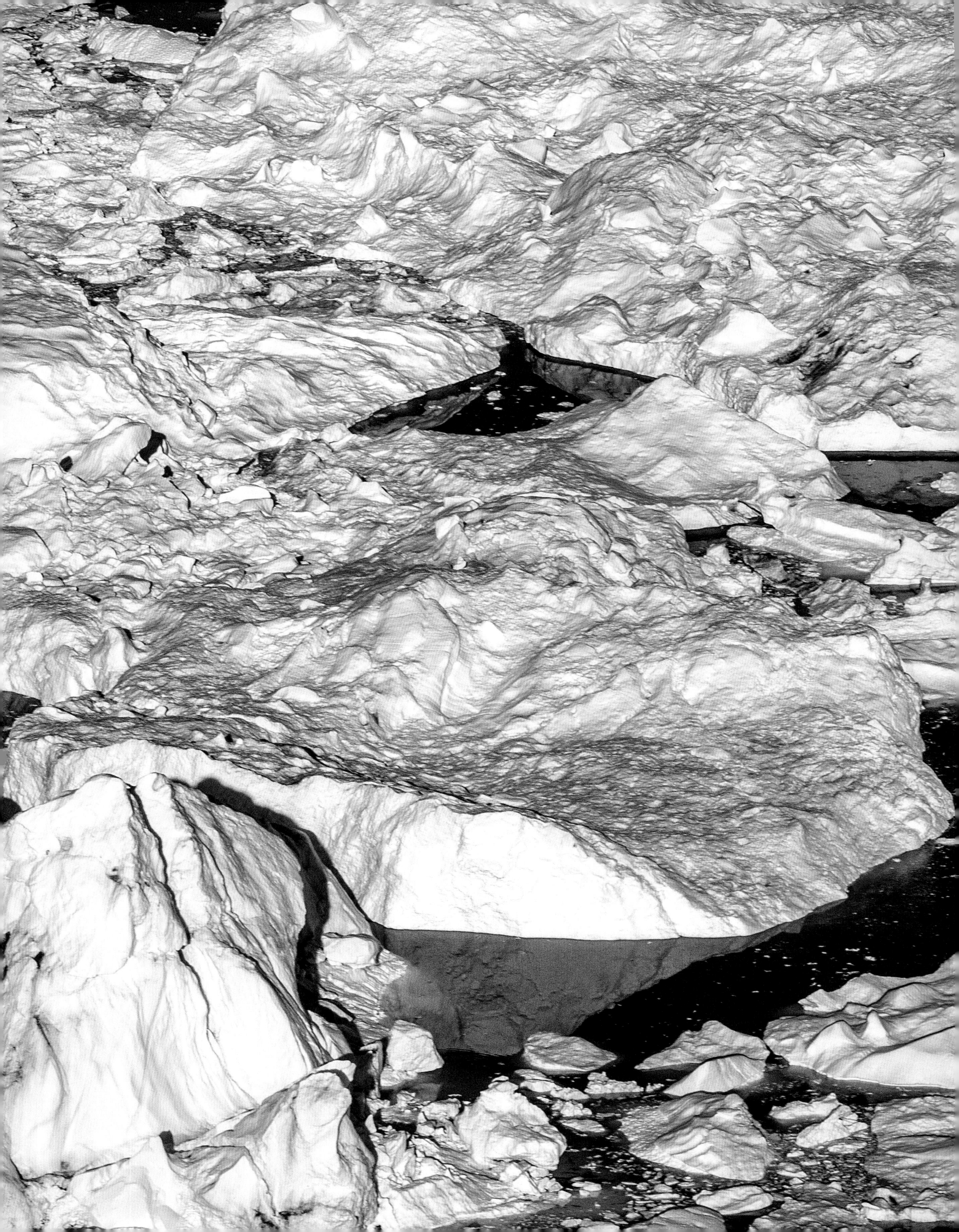

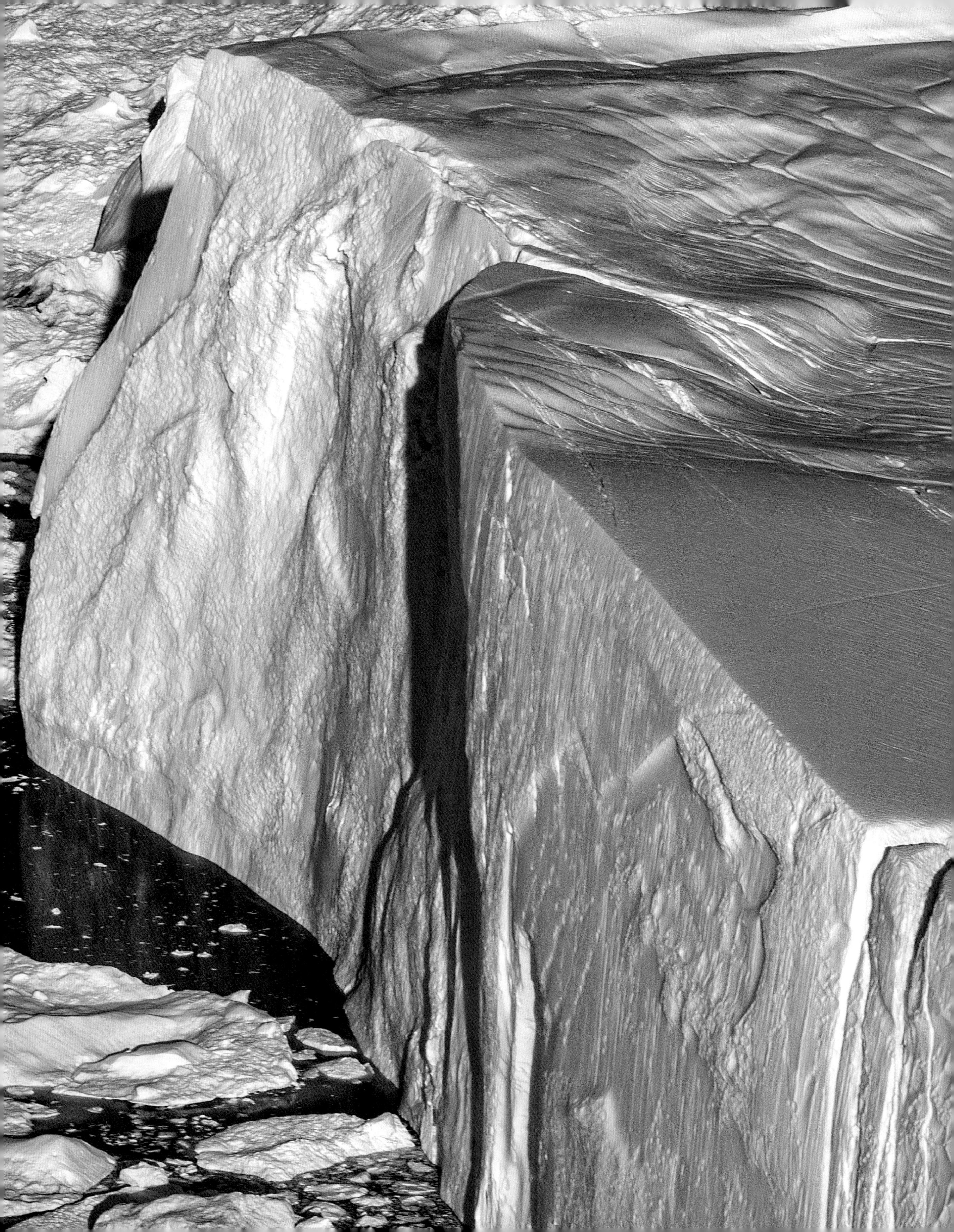

ACKNOWLEDGMENTS

First, I would like to thank the entire science community that has devoted many years researching the effects of climate change on our earth. It is because of their steadfast dedication to the cause and effect of increased greenhouse gases that the world is aware of the catastrophic future our planet will face if we do not address this issue immediately. The Arctic is most vulnerable to the effects of global warming, and its melt will cause unprecedented damage to life on earth.

My journey to Svalbard and Ny-Ålesund, Norway, would not have been possible without the help of Jason Roberts, who secured all of my permits and accompanied me throughout Svalbard. His mountaineering and technical skills proved invaluable in repairing my Leica camera while walking among the glaciers.

I would not have had the opportunity to visit Ny-Ålesund if it were not for Vittorio Pasquali of the National Research Council of Italy, who secured my letter of invitation.

I would also like to thank the other scientists at Ny-Ålesund who were researching various aspects of climate change on the Arctic wildlife and its atmosphere.

They included: William Van de Poll and Gemma Kulk from the University of the Netherlands, who were monitoring the effects of the Arctic Ocean's temperature and amount of ultraviolet light on the phytoplankton population; Dr. Ketil Hylland and Anne Haar of the University of Oslo, who were researching the effects of pollutants on glaucous gulls and other marine birds' DNA structure; Dr. Inka Bartsch and Dr. Katrine Zacher from the Alfred Wegener Institute, who were studying the long-term impact of the Arctic's environment on the

previous pages JAKOBSHAVN GLACIER, GREENLAND, 9:26 PM.

kelp population; and Dr. Uver, an atmospheric scientist working with the Norwegian Institute for Polar Research, who has been monitoring atmospheric gases in Ny-Ålesund since 1987.

The visit to the East Greenland Ice Core Project (EGRIP) would not have been possible without Alan Stoga's invitation to join Tällberg Foundation's seven-member delegation. Dorthe Dahl-Jensen, chair of EGRIP, provided us with information on the importance of the data derived from drilled ice cores. Jim White, director of the Institute of Arctic and Alpine Research at the University of Colorado, also added invaluable information on climate change and its long-term effects on the future of our planet.

My assistant, Kirsty Reeves, was indispensable in helping me manage my cameras and other equipment in extremely adverse conditions. I would also like to thank Bill Megalos, whose video camera provided the coverage of Svalbard and the Arctic Ocean, including interviews with the Arctic scientists.

The team at Assouline—Justin O'Neill, Jihyun Kim, Camille Dubois, Esther Kremer, and Prosper and Martine Assouline—produced not only a beautiful book but one that will be an important documentation of a disappearing landscape.

A special thanks to Joe Romm, who wrote the informative foreword to *The Arctic Melt*.

Most of all, I want to thank my family and friends—my husband, Tom; daughters Erica and Jennifer; son Scott; sons-in-law Michael and Jay; and my grandchildren, Sam, Phoebe, and Casey—for their unwavering support in my quest to capture the earth's fragile beauty.

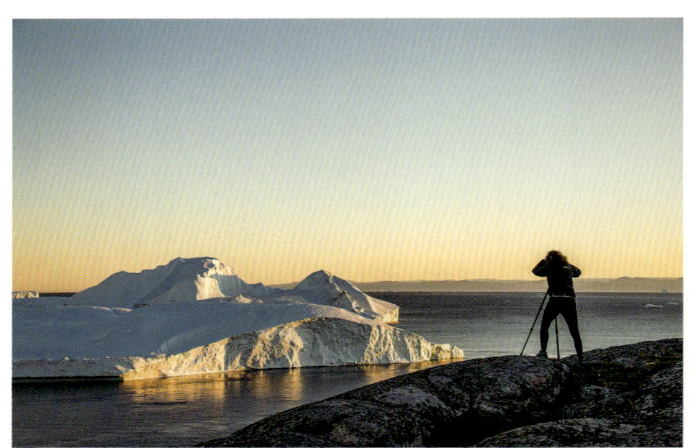

DISKO BAY, GREENLAND
1:21 AM
JULY 14, 2016